on track ...
The Human League
and the Sheffield electro scene

every album, every song

Andrew Darlington

sonicbondpublishing.com

Sonicbond Publishing Limited
www.sonicbondpublishing.co.uk
Email: info@sonicbondpublishing.co.uk

First Published in the United Kingdom 2022
First Published in the United States 2022

British Library Cataloguing in Publication Data:
A Catalogue record for this book is available from the British Library

ISBN 978-1-78952-186-3

Typeset in ITC Garamond & ITC Avant Garde
Printed and bound in England

Graphic design and typesetting: Full Moon Media

on track ...
The Human League
and the Sheffield electro scene

every album, every song

Andrew Darlington

sonicbondpublishing.com

Would you like to write for Sonicbond Publishing?
We are mainly a music publisher, but we also occasionally
publish in other genres including film and television. At Sonicbond
Publishing we are always on the look-out for authors, particularly for
our two main series, On Track and Decades.

Mixing fact with in depth analysis, the On Track series examines
the entire recorded work of a particular musical artist or group. All
genres are considered from easy listening and jazz to 60s soul to 90s
pop, via rock and metal.

The Decades series singles out a particular decade in an artist or
group's history and focuses on that decade in more detail than may
be allowed in the On Track series.

While professional writing experience would, of course, be
an advantage, the most important qualification is to have real
enthusiasm and knowledge of your subject. First-time authors are
welcomed, but the ability to write well in English is essential.

Sonicbond Publishing has distribution throughout Europe and
North America, and all our books are also published in E-book form.
Authors will be paid a royalty based on sales of their book.
Further details about our books are available from
www.sonicbondpublishing.com. To contact us, complete the
contact form there or email info@sonicbondpublishing.co.uk

For Susan, who would probably prefer another band.

on track ...

The Human League,
and the Sheffield electro scene

Contents

Introduction

None of The Human League have any orthodox musical training but prefer to regard composition as an extension of logic, inspiration and luck. Therefore, unlike conventional musicians, their influences are not so obvious.
Fast Product Press Pack, June 1978

Rock 'n' roll was never intended to be about virtuosity. It was more a DIY folk music. Skiffle was a 1950s fad championed by Lonnie Donegan, which ignited a thousand ad hoc austerity groups repurposing household items – a washboard, an old tea chest impaled with a broom handle, tension-strung to create a stand-up bass, and maybe a couple of battered acoustic guitars played with more energy than technique. Two decades later, Sheffield created a new kind of electronic skiffle.

Why Sheffield? The M1 slip road 34 takes you into the small South Yorkshire industrial city that has a greater music tradition than that description would imply. We could start with Wurlitzer organist Reginald Dixon: famous for his radio broadcasts from the Blackpool Tower Ballroom. But we probably won't. Instead, we'll begin in the beat-boom era with Dave Berry, his distinctive creepy stage persona, and hits that included 'The Crying Game', his cover of Bobby Goldsboro's 'Little Things' and the Ray Davies-penned 'This Strange Effect'. Dave was born in Woodhouse – to the southeast of Sheffield – in February 1941.

Then there's Joe Cocker, who took the Woodstock festival by storm with his anguished take on The Beatles' modest sing-along: the Ringo Starr-sung 'With A Little Help From My Friends'. Joe was born at 38 Tasker Road in the Sheffield suburb of Crookes in May 1944.

Tony Christie might've been born in nearby Conisbrough, but his long association with the steel city includes his 2008 *Made In Sheffield* album – produced by Richard Hawley, with contributions from Alex Turner and Jarvis Cocker.

Of course, there's Def Leppard, jazz guitarist Derek Bailey, singer Paul Carrack, jazz drummer Tony Oxley, Pulp, Arctic Monkeys and beyond. But this book is largely centred around the cluster of electro musicians who were feeling their way through the 1970s to upsurge into the 1980s as the 'soundtrack for the second industrial revolution: 45 and 33-and-a-third rpm'.

The first time I visited Sheffield – where now there is the labyrinthine Meadowhall temple to opulent consumerism – there were still foundries you could smell in the air and that shook the street beneath your feet, 'like a metronome, like a heartbeat for the whole city', according to Human League founding member Ian Craig Marsh. 'We all come from pretty strong working-class backgrounds', Ian told me. 'My Dad's a bricklayer, and my Mum used to work at Bassett's Liquorice Allsorts factory. My Grandfather got burned clear down his right side when he was splashed with molten steel at a steel works!'. De-industrialisation left abandoned factory units to colonise as rehearsal rooms and studio space for insurrectionary anti-musicians, who 'discarded natural sound source in favour of synthetic instrumentation because of its convenience, mobility and vast source of as-yet-untapped potential' (the manifesto of 1970s Sheffield electronic band Vice Versa). And there was cheap front-room technology easily adaptable, Skiffle-style, sufficient to bend to purpose: original, in the sense of not using drums – which were just too tedious to learn – or guitars, which were considered obsolete. 'We wanted to sound like a proper pop group, but we were not prepared to put in the five or six years that it would've taken to learn a traditional instrument', explained Human League singer Philip Oakey. The non-Sheffield Nick Rhodes of Duran Duran described his discovery of synths as 'This is a new planet that I could live on'. And yes, that's how it was.

It was a time of dense-black xeroxed fanzines. Sheffield had its own *GunRubber* – produced since February 1977 by Paul Bower and Adi Newton – *Modern Drugs* from Martin Fry, *NMX* from Martin Russian, and the photocopied *Steve's Paper* from Stephen Singleton: all documenting the burgeoning local music scene centred around Cabaret Voltaire and The Future. And there was the cassette underground, where, for the first time, bands, musicians and poets could use their bedrooms to home-record their own experimental sounds, then cheaply reproduce and circulate limited-edition C30s or C60s among a proto-internet of linked like-minded enthusiasts. It was ignited by the punk energy and ethos that anyone could get up and do it. It was new. It was exciting, combining the dissident samizdat self-publishing spirit of insurgency with mischievously incendiary early-Dada art-confrontational energies, supercharged by the relentlessly dark cut-up strategies of beat-generation writer William S. Burroughs and his sci-fi new wave disciple J. G. Ballard. Each bubble-pack package that arrived in the morning mail was ripped open to reveal new bulletins from the innovative edge of luring and sometimes scary tomorrows. *New Musical Express* (*NME*) carried its own weekly review column, with the addresses of more DIY weirdnesses a mere postal order away.

The first experimental synthesizer system had been devised in 1955 by RCA, but it was a certain Dr. Robert Moog who gave his name to the cheaper and more-marketable modular version that began to infiltrate awareness during the late-1960s – as demonstrated on the first entirely synthesized album *Switched On Bach* (1968) by Walter (later Wendy) Carlos, followed by *The Well-Tempered Synthesizer* a year later. Human League producer Martyn Ware recalled hearing Carlos on the *A Clockwork Orange* (1971) soundtrack. Heaven 17 would take their name from the same movie.

Bands such as The Byrds, Pink Floyd, The Moody Blues and others began to dabble in the effects that electronics could produce – with Terry Riley, Tonto's Expanding Head Band and The United States Of America taking it incrementally further, nodding to John Cage as a kind of spiritual godfather. The cosmic synth genre was an extension of the psychedelic music-to-take-trips-by drug culture: an avant-garde trance deployment of otherworldly textures. Then, incorporated into banks of keyboards, the synthesizer became an exotic embellishment to the assault arsenal employed by virtuoso prog rock musicians. Synths were bulky, heavy, fragile and temperamental, utilising voltage-controlled oscillators and related devices that responded to room humidity and temperature. Heat changes from the lighting rig could affect tunings. A Moog required a two-hour warming-up period.

In Germany, Tangerine Dream, Neu and Kraftwerk were not only adapting and developing their own rhythmic variations but were inventing new ones through the use of sequencers. Kraftwerk – 'The most important group of the century', according to Philip Oakey – compressed eccentrically catchy musical ideas into the appropriately stimulating shape of wires, programmes, images, trackers, scanners, impulses and screens.

Championed by DJ John Peel, Tangerine Dream grew out of the Berlin Zodiak Free Arts Lab, where they evolved the hypnotic pulsations of their LP *Phaedra* (1974): the first charting album for them and for Virgin Records. Abstract solo albums by Klaus Schulze and Tangerine Dream's Edgar Froese dissolved into sound pixels, which absorbed the listener into a Rorschach eyelid movie of aural fantasia. The 1977 success of *Oxygène* took Jean-Michel Jarre as close as space music could get to conventional pop, with brisk programmed percussion and melodic synth lines that made it both accessible and relentlessly catchy. Yet, it was closer to soporific mood music, conjuring an aid-to-getting-high mind screen for recumbent sofa surfers. To gonzo music journalist Lester Bangs, 'The men at the keyboards send out sonar blips through the congealing air… three technological monoliths emitting urps, hissings, pings and swooshings in the dark' (in his *Psychotic Reactions And Carburetor Dung, published by* Serpents Tail in 1987).

In Sheffield, it was different. 'We didn't need to spend a lot of money to be creative', said Martyn. The Sheffield answer was to leap obliquely into exploratory voyages to uncharted areas of electronic experiment, sidestepping both conventional musical standards and accepted modes of rock celebrity. It was innovation inspired by the can-do attitude of punk, and the art-school Bowie cool. On one side of town was Cabaret Voltaire; on the other there was The Future – a 'more adventurous but less commercial' version of The Human League, which cannibalised Ian Craig Marsh and Martyn Ware alongside Adi Newton, who operated tape loops and treatments and was destined to form the excellent but much-undervalued Clock DVA.

If there was a pre-existing language, Kraftwerk had utilised tape loops, while Holger Czukay used random bursts of shortwave radio interference for his work with Can. Cabaret Voltaire began in trainee-telephone-engineer Chris Watson's attic, inspired by a brief 80-page book called *Composing With Tape Recorders: Musique Concrète For Beginners* by Terence Dwyer (Oxford University Press, 1971). First Chris – then Chris in cahoots with Richard H. Kirk – played collage sound games with reel-to-reel tape recorders – sped-up, slowed-down, spliced and looped, adding a Farfisa drum machine with rudimentary mail-order ring modulator signal processing patched together by Chris: no keyboard, just knobs to twiddle and tweak. 'I was never a musician', Chris explained: 'I had no interest in playing a musical instrument. I had no interest in that sort of discipline. I just wanted to make some noise ... we didn't really know what we were doing, but we knew we wanted to do it!'.

Later, they acquired an EMS Synthi AKS – its name titling no less than three tracks on their *Methodology '74-'78: Attic Tapes* (Industrial Records, 1980 – expanded for Mute Records, 2002). Where Cabaret Voltaire are concerned, definition remained nebulous – how to classify the one-minute-and-ten-second 'Jet Passing Over' (simply a doubled electronic sound replication of aeroplane jets in the sky: phasey, like a radio tuning itself in and out of focus), or 'Jack Stereo Unit' which is a confusion of conflicting speech. 'Treated Guitar' is splodge sounds. At least the 01:47 'Sad Synth' recognizably utilises a synthesizer, while the 39-second 'Space Patrol' uses cheap TV sci-fi effects in the way The Future would. These were what Chris Watson described as the 'newfound freedoms'.

Adding bassist Stephen Mallinder, their first gig was a Science For People student disco at the university upper refectory on Tuesday 13 May 1975. Percussion consisted of a tape-loop recording of a steam hammer, recorded by Chris in Belgium, while Richard improvised on clarinet, bedecked in flashing Christmas tree lights. Needless to say, the reception was not even mixed – it was hostile, resulting in Mallinder's trip to the A&E department as a consequence of a fracas with the unruly and unappreciative audience. But if there has to be a date for the big-bang ignition of Sheffield electro, this is it: the $E=MC^2$ moment. Martyn Ware and Ian Craig Marsh were taking note.

Lest we forget, there was still a Soviet Union and a Cold War going on; the world seemed breathlessly paused on the brink of mutually assured destruction. But if the crack of doom wasn't to be heard on some hydrogen jukebox, it just might uncoil from that next C60 in the mail.

What semantic references, mythological splendours and glittering epithets can be attached to The Human League? Their career was lived forwards but must be understood backwards, from today back to then: an exercise in de-structuring images and image-making. But all that's really essential to know is that The Human League brought pop from the age of the Flintstones to the age of the Jetsons virtually overnight. This is my chance to set history straight, for they were as original as the solar system.

Sheffield is a small city, and was isolated from what was happening in London, in the same way, that Liverpool had been isolated from the fads and fashions of the southern-based music biz in 1963, or how by the end of the 1970s, simple Casio synths were as cheap and easily-available as guitars.

The participants were:

Martyn Ware – born 19 May 1956: the week 'No Other Love' by Ronnie Hilton was number 1 on the *NME* chart.

Ian Craig Marsh – born 11 November 1956: the week 'A Woman In Love' by Frankie Laine was number 1.

Philip Oakey – born 2 October 1955: the week 'Rose Marie' by Slim Whitman was at *NME* number 1.

Susan Ann Sulley – born 22 March 1963: the week 'Summer Holiday' by Cliff Richard was at *NME* number 1.

Joanne Catherall – born 18 September 1962: the week 'She's Not You' by Elvis Presley was at *NME* number 1.

Ian Burden – born 24 December 1957: the week 'Mary's Boy Child' by Harry Belafonte was at *NME* number 1.

Jo Callis – born 2 May 1951: there was no record sales chart yet.

Adrian Wright – born 30 June 1956: the week 'I'll Be Home' by Pat Boone was at *NME* number 1.

Author's Note

While this book is principally about The Human League, covering the band's entire career, the wider music created by the Sheffield electro scene in the 1980s is vitally important for context, particularly, for fairly obvious reasons, the early work of Heaven 17. As well as touching on other bands that were part of that scene like Cabaret Voltaire, Clock DVA and ABC, the early albums of Martyn Ware and Ian Marsh's hugely successful post-Human League project are covered track by track up until 1984's popular *How Men Are* album. After this, the bands diverge to such an extent that we concentrate on The Human League, although Heaven 17 are certainly worthy of a book in their own right in the future.

Beginnings

The Golden Hour Of The Future – Recordings by The Future and The Human League (2002)

Personnel:
Philip Oakey, Martyn Ware: vocals, synthesizer
Ian Craig Marsh: synthesizer, devices
Adi Newton: vocals, tapes loops, treatments
Cover design: Designers Republic
Release date: 20 October 2002
Recorded 1977
Label: Black Melody Records MELCD4
Duration: 76:53

It was uncompromisingly The Future. A decisive breakaway from the past.

These salvaged Future tapes provide a unique insight into the formative period of the individuals who would etch the sound of The Human League, and also B.E.F., Clock DVA, Box and Heaven 17. It's a glimpse of their novice selves, testing out the range and potential of purely electronic instrumentation, sometimes arty and experimental, flirting with themes and ideas of random chance or playful in adopting dismissive throwaway strategies, with an attractive rawness we'd never encounter again as their ideas became slicker, more mature and targeted. Chances are, if the groups involved had not subsequently achieved success, these tapes would've remained unissued, yet their components would be exactly the same: no more, no less.

Martyn Ware and Ian Craig Marsh were computer programmers. 'ICL 2600 series, I think; the IBM 300 series', recalls Martyn. 'And I wasn't a programmer, I was an operator. Ian was, too, different companies'. Born in Sheffield and educated at King Edward VII secondary school, Martyn bought himself a Korg 700 monophonic keyboard with his first Lucas Services UK wages. Ian, meantime, had replied to a Maplin advert in *Practical Electronics* magazine for a build-your-own modular synth. He'd already worked as part of a performance-art project called Musical Vomit through an association with the Meatwhistle community theatre on Holly Street. With a confrontational agenda located somewhere between the Genesis P-Orridge COUM collective and Alice Cooper's shock-theatrics, the group brought him into contact with Paul Bower – later of 2.3 – Glenn Gregory and Martyn. Paul Bower remembers, 'Early Human League gigs used my 1960s valve Vox AC30 for the synths when playing live. This was also the main amp for Musical Vomit 1974/75. Glenn Gregory was the bass player, and Underpants was a spin-off that played one gig. Martyn Ware was on double-stylus stylophone, playing his first remarkably tuneful debut composition,n 'Wimpy Bar Magnet''.

While Punk was erupting in the music world outside Sheffield, Ian and Martyn were taking a contrary approach by forming an analogue synthesizer-

and-tape trio, completed by intense 'sonic and kinetic engineer' Adolphus 'Adi' Newton. They lifted a name from the Starforce sci-fi board game, first becoming The Dead Daughters for a one-off set performed at a private party in a bar at Sheffield University. Then they became The Future, around June 1977. It was during that same summer that they recorded some ten tracks at Studio Electrophonique: the home studio of recording engineer Ken Patten, in Handsworth Crescent, Ballifield, east of Sheffield – limitless dreams conjured from limited resources.

I once asked the personnel what type of sound The Future was making. 'Like a less adventurous version of early Human League', suggested Martyn: a pronouncement that brought howls of protest. 'Not *less* adventurous!' insisted Glenn Gregory. So Martyn adjusted his verdict to 'More adventurous, but less commercial', which seemed to be the consensus view, because when they hawked the demo tape around various record labels on a trip from Sheffield down to London – 'Nine meetings with nine different record companies', according to Martyn – they got no positive response. So, with no future in sight, Adi shifted sideways, after toying with Veer, to become Clock DVA, alongside Steven 'Judd' Turner (bass) and Roger Quail (drums).

After briefly persisting as The Future in duo form, Ian and Martyn cast around for a new frontman vocalist. They wanted blonde Glenn Gregory: a charismatic bass player who'd worked in casual bands with Ian since 1973. There's a reference to a one-off assignation called The Studs – which included not only Glenn with Ian and Martyn but Adi Newton alongside Richard H. Kirk, Chris Watson and Stephen Mallinder of Cabaret Voltaire. The Studs played one anarchic 19-minute performance at Sheffield Art College, supporting Manchester punk group The Drones, in a set that included versions of the *Dr. Who* theme, 'Louie Louie', Lou Reed's 'Vicious', Iggy Pop's 'Cock In My Pocket' and an improvised 'The Drones Want To Come On Now', which were salvaged onto a hard-to-find bootleg recording.

But since then, Glenn had moved south from his native Sheffield. 'He came from Sheffield, but went down to London at an early age', Ian told me. Glenn joined a London band initially called 57 Men: 'It wasn't a particularly good band, and that's why we split up. We just played gigs 'round London. We played the Marquee and all those places, the pubs and that. They were called 57 Men. In fact, you're the only person in all these interviews who's even asked me that! Which shows how fucking ignorant they are!', said Glenn, more in humour than belligerence. Maybe the cost-effective problems of keeping a 57-piece personnel on the road, led to their eventual demise! 'We had to economise down to just 17', Glenn quipped. 'The band were subsequently renamed Wang Chung', he told me.

So instead, once the days of Future passed, Martyn brought in schoolfriend Philip Oakey, who worked as a porter at Sheffield's Thornbury Annex hospital, although he'd also been a university bookshop assistant and a filing clerk at the Sheffield dole office.

Though Philip had been born in Hinckley – a market town in Leicestershire – his father's position with the Post Office necessitated regular family relocations – to Coventry, to Leeds in 1960, and to Birmingham four years later, around the time The Beatles were spearheading the first British invasion of the American charts. It was not until he was 14 that Philip arrived in Sheffield, where he found himself attending the same King Edward VII secondary school as Martyn Ware. In Leeds, Philip was transfixed by the sound of Lovin' Spoonful's 'Daydream' coming from a nearby disco. 'At school, we liked King Crimson, Van der Graaf Generator, The Moody Blues', and the first gig he attended was Jethro Tull supported by Procol Harum with Irish folkies Tir na NÓg at Sheffield City Hall. He quit school in 1973 without completing the exam syllabus, in much the same way that he'd bought a saxophone but could never be bothered to learn how to play it.

There's a story that Martyn went around to the Oakey household in order to invite Philip to join their embryonic group, less due to his musical experience – because Philip had none – but more due to his flamboyant dress sense that had made him a recognizable presence on the local Sheffield scene. From a 21st-century perspective, that moment shapes up as potentially as significant as the 1957 Woolton village fete where a young Paul McCartney first watched John Lennon's skiffle group The Quarrymen, although, at the time, it would've been no big deal. Anyway, Philip wasn't even home. He'd gone out. So Martyn stuck a note on the front door instead, posing the invitation. Philip responded with a 'yes', and joined the lineup.

Throughout the history of pop, hair has formed the flash point for generational conflict – from the Elvis Presley sideburns and greasy slicked-back pompadour through the moptop comb-down fringe and hippie 'Almost Cut My Hair' excess, into punk spiky-top, skinhead and suedehead beyond. Philip Oakey contrived an asymmetrical variant with a peek-a-boo bang that obscured three-quarters of his face, both seizing and teasing the eye. It was a useful, attention-grabbing strategy. Where there were dense industrial-black fanzine layouts and cassette-insert images collaged together from thin, young identikit intense men and punkish girls with attitude, he supplied the focus.

This is an album of lost formative tracks from the very start of the story.

'Dance Like A Star' by The Human League (Oakey, Marsh, Ware) (4:48)

This track was also the title of a 12-inch EP (MEL3) issued in a limited-edition 2000 copies in September 2002 as a promotional tie-in for the CD, with production credits going to Tim Pearce and The Human League. With a total running time of 23:23, the track-list was as follows:

'Dance Like A Star' (Version 1) (Oakey, Marsh, Ware) (4:23)

'We are The Human League, and we are much cleverer than you', announces Philip confidently, leading into a catchy 'Dance dance dance' lyric over programmed drums and twittering electro. 'Hear the guitar' – there is no guitar! It may be a throwaway tongue-in-cheek piece, but all the basic Human League elements are already in place. Ian had conjectured the group as the 'first electronic pop band', while, to Martyn, The Future was 'an interface with the real world'. And dance can be a weapon – the danceable solution to teenage revolution.

'C'est Grave' (Trad arr. Marsh, Ware) (3:04)
A macabre dance with the dead featuring demented high-pitched vocals from tour manager and engineer Timothy Pearce.

'Titled U.N.' (Marsh, Ware) (3:06)
An upbeat instrumental with a sharp drum track. It was the backing track for an untitled and unfinished song which was rediscovered by the League's engineer David Beevers in 2002 while searching for material for the *The Golden Hour Of The Future* project. Had the track been completed, it might've made for quite a catchy pop song. Martyn and Ian later issued a slightly different version as part of their B.E.F. cassette *Music For Stowaways,* under the title 'Wipe The Board Clean' (according to www.blindyouth.co.uk).

'Dance Like A Star' (Version 2) (Oakey, Marsh, Ware) (3:14)
An alternate version of the cut that was included on the album.

'Morale' (Marsh, Ware) (2:27)
A hypnotic meditative early instrumental demo with twittering synths and a neoclassical electronica feel; mistitled 'Treatment' on this EP (and also referred to as 'Depression Is A Fashion', with rough vocals by Martyn). A revision would later feature as the prelude to 'You've Lost That Loving Feeling' on *Reproduction*, although the B.E.F. team reworked it further as a track for Arlene Phillips' dance group Hot Gossip on their 1981 album *Geisha Boys And Temple Girls*, with her talk-sung voice run over distinctive Martyn and Ian electro.

'The Last Man On Earth' (Excerpt) (Marsh, Ware) (6:16)
The EP closes with an edit of the full ten-minute version which was included on the 12" EP and the album. It seems unlikely that the sci-fi-literate Future were unaware that the title was lifted from the first movie of Richard Matheson's post-apocalypse novel *I Am Legend* starring Vincent Price (1954), remade with Charlton Heston as *The Omega Man* (1971), and again with Will Smith in 2007.

'Looking For The Black Haired Girls' by The Future (Ware, Marsh, Newton) (3:40)
This opens with screams and crashing synths, enhanced by swooping electro gunshot effects with a dark sexual voice-over: 'my young Brooklyn mind ...

young and violent'. There's a version on the Clock DVA *Horology* collection
that reflects Adi Newton's input and the way his work would evolve. There's
an influence from the existential black humour of William S. Burroughs'
routines, which were circulating in much-duplicated bootleg-cassette form
– *Nothing Here But The Recordings* and *Call Me Burroughs* – with Adi's dry
voice delivery ascending into frenzy overload in an extremely disturbed way
that The Human League would seldom revisit. A million parsecs from pop,
with little to do with the more-improvisational aspects of rock, this carries
the frisson of something subversive, new and dangerously innovative. There
had been experiments with a home-devised computer program called Carlos,
which auto-generated lyrics from input words and phrases, which might
explain some of its genesis.

'4JG' by **The Human League** (Ware, Marsh, Oakey) (4:36)

With the titular tribute being 'For J. G. Ballard', with whining distortion,
analogue bleeps and snarling Korg 700 and 770, Roland System 100 and
Jupiter-4 filters, this simple recurring motif repetition is moody and upbeat,
with advance trace elements of the Detroit techno to come, and a bizarre
treated child-voice in the fade, reciting '(How Much Is) That Doggie In The
Window?' and 'Baa, Baa Black Sheep' (maybe a sideways reference to M. John
Harrison's *New Worlds* (#184) story 'Baa Baa Blocksheep'). Used as part of the
incidental soundtrack for the *Made In Sheffield* DVD (2005), the title is part
of a homage theme that also includes the 1972 Roxy Music track '2HB', which
dedicates Humphrey Bogart, and David Bowie's largely instrumental *Heroes*
track 'V-2 Schneider' which acknowledged Kraftwerk's Florian Schneider.

'Blank Clocks' by **The Future** (Ware, Marsh, Newton) (3:20)

A track constructed from a set of lyrics seemingly assembled by a random
shuffling of words, in a mathematical permutation of phrases. After ambient
background sounds, there's a brief spoken introduction: 'I stand alone on
Westminster Bridge, amid acoustic distortion. I turn towards Big Ben; there is
no time...'. Why the London location? Maybe it's intended to be more universal
than a corresponding Sheffield landscape, and the chimes of Big Ben have
been associated with a BBC radio call sign signifying the passage of time since
the iconic bongs of the World War II years. Then, Martyn, Ian and Adi take
turns to recite the cut-up 'Your face, the clock, my mind', which is rearranged
into 'My time, blank face, your clock' and so on, until all combination variants
have been exhausted. As an exercise in games of artistic chance, this is a unique
experiment. The oscillating background synths are almost incidental.

'Cairo' by **The Future** (Ware, Marsh, Newton) (3:08)

The Future recorded this demo in mid-1977 at Studio Electrophonique.
Desert winds blow, or at least a synth facsimile of desert winds, with vaguely
Arabic-sounding lines resembling something that might've been contrived by

the BBC Radiophonic Workshop. There is a clear and precisely-enunciated poem tacked onto the final moments of the track, with words by J. G. Ballard – 'This Venus of the dunes, virgin of the time slopes/Rose above into the meridian sky/Diffused upon its crests, into the wind' – edited from the 'The Assumption Of The Sand-Dune' sequence in 'You: Coma: Marilyn Monroe' from Ballard's groundbreaking *The Atrocity Exhibition* (originally published in the *Ambit* arts magazine: number 27, spring 1966). Ballard's hard fetishistic urban imagery was a shared sub-cult fascination. Joy Division plundered the same book for the title of a track on their 1980 *Closer* album, while Sheffield's Comsat Angels took their group name from the Ballard mythos. Did J. G. Ballard ever comment on The Future's appropriation of his words? Martyn tells me, 'No'.

'Dominion Advertisment' by The Human League (Ware, Marsh, Oakey) (0:25)

A briefly spoken infotainment spoof advertisement, with Philip doing the sales pitch for a new non-habit-forming drug for use when 'the pressures of modern life can bring you down', with the percolating electro sounds tacked on as an afterthought. Humour is the intention; the pharmaceutical industry simply offers the wheels. Various takes were included on what's called *The Taverner Tape*: a set of demos recorded in 1979 and distributed free by Fast Product in return for sending in a blank cassette. And Dominion will recur as 'The narcotic that forges their union', in 'Circus of Death'. Whatever indulgences Martyn, Ian and Philip may or may not have been imbibing at the time, is another issue entirely.

'Dada Dada Duchamp Vortex' by The Future (Ware, Marsh, Newton) (5:49)

There's an argument that every art movement that erupted throughout the 20th century – from abstract expressionism to conceptual art and pop art, has its origins in the incendiary Dada explosion. Marcel Duchamp (28 July 1887-2 October 1968) was one of its prime architects. He inked a moustache onto the *Mona Lisa*. He autographed a urinal 'R Mutt' and submitted it as found art, in the same way that musique concrète would sample and reconfigure natural sounds into new shapes. Whether the moody swirls of this instrumental were always intended to reference the art dialogue and arsenal of techniques offered by Duchamp and his Dada co-conspirators or whether it was simply an appropriate title added later is something known only to Martyn, Ian and Adi. There's no drum track; it relies purely on intertwining textures to create a strange but serene effect that some might regard as *ambient*. And yet, it works. I asked Martyn if all three members were interacting in their enthusiasm for J. G. Ballard and Marcel Duchamp, or was that input primarily from Adi? Martyn said, 'All'. Philip concurs: 'Everyone would talk about politics, see arty films and read things by William Burroughs'.

'Daz' by **The Future** (Ware, Marsh, Newton) (3:40)

Daz was a heavily TV-advertised brand of laundry detergent. New! Improved! Boils Whitest Of All! Which probably has little to do with this track, except in the loosest Andy-Warhol-consumerist-satire sense. Interjected with the occasional deadpan and heavily-Echoplexed pronunciation of the song title, it consists of little more than sharp electronic noises processed with short, receding echoes.

'Future Religion' by **The Future** (Ware, Marsh, Newton) (3:44)

Bells. Drones. What will be the shape of future religions? Tinkling and clanging over the neural structure of a minimal pulse, riddled with machine auto-spirituality, an artificial intelligence on the brink of self-awareness?; Michael Moorcock's *Behold The Man*, in which a time traveller becomes Jesus; the robotic pope of Robert Silverberg's 'Good News From The Vatican'; all of this, none, the left, right or the ambidextrous. This is an immaculately-conceived instrumental with playful doom overtones, too nervy and dissonant to be considered a meditative sanctuary.

'Disco Disaster' by **The Human League** (Ware, Marsh, Oakey) (5:06)

There had been a 'Disco Inferno', 'Disco Nights' and even 'D.I.S.C.O.'. Now, with tongues only partially in collective cheeks, The Human League strike stylish dance moves here, programmed for our listening pleasure, an innovative foray fusing electronics with dance rhythms. 'Running with the endless beat/Looking at the teenage heat', with just a hint of impending violence as they rhyme 'future light' with 'senseless fight'. It's a blueprint for the bigger and better things to come, a rehearsal for throwing shapes at the Crazy Daisy discothèque at the corner of Sheffield's York Street and High Street. And why not? – they were young men with testosterone-driven appetites and the stirrings of strange chromosomal whims, and dance is a seductive strategy into new energies.

'Interface' by **The Human League** (Ware, Marsh, Oakey) (2:59)

A demo that opens with a slow bleeping sequence that rapidly accelerates into a sandfire-storm of busy swirls and dancing rhythms that glide and clide into and over one another in a quite seamless way, with an ascending chord progression that might suggest the alien call-sign from the 1977 Steven Spielberg movie *Close Encounters Of The Third Kind*, before it decelerates into the close. It's not a million miles from what Faust had been doing or what Jean-Michel Jarre would be doing for hugely lucrative returns in a few year's time.

'The Circus Of Dr Lao' by **Philip Oakey** (Oakey) (3:58)

Although the title is lifted directly from the 1935 fantasy novel by Charles G. Finney, it's likely that the nudge came from the 1964 George Pal movie adaptation *Seven Faces Of Dr Lao*, in which the travelling Chinese showman's mythological exhibits are cleverly stop-motion animated. There are fast shuffling ripples, doomy crashes, whistles and spooky quaverings over a walking electro bass line, interrupted by Philip's punning telephone voice: 'Hello, Doctor What? Sorry, Doctor Who... Hello, Doctor Lao, Hello?'. It can only be a coincidence that David Bowie's experimental 1977 album was called *Low*.

'Reach Out (I'll Be There)' by The Human League (Holland, Dozier, Holland) (3:55)

Northern soul exerted a subliminal effect, one not frequently acknowledged. Marc Almond was listening to Gloria Jones' 'Tainted Love' and keeping it on the back-burner, ready for use by synth-pop duo Soft Cell, while the earliest incarnation of The Human League messed around with the Four Tops' signature Motown number-1 hit, translating its distinctive soulful sweeps into a crude electro instrumental. In most respects, it's a throwaway dabble into the shallows of dance, but it indicates previously unsuspected inputs into the group's genetic structure.

'New Pink Floyd' by The Human League (Ware, Marsh, Oakey) (2:14)

So, what's wrong with the old Pink Floyd? From their earliest Syd Barrett days, they were open to weird hallucinogenic electronic experiments, and although they became the target of punk derision, there's much that's uniquely innovative in the Floyd's black vinyl grooves. That being said, this discordant 142-bpm instrumental has no real Floydian dynamics to it. There's little in the way of conventional melody either. It's a harsh work-in-progress demo that prefers metallic sounds, betraying more than a passing resemblance to a *Doctor Who* soundtrack. It ignores the rules, to see only the possibilities: a saucerful of secrets.

'Once Upon A Time In The West' by The Human League (Ennio Morricone) (1:53)

Italian composer Ennio Morricone was one of the less celebrated heroes of the era, with his 1966 *The Good, The Bad And The Ugly* in particular being quoted, sampled and referenced across a countless number of records. He also scored the iconic theme for this 1968 Sergio Leone spaghetti western starring Claudia Cardinale and Henry Fonda. Announced at the opening as 'Funeral March: Mix One', The Human League invest the brief ritual with a stately, dignified pacing appropriate to Morricone's elegiac orchestral arrangement.

'Overkill Disaster Crash (v.1)' by The Human League (Ware, Marsh, Oakey) (2:02)

Crash was not only the title of The Human League's fifth studio album but was also a fetishist J.G. Ballard novel. This discordant jangle falls vaguely into a three-section triptych corresponding to the charged three-keyword title. The first 28 seconds are a dazzling barrage of bleeps and seemingly random sonic stabs impersonating the raster of radio-static, with a vague submerged voice talking deep in the mix. The voice belongs to chess champion Garry Kasparov, who just happened to be on TV in the background. When Cabaret Voltaire used a similar technique on their April-1981 'Sluggin' For Jesus' track on the 'Three Crépuscule Tracks' 12" EP, the voice of televangelist Dr. Gene Scott was purposefully selected and sampled, but here, it was simply happy happenstance. For the next phase, there's a solo voice – sampled from John Carpenter's *Dark Star* (1974) – that says, 'Hi guys, glad we got your message. You'll be interested to hear it was broadcast live all over Earth, prime time' (Another sample from the same media sci-fi source would soon close the single version of 'Circus Of Death'). Finally, at the 42-second point, the third section hits a fast chugging locomotive breath that skips relentlessly through to the close. Whatever it means, there are ideas aplenty crammed into the track's compressed time-space. Recorded in a number of forms, the seed of the *Reproduction* track 'Introducing', lies within.

'Year Of The Jet Packs' by The Human League (Ware, Marsh, Oakey) (5:26)

In the quirky line-illustrations of 1950s pulp sci-fi magazines, all the future projections foresaw robots, tinfoil suits, a diet of coloured pills and jet packs. 'Lifted straight from Buck Rogers', who uses a jet pack. Styled for 21st-century living, the fact that jet packs as they are imagined here have yet to happen has become a regular focus of jokey ironic disillusionment.

With a faux finger-clicking introduction vaguely reminiscent of the 1965 Buddy Greco/Morgan James song 'Sweet Pussycat' – or the *West Side Story* 'Jet Song' – this catchy instrumental choreography is based around fast zippy synth figures that twirl and pirouette, repetitively orbiting and re-entering the signature phrase. Infinitely extendable, having longer edits up to 7:40 in length, this was the first track to be played live on Monday 12 June 1978 as part of The Human League's debut live set at Wham Bar (Bar Two) at Psalter Lane Art College. There is now a blue plaque on the wall to commemorate the event.

'Pulse Lovers' by The Future (Ware, Marsh, Newton) (4:02)

A bass pulse, a whipcrack synth and a twinkling motif spiral that burbles in and around itself pleasantly. At the 1:45 point, Martyn and Ian's voices intone 'Pulse, pulse'. Then at 2:01, Adi recites the brief low poem/lyric, 'Their pulse is stronger, pulse bodies feel fear', after which the 'Pulse' repetition goes on ad infinitum. Composer Igor Stravinsky said, 'There is music wherever there is rhythm, as there is life wherever there beats a pulse'. Pulse is the essential rhythm of the human organism. Pulse is the essential rhythm of the cosmos. Pulse is the rhythm of dance.

'King Of Kings' by The Human League (Miklós Rózsa) 1:56

There's a long sequence of white-noise audio static. They liked it. It liked them. It's followed by stately scene-setting, vaguely alluding to the grand theme of Nicholas Ray's 1961 biblical movie epic from MGM – *King of Kings* – the one with an uncredited Ray Bradbury as one of the scriptwriters adapting stories from the four Christian gospels. 'Respect to Miss Piggy', says Philip, apropos of nothing in particular. Then there's bantering studio dialogue – 'OK?'. 'Now?'. 'Yes'. – and a series of shrieks. Laughter. 'Do you want this… I mean, really loud?'. 'Completely. Is this switched on?'. A shriek. 'Better?'. And laughter into the fade. What this means is anyone's guess, except that it supplies circumstantial evidence that The Future tracks featuring Adi tended to be arty, more menacing and intense. Whereas Future sessions featuring Philip tended to be more lighthearted and fun.

'The Last Man On Earth' by The Human League (Ware, Marsh, Oakey) (10:01)

Quivering and twittering in dream streams of swishing layered sound, the hypnotic repetitions are contoured with minor textual variations into a web of introspective contemplation. Be-Bop Deluxe's Bill Nelson was experimenting with similar electronic landscapes – maybe intended to suggest the vast emptiness and yearning loneliness of 'The Last Man On Earth', or maybe not. Unlike the edit on the 'Dance Like A Star' EP, the album version extends out to the full ten minutes.

The final hacksploitation sequence on 'Circus Of Death' is 'a shortwave radio message from the last man on Earth.' As cyberpunk author William Gibson claimed, 'The Future is already here – it's just not very evenly distributed'.

Contemporary Singles

'Being Boiled' (Marsh, Ware, Oakey) (3:48) b/w 'Circus Of Death' (Marsh, Ware, Oakey) (4:47) by The Human League

Personnel:
Philip Oakey: vocals
Ian Craig Marsh, Martyn Ware: synthesizer
Producers: The Human League, at Devonshire Lane Studios, Sheffield
Label: Fast Product FAST 4
Release date: 30 June 1978

'Okay, ready! Let's do it!'. A stunning debut. One of the most accomplished first vinyl incarnations in the history of UK pop; an immaculate burn, punched out by the snarling bite of precise analogue synths, the whine of insects, frozen worms of sound, bleeping and pinging in soulless cybernetic precision. The exact interplay of programmed bass and fizzing, popping futuristic warp and weft, legato, staccato, a tempo and decrescendo form a quantum leap of angry wasps away from anything else in the relativistic continuum. Are the dark menacing info-vandalistic use of the keywords' slice', 'torture', 'slaughter' and 'boiled alive' really a condemnation of the silkworm industry? Supposedly so. There's no excuse for thoughtless slaying! Buddha's watching, Buddha's waiting.

The B-side is an even stranger collage of sequences, written in just seven minutes, according to Martyn. It's introduced by Philip's opening line, 'The true story of a circus we met,' with jet-stream sounds linking into Commissioner Steve McGarrett's arrival at Heathrow airport by Trident from Hawaii. *Hawaii Five-O* with Jack Lord as McGarrett (the central former-Navy-SEAL character) was a popular police procedural TV show from 1968 to 1980, rebooted in 2010 with Alex O'Loughlin taking the role.

The track's next *sequence* – taken from *The Guardian* (19 March 1962) – concerns dominion: 'The fictitious drug administered by the ringmaster/clown to subjugate those who fall prey to his powers'. Philip's voice rises to previously unexpected highs, and drops into recitation until the single closes with another sample from the *Dark Star* movie: which is edited out of subsequent versions. The question: 'Do you think we'll ever find any real intelligent life out there?'. And the answer: 'Who cares?'. J. G. Ballard lists *Dark Star* as one of his ten favourite sci-fi movies in *Interzone* number 27.

Recorded in Sheffield's Devonshire Lane studio in January 1978 – for just £2.50! – the trio began hawking the three-track demo ('Being Boiled', 'Toyota City' and 'Circus Of Death') around various UK indie labels, to largely negative response, until it eventually attracted the attention of Bob Last of the Edinburgh-based Fast Product Records. A former Rezillos roadie, Bob signed The Human League and became their manager. On its initial release, the soft mud-orange postmodern retro but futuristic cover showed a trendy couple dancing, superimposed over a New York skyline with its skyscraper peaks notated as Letraset musical figures. Guest singles reviewer John Lydon dismissed the band as 'trendy hippies'. It was too strangely off-the-map to be easily pigeonholed, and failed to register with the masses, despite being nominated as *NME* Single Of The Week and allegedly sold only 2,000 copies. Although, this single would return: with a vengeance!

To *Melody Maker* journalist Steve Sutherland, the track bubbles with promise and the thrill of expectation – an 'art-lab eruption when thinking people, students, still thought pop was something worth bothering with, worth debating, worth infiltrating. Some of us still feel that way'. (*Melody Maker*, 29 October 1988).

On 25 July 1978, The Human League played a gig at Sheffield's The Limit club, with Clock DVA supporting in their live debut – Roger Quail noting that Ian Craig Marsh 'wearing headphones the size of oven gloves, stands in front of a small telephone switchboard of snaking wiring, prodding the beats along, dutifully keeping an eye on the two Revox tape machines churning out the backing tracks'. In September of that same year, The Human League topped Monday's bill as part of The Limit's Band Festival, supported by a unit that appeared on the poster as Defleppard.

Extended Play - Cabaret Voltaire EP (1978)

Personnel:
Richard H Kirk: guitar, vocals
Stephen Mallinder: bass, vocals
Chris Watson: keyboards, vocals, tape operation
Cabaret Voltaire: production and sleeve design
Label: Rough Trade RT003
Release date: November 1978

The Cabs were over in another part of Sheffield. 'People were genuinely interested in what everybody else was doing creatively. That is, in essence, distilled, what a scene is', recalled Martyn Ware. 'And Cabaret Voltaire were very generous people in terms of their time and their encouragement to other people; they encouraged creativity in everybody around them'.

'We all liked the Cabs', agreed Philip Oakey. 'They were really the great band of the decade for Sheffield. Although, we weren't like them'. Instead, The Cabs were taking an oblique perception and applying it to the same vital impulse, utilising repetitions and dissonance to build a dislocated trance state.

Cabaret Voltaire had consciously adopted their name from the anarchic Dada club – founded by Hugo Ball in the neutral Zürich island of peace within the continent-wide atrocity of The Great War – in February 1916, with misfit art-subversive collaborators Tristan Tzara, Jeap Arp, Richard Huelsenbeck, and later, Marcel 'Dada' Duchamp. The band's chosen name was a deliberate exercise of informed intention. 'Cabaret Voltaire were always much more subversive than anybody else', claimed Chris Watson. 'We weren't interested in any sort of cult of personality. Who we were didn't really matter. It's what we did and what we produced ... we didn't form a band to make music. What we did through Cabaret Voltaire was simply an outlet for what we were all interested in doing ... it fulfilled my ambition of making music without musical instruments'.

Recorded at Sheffield's Western Works with the original lineup of Chris, Richard H. Kirk and Stephen Mallinder, this EP issued through the indie Rough Trade label is made up of four tracks – the Velvet Underground cover 'Here She Comes Now' (4:30), reinterpreted and translated way beyond Lou Reed's nightmare recognition; three original constructions, including the eerie, pulsing electronic 'Do The Mussolini (Headkick)' (3:03) with submerged dubwise voices fading in and out; 'Talkover' (3:22) and 'The Set Up' (3:03). The inclusion of Velvet Underground is a useful indicator. Channelled through an Andy Warhol art project, the Velvets inflicted pure noise and dissonance, albeit within a vague rock-'n'-roll sensibility. Flirtations with extremism were not restricted to the ring modulators or Bode Frequency Shifters of classicist electro-experimentalists John Cage or Karlheinz Stockhausen. In the Thomas Mann novel *Doctor Faustus* (1947), a Schoenbergian composer called Adrian Leverkühn liberates dissonance in a symphony called 'Apocalypsis', and in so doing, he sabotages cosmic order. Experimentation was contagious.

Cabaret Voltaire used slides and films in ways that The Human League would. 'I'm a child of the TV generation', admitted Richard H. Kirk. Oakey told him, 'It made your shows an event for two or three years: I never missed one ... you're the only band we can't accuse of stealing our idea of the slides, because we stole it off you'. (From a cross-band dialogue in *Sounds*, 10 August 1985).

There are teasing suggestions that the early Human League recorded at the Cab's Western Works studio, although nothing survives, and the rumour – though intriguing – is probably apocryphal. After all, The Human League already had their own Devonshire Lane studio, located within strolling distance of Devonshire Green.

The *Cabaret Voltaire* EP was followed by the perfect freakbeat garage-psychedelic single 'Nag Nag Nag' b/w 'Is That Me (Finding Someone At The Door Again?)' (Rough Trade RT018, June 1979), which rivalled 'Being Boiled' as the project with the strongest chart potential to emerge from Sheffield's burgeoning electro subculture.

Reproduction (1979) – The Human League

Personnel:
Philip Oakey, Ian Craig Marsh, Martyn Ware: vocals, synthesizer
Philip Adrian Wright: slides and films
Producers: The Human League, Colin Thurston
Recorded 4-21 July 1979 at Workshop Studio, Love Street, Sheffield; mixed and overdubbed at London's Red Bus studio, with engineers Gordon Milne and Richard Lengyel
Label: UK: Virgin V2133, USA: Virgin 7-90881-1 (1988)
Release date: October 1979
Running time: 43:33
Chart position: UK: 27

As early as the 23 August 1979 issue of *Smash Hits,* Martyn Ware had contributed a 'Sheffield Rising' feature 'traveloguing' the innovative steel-city music scene, taking advantage of the opportunity to describe how 'The Human League rebel against the convention that electronic groups have to translate the modern world as a dull, depressing and alienating place. They use a sly, tongue-in-cheek approach that confuses many less flexible people'. They were already widely known to a select few. Although reaction from those less-flexible people was muted, Human League played Tiffany's in Coventry (24 October 1978) as third on the bill to a headlining Siouxsie and the Banshees and Spizz Oil: all for just £1.80. They toured Europe with Iggy Pop (12 dates opening 7 April at London's Rainbow Theatre, taking in Brussels (17 May), Amsterdam (18 May), Munich (22 May), Berlin (24 May) through to Barcelona (31 May). Then the band went one better: after negotiating with Fast Product, Virgin signed them.

Despite the label now being seen not only as ubiquitous but mainstream, Virgin had come from both humble and daring origins. Richard Branson and Nik Powell started out with a small Notting Hill Gate specialist record-and-tape shop. They took a chance issuing Mike Oldfield's *Tubular Bells* when no major label would touch such risky eccentricity and were rewarded with massive success, accelerated by the music's incidental use in the 1973 movie *The Exorcist*. Virgin following it with German electronica from Tangerine Dream and Faust's *The Faust Tapes* – released in a special 49p edition that gave the previously unmarketable Faust an accessible breakthrough – positioned the label as an attractive proposition. That Virgin took the Sex Pistols provocation on board was further vindication.

The 12" Human League vinyl art is a striking knee-downward view of three smart dancers: one girl in stylish high heels, another in a floral minidress and radiating strappy shoes, and a guy in sensible slip-ons – except they're dancing on a cracking glass surface beneath which are an assortment of naked babies – visibly of both genders – crying and squirming. The reverse art is a single close-up baby face, with the song titles listed bottom-right across its cheek. What this represents is open to interpretation. To *Vox* magazine, 'You see the message, don't you?: First we were babies, then we become adults. And yet, once we *were* babies: we who are now adults. This whole baby/adult thing makes you think'. Maybe it's simply the role of dance as a courting ritual in the cycle of sexual reproduction or just an eye-grabber in itself. The art is less striking when it's shrunk down to CD size. Though by way of compensation, the foldout insert includes four distorted centre-spread panel photos – one of each group member, plus a smaller moody black-outlined lineup photo at the foot of the insert.

As Philip remembers, 'We did the whole thing in two weeks, recorded and mixed, and we took the weekend off as well!'. The original vinyl release of the album also included musique concrète-style vocal recordings – seemingly taken from radio or TV – inserted between some tracks. Of note, 'Knit one, purl one' can be heard on side one. These elements were not included in subsequent CD reissues.

Another quantum step forward was that Adrian Wright was now listed in the credits as 'film technician' or 'Director Of Visuals' – involved with planning the lighting, slideshows and all visual aspects accompanying The Human League's live performances. 'We've always designed our own singles and LP sleeves', Oakey adds. 'We used to take all our own publicity photos'. Going to a Human League gig meant also attending Adrian's Saturday morning movie show with slides of bubblegum cards, scans from *The Man From U.N.C.L.E* annuals, Dalek toys and the Batmobile. Adrian stands 'studiously attentive at his work station, ring binders of slides illuminated by an Anglepoise lamp, cueing and triggering the imagery which continues to mesmerise the audience'. But Roger Quail is also 'fascinated by the juxtaposition of futuristic-sounding music, and visuals which evoke the recent past'.

In a *Smash Hits* comic strip telling the Human League story, 'Adrian signed up, and soon the trendy papers became impressed'.

In another continuum, Jefferson Airplane had also used movies as an integral part of their Haight-Ashbury light show. But these slideshows really made The Human League stand out amongst other synth bands: there was nothing quite like it around at the time. Soon, all the electro bands were doing it, of course, and on a much grander scale. But it really started with Adrian's little bunch of slide projectors and screens.

The robust self-sustaining all-singing/all-playing/all-writing beat-group model had in itself been a resilient evolutionary miniaturization on the previous unwieldy and expensive big bands that went before. Since the very dawn of rock 'n' roll – with The Crickets, through The Shadows and The Beatles – the conventional lineup showed the drum kit on the riser to the rear, lead and bass guitars to left and right, and the vocalist out front. The vocalist might also play guitar. There might be a rhythm guitarist or keyboard player, or even a saxophone. Yet that basic instrumentation remained constant. Even when the Sex Pistols supposedly tore up the rule book and declared year zero, they did it with the same drums/lead guitar/bass/vocalist lineup. That The Human League were two synths and a singer was in itself sweeping the old into the dumper of history and ushering in the shock of the new. That Adrian Wright was listed essentially as a non-playing member was a further step. Pop bands simply didn't look like that. This in itself was a step over the event horizon. Philip recalls: 'Martyn and Ian weren't going to learn guitars. So we did it with synths. Because it was approached quite intellectually. Really, by Martyn and Ian. And I took the idea on. They were quite dogmatic about it for a while. Especially Ian, actually. Ian's always got theories going. It was a selling point. We don't use guitars or drums'. It was the miniaturisation that King Crimson guitarist Robert Fripp defined as operating as 'a small, independent, mobile and intelligent unit'. All systems were GO! Now was calling!

Reproduction's ten tracks placed them square on every scene-mongering trendy's music centre, and established The Human League at the epicentre of what later became known as synthcore as a blueprint for a plethora of plagiarists. And yet, Tubeway Army – with Gary Numan – hit number 1 in the UK for four weeks from 30 June 1979 with 'Are Friends Electric?', followed by a second number 1 for Numan solo on 22 September with 'Cars'. Numan was magnanimous enough to credit The Human League as a major source of inspiration, but even Human League vocalist Susan Ann Sulley admits, Gary Numan 'was the first time I heard an electro record that was also an archetypal pop song'. It looked as though Gary's album *The Pleasure Principle* was already opening up the electro sci-fi scenario. *Philip said ruefully:* 'We'd done really well on an indie label (Fast Product), and suddenly we signed to Virgin, and the first LP that everyone thought was going to be huge, only sold 11,000'. *Reproduction* reached number 27 on the album chart, until – following the success of *Dare* – it re-entered the chart, reaching number 51. The BPI eventually certified it gold in 1988.

Side One
'Almost Medieval' (Marsh, Ware, Oakey) (4:43)
There's a slow count-in, with vague weaving synths of some madrigal delicacy. The lyric slips in and out of time. It's a long and complex text resembling a short story or poem, from humour – 'There's no stagecoach speed limit' – to the macabre: 'Outside the office hangs the man on the gibbet'. The melody that conveys the tale is more than a little repetitive, although that accumulating repetition is used to build a certain momentum of intensity, with a scream to amplify the 'Falling off this rotting ladder' phrase. Much later, Martyn Ware commented, 'The opening track 'Almost Medieval' was meant to be a shock to the system. It was meant to sound punky, angular and aggressive. He (producer Colin Thurston) rinsed that all out – on the album, it was nicely produced but sounded a bit polite and made us sound like a fucking chamber orchestra! When the album was properly mastered in 2003, it sounded much, much better'. It was recorded using only a Roland System 100, a Korg 700s and a Roland Jupiter-4, while Ian played a Korg 770.

'Circus Of Death' (Marsh, Ware, Oakey) (3:55)

If *The Golden Hour Of The Future* dabbled in the conceptual insurrectionist anti-art of the early 20th century, this new recording of the song – included as part of the original 'Being Boiled' demo – advances into the mid-century pop-art stripped-collage technique of mixing and matching images from popular TV culture, with a catchy rhythm.

It's a high-octane flying visit through Todd Browning's freakish Cirque du Soleil – a cool in-flight romp through the menace doom-dream territory of fan fiction. On the principle that there's maybe an excess of ingredients here, the surfeit of ideas are edited down from the version issued as the 'Being Boiled' B-side. Philip's introduction is replaced by a more concise TV-continuity voice, merged into a cabin-crew announcer recording, while the closing movie clip is deleted. Tighter and more integrated, it works even better than before.

'The Path Of Least Resistance' (Marsh, Ware, Oakey) (3:33)

Lyrically, it's a refutation of taking the easy path in favour of self-belief. 'Comfort kills', indeed. Featured live on a BBC-TV programme called 'Mainstream' (6 November 1979) – with the clip subsequently replayed as part of the *Sounds Of The Seventies* retro-series – Philip closes his eyes in serious emphasis, glancing back to where Ian and Martyn operate keyboards in sound booths with revolving Revox spools, while Adrian triggers a series of slides of lightning, tornados, surfers, and the shiny pornography of military hardware. It was punched out by a hard programmed drum pulse. An earlier demo would later be salvaged onto disc three of the deluxe edition of *A Very British Synthesizer Group* and varies only slightly, while the version included on the 1989 CD edition has a variant opening, with the vocals channelled differently on the song's second half.

'Blind Youth' (Marsh, Ware, Oakey) (3:25)

The Human League recorded a studio session for the BBC Radio 1 John Peel show (8 August 1978) broadcast on 16 August. It was made up of four songs – 'Being Boiled', a strained 'You've Lost That Loving Feeling', a semi-spoken song called 'No Time' ('Surrounded by old imagery, his brain bypassed, the eternal moment laid bare, no time to heal, continuum continuum continuum'), which is an early version of 'The Word Before Last' (also sometimes listed as 'Again, The Eye Again'), and a raw 'Blind Youth'. The tracks later appeared as part of a bootleg album called *In Darkness* (1981, RTS003), which also featured unreleased material from the 1978 *Human League Cassette*. 'No Future, ' Phil says, quoting the Sex Pistols, before turning the nihilism neatly around with 'humanisation': the time of blind youth is due. We've had it easy; we should be grateful; high-rise living is not so bad. It has an anthemic rising tension, with marching effects punctuated by hard rhythms; a rallying call, with just a hint of J. G. Ballard.

'The Word Before Last' (Marsh, Ware, Oakey) (4:04)

'The tape was running', for this is a song evolved from the earlier demo 'No Time', with twanging, soaring synths, while Philip recites in a flat monotone, about 'this man I saw'. The demo would also be salvaged onto *A Very British Synthesizer Group*. For this album, there are more-clearly-defined synth lines. Reflections on a TV screen, 'Of course, of course, of course'. Philip's voice is more modulated, although the melody remains minimalist, carried more by the surrounding instrumentation, 'Continual pain continual pain' replacing the earlier 'continuum continuum'. In this incarnation, the track is topped-and-tailed with indistinct low-fi TV voices – first about being left-handed and finally about Mrs. Thatcher's disastrous first three months.

'Empire State Human' (Marsh, Ware, Oakey) (3:17)

Two ideas come to mind – a movie poster for *Attack Of The 50 Foot Woman* (1958), with her legs astride the freeway, stooping to pick up puny automobiles; and scrawny weakling Charles Atlas (30 October 1892-24 December 1972), who was the guy getting sand kicked in his face by ripped alpha-males, until in retaliation he devised the Dynamic Tension programme for bodybuilding, and made his fortune advertising with the slogan 'You Too Could Have A Body Like Mine'.

If 'Being Boiled' was the first shock indication of just how astounding Human League could be, 'Empire State Human' must register as the second – the immaculate fusion of a ludicrously surreal lyric (evidence of Philip's sarcastic and self-deprecating humour) balanced by an alchemical equation of synths and a catchy memorable chant, emphasised by traces of South Yorkshire in Philip's pronunciation during the talking insert. There are talkback voices from Ian and Martyn: 'and now I'm fourteen stories high', with an added qualifying 'at least'; the answering 'Fetch more water, fetch more sand/Biggest person in the land' as the lead voice urges 'Tall tall tall, I want to be tall tall tall/As big as a wall wall wall', driven on relentless machine percussion. It was subject to a one-pill-makes-you-larger Alice-in-Wonderland logic.

For Chris Westwood in *Record Mirror* (13 October 1979), the track was 'a product of Phil Oakey's halcyon height complex, and stretches matters to hilarious ends, tongues rigid in cheeks and all that'. It became the third Human League single, the only one to be lifted from *Reproduction*. To me, this still sounds like the future. One day, *all* pop will sound like this.

Side Two
'Morale... You've Lost That Loving Feeling' (Barry Mann, Cynthia Weil, Phil Spector) (9:30)

When Beatles manager Brian Epstein was on a December 1964 New York promotional trip, he happened to hear the newly-released Phil Spector production 'You've Lost That Lovin' Feelin', which he promptly whisked back to London, where he rushed Cilla Black into the studio to record an opportunistic cover in advance of the original's release. Cilla's version entered the chart first. But once the Righteous Brothers' wall-of-sound classic appeared on the black-and-silver London-American label, it promptly leapfrogged Cilla to snatch the number-1 position. There have been many subsequent recordings of the song: even Elvis Presley took a shot at it. But as if to emphasise their superiority, the 'Brothers' Bobby Hatfield and Bill Medley returned to the top ten in February 1969 and then again to number 3 in December 1990.

Philip Oakey's admittedly-limited vocal range and technique was ideal for 'Empire State Human', but it's strange that The Human League dared to suggest he was up to the task of taking on this definitive Phil Spector classic. Yet, as Adrian explained to *Soundmaker* magazine (11 December 1982), 'Martyn's idea was to do an accessible song to start the set from, and to give the audience a recognisable base so they could say 'I recognize that', and then hopefully they'd think the rest of the set was worth listening to'. So, with Martyn adding vocal support, they performed the song in a number of prominent promotional slots – including the 8 August 1978 John Peel session; on this *sweetener*, the principle sense being that they saw the song's familiarity as providing some kinds of potential conduit into the mainstream.

Treated as a medley, the 'Morale' sequence opens with reflective synths and verses about being an old man in a poor little room with a view of the corner, looking back with regret at how 'I never met anyone who used their knowledge to avoid those mistakes made again and again'. This dissolves into industrial clinks and clanks, with dense voice textures resembling those of György Ligeti's 'Atmosphères', before feeding into the doomy funereal tones and histrionic vocals of the song that Phil Spector wrote with the golden pop-songwriting duo of Barry Mann and wife Cynthia Weil – the duo who also wrote 'We Gotta Get Out Of This Place', The Crystals' 'Uptown' and 'I Just Can't Help Believing', a hit for both Elvis Presley and B.J. Thomas amongst others.

Cover versions – reformatting the classic pop of earlier times – have always been an aspect of new musics, yet this still seems like a misstep to me.

'Austerity/Girl One (Medley)' (Marsh, Ware, Oakey) (6:44)

This has a fast rhythm track and a strong melody line with a sharply-observed lyric: 'We don't choose who we love'; 'Malice is so human'. There are contrasting voices; the 'Austerity' sequence seeming to express an ageing man's baffled bewilderment with the waywardness of youth, with a seamless rise into 'Girl One', which articulates his daughter's point of view: her modern life is both as hectic and frazzled as it is exciting. The lines 'When the best of men take bribes/Isn't it the fool who doesn't?' sounds good enough to be a quote from somewhere else, but it isn't. Did Philip write the lyric for The Human League? 'That's a bit myth', Ian told me. Martyn conceded: 'He wrote perhaps half of them, perhaps not even that much, more like a third. People automatically think singers write lyrics, which isn't the case. Everybody wrote'.

There had already been a number of shots at reformatting the bare sterility of the 'Austerity' theme, including 'Depression Is A Fashion' and 'Treatment'. But this track must represent its most perfect consummation.

'Zero As A Limit' (Marsh, Ware, Oakey) (4:13)

A song about a motorist ramming into a pedestrian – 'the stranger crashing into you' – an image predicted directly from a deconstruction of the controversial movie of J. G. Ballard's *Crash* (1996), itself lifted from his 1973 novel. 'See the blood now overflowing'. Speed, motorway, freeway, overpass, the swirl of ruby taillights, orbital, asphalt, satellite, concrete struts and flyovers. Pulsing direction lights red-shifted through spectrums of terminal velocity. The shock sequenced crack-crack-crack punctuation. QED – the Latin 'quod erat demonstrandum': a legal term which translates as 'which was to be demonstrated'... as the accelerating sound intensifies, the momentum increases, and the impact climaxes into pure whiteness. There was a time when pop songs were catchy jingles about jukeboxes, soda pop at the teenage hop, holding hands at the drive-In movie show, twisting, and a sweet 16's first kiss; doobie-doowah. To close the album, this track is nothing like that.

A short Adrian Wright film called 'Zero As A Limit' was screened during Human League concerts through late 1979.

Bonus tracks added for the 1989 CD (Increased running time: 74:38)

'Introducing' (Marsh, Ware, Oakey) (3:19)

Sirens, machine-gun fire, separating out, mapped by a throbbing, pulsing bass synth. War breaks out between your ears, in panic, chaos and confusion. A car chase that hurtles from right channel to left channel, with treated voices and a scream, 'what's going on?'

This is the original B-side of the 'Empire State Human' single, although a remaster of the vinyl recording – not the stereo master tape (which had somehow gone missing) – was used for the CD. A reminder – as if we need reminding – that The Human League flirt with the outer limits of the avant-garde.

The Dignity Of Labour EP – The Human League (1979)

Personnel:
Philip Oakey: vocals
Martyn Ware, Ian Craig Marsh: synthesizer
Adrian Wright: director of visuals
Producers: The Human League, at Devonshire Studios, Sheffield, January 1978
Chart position: UK: -
Four tracks that were issued as a June 1979 instrumental 12" EP (Fast Product Fast 10, VF.1)

'The Dignity Of Labour (Part 1)' (Marsh, Ware, Oakey) (4:21)

The sleeve photo shows cosmonaut Yuri Gagarin – the first human being to boldly go into space – marching across Red Square as part of his triumphal post-orbit tour. Martyn Ware recalls: 'Conceptually, after we signed to Virgin Records, we wanted to stamp our authority, because we were concerned about losing our independent status. So the first thing we did after 'Being Boiled' on Fast Product, was *The Dignity Of Labour* – a completely instrumental twelve-inch EP – to show our fans that we had not abandoned our principles'. And the EP fully embodies that intention, although Peter Nash pronounces it as 'swathed in arty pretence and foppery'.

The first track is from *The Tavener Tape*. There are busy machine sequence patterns, chip-chip hewing noises, and repetitions that drone and spiral in and around the main melodic thrust. There is no concession to commercialism. 'If you care about money, you don't think in a creative way, you think in a financial way, which doesn't work', Philip explained. A comment on the original demo cassette refers to the three-part story arc of Yuri Gagarin's Soviet Vostok One capsule: 'The first part has the miners underground in Russia, digging up the coal to make the steel'; 'The second part shows gantries being made from the steel, for Yuri Gagarin's spaceship', and 'The third part is an instrumental tribute to Yuri Gagarin'. Yet, on the flexi, Philip clearly states 'It's not about facts, it's not about Yuri Gagarin', before going on to relate the true story of Gagarin's parachute return to Earth when he was greeted by a farmer who invited him in for a cup of tea! Whatever, the amiable soft-featured space adventurer was a cult hero for many. *Bring Me The Head Of Yuri Gagarin* is a 1985 Hawkwind album recorded live at the Empire Pool on 27 May 1973.

'The Dignity Of Labour (Part 2)' (Marsh, Ware, Oakey) (2:46)

'Part 2' uses the extreme chill of crystalline timbres, the clinking of celestial dreams, mechanical and dissonant, strangely inhuman, yet still the cling-clang of a working methodology that reminds a lot of what fellow Sheffield experimentalists Cabaret Voltaire were doing in their early years. If 'Part 1' is the EP's peak – its stark, foreboding Maschine musik recalling the innovations of German practitioners such as Conrad 'Conny' Schnitzler of Kluster, and Eckhard Seesselberg (Seeßelberg of *Synthetik 1* (1974)) – 'Part 2' is remote and detached from gravity, with figures ascending and accelerating towards a mid-point heliopause, after which it continues.

'The Dignity Of Labour (Part 3)' (Marsh, Ware, Oakey) (3:49)
Fast Kraftwerkian shapes enter deep teutonic territory with spacial interjections, showing an alternate side of the band's instrumental electronics; heavily influenced by the German cosmic school of Tangerine Dream and Klaus Schulze. This separates out into spooky, keening, tidal tsunamis of almost human vocal tones, a dizzying whirl of high-pitched theremin-style synth, and vibrant arpeggios reminiscent of Harald Grosskopf's and Tangerine-Dream-member Peter Baumann's work, diving into the close.

'The Dignity Of Labour (Part 4)' (Marsh, Ware, Oakey) (3:49)
A slow arc of descent with doomy undertones threaded by quivering synth lines picking their way through the shimmering eerie notes of BBC Radiophonic Workshop-like atmospheres. A few bars poke their backbones above the white smother and hum of the deeper drone – a storm of images that wrench across the inside of your head from ear to ear, evolving into a pulsing theme a million light-years away from anything The Human League would be doing on 1981's *Dare* or even 1980's *Travelogue*.

Other Contemporary Releases
'Flexi-Disc' (Marsh, Ware, Oakey) (4:11)
A tongue-in-cheek studio recording of a meta-conversation between their manager Bob Last and the band members about their plans to include a flexi disc with the EP, and what to include on it. It provides a reality-TV-like glimpse into the internal politics operating within the group. 'We want to get this record out', complains Philip. 'It's never gonna get out at this rate, what with Bob wanting this on and that on'. 'Don't blame me', says Bob defensively. Then later, when discussing the proposed duration of the flexi, he tells Philip, 'You're being really silly on that. You're just trying to find things to make things difficult on that score'. Talking through the logistics of the flexi, 'You could put '+ Commentary' on the sleeve somewhere', suggests Bob – 'I really like the idea actually', and 'People could throw it away'.

That the participants are happy to put this amiable banter 'on record', says something about the group's democratic lack of pretence. To make a closing statement, Philip says, 'What we've got in this is not simple, like everything else, and it's not even complex, it's multiplex!'. (The concept of simplex/complex/multiplex is from the Samuel R. Delany novel *Empire Star*). Philip continues, 'It's about the individual as opposed to the group, and it's about human frailty: no matter how big you are, you're gonna be dead pretty soon'.

'Good', says Bob, evidently happy with the results. This was then issued as a free flexi disc included in the *The Dignity Of Labour* package.

'Being Boiled (Fast version)' (Marsh, Ware, Oakey) (3:54)
The A-side of the single released before they'd signed to Virgin. It becomes the 'Fast version' because it was released on the Fast Product label. Recorded in demo form even before Philip had officially joined, the basic track was done in mono on a domestic tape recorder in an empty Sheffield factory, at a cost of just £2.50. It was Philip's lyric that clinched his acceptance as the replacement for Adi Newton. The sleeve is tagged 'Electronically yours...'.

'Circus Of Death (Fast version)' (Marsh, Ware, Oakey) (4:38)
The B-side of 'Being Boiled', but a shorter edit than the original single version, due to the deletion of the spoken voice at the end of the song. Again, the 'Fast' refers not to the tempo but the label it was issued on.

'I Don't Depend On You' (Marsh, Ware, Oakey) **(4:31) b/w** 'Cruel' (Marsh, Ware, Oakey) (4:41) **by The Men**
Personnel:
Philip Oakey: vocals
Martyn Ware, Ian Craig Marsh: synthesizer
Adrian Wright: director of visuals
Mystery Girls: backing vocals
Produced and engineered by Colin Thurston and The Men
Label: Virgin Records VS269
Release date: February 1979
Chart position: UK: –

Funk bass lines, a flooshing flux capacitor of synths, with chanted backing vocals by the Mystery Girls (Katie Kissoon and Lisa Strike), to provide a temporal flash-forward to the *Dare* format. Technically The Human League's first release under the new Virgin contract, it was produced by Colin Thurston. Yet the blatant commercial dance floor slant determined that they issued the single under the convenient guise of The Men. Allegedly, there was pressure from Virgin to come up with more-marketable product, and this was the compromise they contrived. Although wary of their 'credibility', Martin had already confessed, 'We were concerned about losing our independent status', because yes, it's pop and catchy in ways that nothing on *Reproduction* comes close to. But *dance* can simply be another kind of groove, with its own levels of cool.

The B-side is a doctored instrumental mix of the song, with a thumping drum track and strong ribs of bass, while the synths sigh and flicker like shafts of reflected light from a mirror ball across the disco dance floor. Katie and Lisa repeat the 'It's cruel but it's true/I don't depend on you' refrain into the final moments. Meanwhile, The Human League's March tour with Siouxsie and the Banshees climaxed with a charity show for MENCAP (at the Rainbow, 7 April 1979), the profits whittled away by fire damage perpetrated by a moronic section of the audience. B.E.F. later produced a version of 'I Don't Depend On You' as part of their 1981 Hot Gossip project, while Katie Kissoon and Lisa Strike went on to work with Pink Floyd.

'Empire State Human' (Marsh, Ware, Oakey) (3:10) (Producer: Colin Thurston) b/w 'Introducing' (Marsh, Ware, Oakey) (3:13) (Producers: Marsh, Ware, Oakey) (Dutch B-side was 'You've Lost That Loving Feeling')

Label: Virgin VS 294
Release date: 12 October 1979
Chart position: UK: 62

Taste the energy that hits with the power of a ton of assorted lightning rods.

1979 was a peak year for the 45-rpm single format. Introduced by RCA Victor records in 1949, it gradually replaced the 78-rpm shellac through the 1950s, was accelerated by the 1960s beat boom, and finally hit 79,000,000 across-the-counter sales by the late-1970s when affluence meant kids could buy them, play them, and then use them as a frisbee. *Top Of The Pops* was the leading promotional tool, watched by 19,000,000 potential record buyers. The single was an access point to fame and fortune.

But 'Empire State Human' was not destined to be a success. On its initial release, it totally failed to register on the chart. Reissued in June 1980 (VS 351), it finally achieved a peak of 62, with the added incentive of a bonus single 'Only After Dark' b/w 'Toyota City' (produced by The Human League with Richard Manwaring) gifted with the first 15,000 copies. There was also a 12" edition of 'Empire State Human' b/w 'Introducing' (VS35112). Adrian admits, 'It really downhearted us, we just couldn't fathom it out, 'Cause Gary Numan was having all these hits, and we had started before him, and there we were trying to work out what we were doing wrong'. The B-side 'Introducing' is an instrumental produced by The Human League, and though Oakey sings on the original recording, his vocals were not used on the released version.

Human League live performances still consisted of dour slim pale young men crouched over electric keyboards, with song titles flashed up on the on-screen slides, rather than being announced. Yet, word was percolating. At a gig at the Nashville pub in West Kensington, David Bowie was glimpsed in the audience. He came backstage after the gig, effusive with compliments about their set. Adrian recalled how during their conversation, Bowie confided that at a certain point in his career, he'd vowed never to play support to other acts, and he advised The Human League to do the same. He said playing as a solo name – even to smaller audiences – was more healthy for a band's identity and long-term growth than calculating on jumping someone else's bandwagon, which was problematic.

Reproduction was selling below expectations. Keen to gain maximum exposure for their charges, Virgin were negotiating a support spot for Human League on a Talking Heads tour! Talking Heads were art rock, weren't they? There would be likely audience crossover points, wouldn't there? There was talk that The Human League sat around discussing ideas, and contrived a conceptual set involving four screens simultaneously showing a dazzling sequence of Adrian's slides, accompanied only by prerecorded tapes, while the band themselves would be sitting in the audience as spectators! Talking Heads seemed initially agreeable but later changed their minds, and the tour deal fell through. Perhaps the story is apocryphal because it was repeatedly told in subsequent interviews. Although, a later Human League tour opened immaculately with 'Being Boiled', played over an empty stage, with only screens and instruments.

The 1980s
Early Compilation Albums
1980: The First Fifteen Minutes (Compilation EP) (1979)
Neutron Records NT003

Chris Westwood had reviewed electronic trio Vice Versa debuting unpaid as support for Wire at Doncaster's The Outlook (*Record Mirror*, 20 May 1978). Soon afterwards, the threesome were supporting The Human League at Sheffield University's bar two Now Society, the 45p ticket proclaiming 'Electronic Pop: No Drummers'.

Vice Versa – who originally consisted of Stephen Singleton, David Sydenham and Mark White: until David was replaced by Martin Fry – had launched their Sheffield DIY Neutron label. They devised this beautifully-produced 7" EP featuring the martial drumming and chaotic discord of Adi Newton's Clock DVA and their track 'Brigade' – a hard metallic anti-war diatribe that remained my prime listening input for the year (later collected onto *Horology*). Plus, there was the more-punk-guitar-orientated Stunt Kites' 'Beautiful People'; I'm So Hollow with 'I Don't Know' (which also features on the *Hicks From The Sticks* regional multi-artist album), and Vice Versa themselves referencing the movie *Dr. Strangelove* on their pure-electronic 'Genetic Warfare'.

The four tracks on the Vice Versa EP *Music 4* (1979, Neutron PX1092) also form a perfect souvenir of the cool synth crucible of sound fermenting in Sheffield in the countdown to the new decade – from the thalidomide buzz of 'Science Fact', to the totalitarian urban imagery of 'Riot Squad' (which rhymes 'Quatermass' with 'tear gas'), to 'Camille', which has TV atrocity voices from the Flixborough chemical plant explosion of 1 June 1974, and sets them against insistently-pulsing electronics.

An intriguing cassette compilation called *Sheffield Now Society Greatest Hits-1 1978* (1980) also included live material by I'm So Hollow, Cabaret Voltaire ('Oh Roger') and 2.3 ('Beats Are Back' and 'London'), with They Must Be Russians ('Beat Goes Off', 'Nagasaki's Children') and The Extras ('Good Time Girls' and 'What More Can I Say').

The First Year Plan (Compilation)
Label: Fast Product F-11, EMI EMC3312
Release date: January 1980

A 'mutant pop' compilation of material from the Fast Product label, five tracks by The Mekons (including 'Never Been In A Riot' and 'Heart And Soul'), three by Gang Of Four (including 'Love Like Anthrax' and 'Damaged Goods'), two by The Scars, and two by 2.3 (both sides of their only single: 'All Time Low' b/w 'Where To Now?'). 2.3 were a Sheffield band featuring Haydn Boyes-Weston, Paul Bower, John Clayton, Paul Shaft and Kevin Donoghue. Paul Bower – 'the fulcrum of the Sheffield scene' – had produced the *Gunrubber* fanzine with Adi Newton. Formed in May 1977, 2.3 were the first band of the new Sheffield generation to sign to a record label – an association through which Paul helped arrange Human League's first gig at Psalter Lane Art College, and introduced the group to Bob Last of Fast Product.

This album also features both sides of The Human League's 'Being Boiled' b/w 'Circus Of Death'. The album was reissued in January 1982, following the success of *Dare*.

Travelogue – The Human League (1980)

Personnel:
Philip Oakey, Ian Craig Marsh, Martyn Ware: vocals, synthesizer
Philip Adrian Wright: slides and film technician
Produced at Monumental Pictures Studio, Sheffield, in March (Except 'Toyota City' recorded at Devonshire Lane in April 1978)
Producers: The Human League, Richard Mainwaring, John Leckie
Label: UK: Virgin V2160, USA: Virgin International VI 2160
Release date: 14 May 1980
Chart position: UK: 16
Running time: 39:24

There's a photograph in *National Geographic* magazine (Vol.124, number 3, September 1963) – of a sleigh being drawn across the ice by three huskies. It portrays an epic journey through extreme climates; a travelogue into wonder beneath bright new constellations. The sleeve design for the album *Travelogue* is credited to The Human League but was realised by Angular iMaGes.

For much of the first half of the 20th century, jazz had been the great subversive music force that turned the world around to confront racial injustice and civil rights issues while busting social deference wide open with an irresistible dance rhythm. When it became stale and conformist by the mid-1940s, it wriggled itself around to become bebop, with a new uncompromising hard-line intelligence, before it was in turn eclipsed in the mainstream by the meteoric rise of rock 'n' roll. By the late-1970s – despite the efforts of punk – mainstream rock had become stale and conformist. It seemed to many that electropop was the bebop of rock: the birth of a new cool.

Think of it this way – rock 'n' roll was patented and went global in the 1950s. Then during the 1970s, punk confronted rock 'n' roll's internal contradictions, ridiculed its pomposity, and reverted it back to its basest primal impulse. End of cycle. Time for a new evolution. As bebop had convulsed up and out from jazz, so there was space for a new music. The new templates would come from new technologies, from Kraftwerk, from the theremin quivers in sci-fi shock movies, from Bowie's *Low* instrumentals, Eileen Darbyshire's *Doctor Who* sound workshop, and from electronic pioneers such as Karlheinz Stockhausen and John Cage. With the proliferation of accessible drum machines, it was anti-musicians who inherited the punk DIY play-in-a-day ethic by way of cheap Casio keyboards. It arrived in multiple guises – it was Cabaret Voltaire; it was Soft Cell. Sometimes it even seemed to be Tubeway Army. But more than anything else, it was The Human League.

Clear through the 1976/1977 period when the rest of the UK – in favour of minimalist punk – was embroiled in a systematic rejection of all artistic and musical pretensions, Sheffield alone was laying the ground rules for all the movements that were to dominate to the end of the decade and beyond. Of course, it was argued at the time that punk was a necessary and essential shedding of all that had become phoney and turgid in rock: syringing the aural rubbish from the ears of a nation. But stomping on the concept of goal and objective, be it strictly musical or even crassly commercial – if the greatest notoriety a band could generate was mythologised self-destruction in the Sid Vicious or Iggy Pop mould – also removed the element of motivation. If stardom was immoral and proficiency was suspect, then all endeavour was rendered redundant.

In Sheffield, it was not so much redundant as sidestepped. Philip told *Melody Maker* in the 29 October 1988 issue:

> I was astonished when I heard my first proper acid house song and discovered it was exactly the same as Ian Marsh was doing on *Travelogue* back in 1981. I love all that stuff. For all those techno groups, The Human League are *it*. The trouble is, each time an opportunity arises to capitalize on our success, we've moved away from it because it was too obvious. Then again, the fact that we've had any success at all still amazes us. It's all been guesswork.

On the *the-black-hit-of-space.dk* website, producer Richard Manwaring recalls how he initially met Philip, Martyn, Ian and Adrian in Sheffield over 18/19 March 1980:

> It was a new experience for me, working and getting to know the Sheffield band. They had previously recorded in The Townhouse, so having their own studio was a logical step. They found a room in Sheffield. The setup was a Trident Fleximix console audio desk with an Ampex 440 8-track recorder which at times only had six useable tracks and Revox 2-track recorders. We must have had some outboard gear like a compressor, a delay unit and a reverb, but I can't remember the specifics. One example of their self-deprecating humour is the name they chose for the recording setup financed by their Virgin advance. Monumental Pictures is a great name for a studio. There's a nod to Hollywood, with the image of an enormous and unstoppable production powerhouse. In fact, it was two rooms on the first floor of an empty building, above a disused veterinary practice on the ground floor, complete with metal trolleys where I assume the unfortunate animals were examined or operated on. You didn't wish to look too closely at what else had been left behind. The stairs at the back of the ground floor led up to the first floor and the studio. The ground floor electricity had been cut off, so in the evenings, we staggered through the dark to get to the studio. Sessions started from 22 to 30 March, and 12 to 14 April, and the album was mastered by Denis Blackham at Tape One on 15 April.

There are four liner photos on the rear of the vinyl edition, which are Polaroid SX70 snaps taken by Brian Clark. They adorn the first Human League album to be made available in the United States.

But critical reception was muted. Chris Westwood called the album 'electropop tiddlywinks ... tripping over their own streamlined quirkiness' (*Record Mirror*, 17 May 1980). And if there were accusations of a certain production muddiness, the digitally remastered reissue sounds pristine.

Side One
'The Black Hit Of Space' (Marsh, Oakey, Ware, Wright) (4:11)

This is electro's ceiling of the Sistine Chapel; its Venus de Milo. This is everything that electropop could and ever should be. This is the consummation of the promise and the lie – a huge marching percussion, a feed of snickering synths that build a sense of impending menace, futuristic sounds warbling off and on, into a launch take-off swoosh!

Philip has been out all night, he needs a bite, but while he fills his sandwich, he decides to put a record on. He selects the one with the ultra-modern label and the futuristic cover lifted straight from *Buck Rogers*. It is, of course, a vinyl record, operated by the autochanger switch; the revolving black bands of a long-player ignited as the stylus drops onto the intro groove. This image is lost in the subsequent CD and MP3 formats, so it's entirely appropriate that *Travelogue* was reissued in a 180-gram vinyl edition in July 2016 (Universal 4777481). Meantime, it's evident that the record he's chosen is a kind of black hole singularity, drawing everything into the inexorable maw of its devouring event horizon; as it climbs the chart, every other record is swallowed up until there's nothing else left to buy – as well as the record shops that sell it, then it's sucking in the human race itself. It gets to number 1, and goes into minus figures.

The track drops into a spoken recitation, like the voice-over from an apocalyptic sci-fi movie. He tries to stop the record, which has now assumed a doughnut shape with the label revolving around its outer rim: assuming the form of the accretion disc of a forming solar system. But the play arm – though less than one micron long – weighs more than the planet Saturn. He tries to flee but can't escape because the record is always there ahead of him. There's a quip: 'Get James Burke on the case'. (He was the BBC science populariser and presenter of *Tomorrow's World*.) The track ends with a smart edit; this is the hit record that's never gone, and 'time stops when you put it...' Stop. Silence.

This is a complete episode of *The Twilight Zone*; a vignette lifted from Michael Moorcock's *New Worlds*; a short story by Robert Silverberg, taken from Harlan Ellison's *Dangerous Visions*, clawing its way through your earbuds.

The Human League played the students' union at the University of Manchester (Wednesday 19 May 1980, rescheduled from 14 May, with a second gig at Derby Assembly Rooms, 21 May 1980), supported by Edinburgh-based Fast signings The Scars and Clock DVA. Roger Quail recalled:

Three huge screens dominate the stage as the intro tape gives way to the ominous creep of 'The Black Hit Of Space'. The song explodes into life – John

Barry meets James Burke atop a synthetic sledgehammer beat. Suddenly the screens are alive, a constantly-rotating, pulsating patchwork of imagery – JFK, B-52 bombers, radio transmitters, John Wayne, Vargas girls, the Moon-landing, Lolita and more; sex, money and power; a bewildering myriad of pop culture imagery endlessly shifting in front of the eyes; Disney's **Black Hole**, Janet Leigh, helicopter gunships, Lauren Bacall. All coupled with the tumultuous torrent of sonic energy pouring forth from the PA. I am instantly utterly transfixed and amazed by the sensory overload. This, then, is the gift of sound and vision I have been waiting for.

Martyn Ware told David Buckley in *Mojo* number 119 that tracks like 'The Black Hit Of Space' are way ahead of their time: 'Pumping the synths through massive distortion, and overloading the desk. How prescient is that? The ethos of what we were doing was to kind of future-proof it all. We were envisaging people playing this music in 10 or 20 years' time'.

He is correct. It's the equivalent of sticking your tongue in a mains electric socket. Elsewhere there's been a slippage of pop progress. But this, it still sounds fiercely modern. We are still listening. The Human League seldom got better than this.

'Only After Dark' (Scott Richardson, Mick Ronson) (3:51)

It fades in gradually, then up-switches into a tight mid-tempo, with Philip's lead vocal answered by Ian and Martyn's supporting voices. Written by the Hull-born Mick Ronson (guitarist, songwriter, multi-instrumentalist, arranger, producer and one-time member of Mott The Hoople) with Scott Richardson, 'Only After Dark' was on Ronson's 1974 debut solo album *Slaughter On Tenth Avenue*: released shortly after he'd quit Bowie's Spiders From Mars. The song was also the B-side to Ronson's second solo single: a cover of Elvis Presley's 'Love Me Tender'. To further complicate the story, Def Leppard made 'Only After Dark' the B-side of their massive 1992 single 'Let's Get Rocked'.

Does this song stand out as being significantly different from The Human League's original compositions? No – it sequences directly and seamlessly into the continuum, although they were initially dubious about its inclusion on the album.

'Life Kills' (Marsh, Oakey, Ware, Wright) (3:07)

A frantic pace counters the bleak message for one of the very few Human League songs where the words came first. This track carries a dark socialist-realist lyric about lives driven by the necessity to work hard shifts in order to simply pay the bills. Sheffield was an industrial city where people endured a gritty monochrome *Saturday Night And Sunday Morning* existence. It's a flash-forward to the 'Work all day or work all night/It's all the same if you want the pay' of Heaven 17's 'Crushed By The Wheels Of Industry'. Although, it's taken at the compressed danceable speed of a weekend escape and bursts into blossoming synths at the close.

'Dreams Of Leaving' (Marsh, Oakey, Ware, Wright) (5:49)

There's a brief ticking countdown to departure, then a piping of synths, disrupted by slams as if of cell doors. Philip's lyric deals with activists escaping from South Africa's apartheid regime: 'Our lives are in his hands/We pay with Krugerands'. The repressive apartheid system was dismantled only when the ANC (African National Congress) assumed power following the first free elections (held in April 1994), but the migrant agony endures to this day in other theatres of crisis.

There's a distinctive mid-point break with a twisting and hypnotically-undulating keyboard figure that opens up into a roaring of storm clouds. When the vocal resumes, it's only to discover that the exile's new life elsewhere is also uncertain and resented. This is a strong, involved, engaged, political track fraught with drama and tension: a level that The Human League would seldom attempt again. For Roger Quail, 'Phil, with extraordinary prescience, dusts off his crystal ball to foresee a distant 21st-century future of civil wars, human trafficking, desperate refugees and displaced immigrants'. Much later, 'The Lebanon' would tackle the humanitarian crisis of political refugee camps: albeit in a less forceful form.

Some critics have claimed that 'Dreams Of Leaving' is also a metaphor for young adults leaving the comforting security of their parental home: which is also an interpretation. Good art should always be open to multiple theories.

'Toyota City' (Marsh, Oakey, Ware, Wright) (3:24)

A slow and mystical instrumental, with icily hypnotic repetitions that hint at Japanese scales. Taken from mono tapes recorded at Devonshire Lane in April 1978, this was the album's only track to be circulated in demo form prior to the album sessions. A longer 5:38 version was issued as the B-side of the 'Only After Dark' single, included as part of the 'Empire State Human' package.

Japan was considered all-things *Blade Runner* and techno-future – the cyberpunk hi-tech low-protein squalor of environmentally-degraded but shiny digital tomorrows. A remembrance of things to come. The album sleeve proudly bears the legend 'Contains synthesizers + vocals only': a manifesto and a statement of intent. It's placed halfway through the album, and already it's spanned a variety of moods and styles as if to assert that electronics have just as expressive a range as more-conventional instrumentation; templates for future music genres that have yet to be invented.

Side Two
'Crow And A Baby' (Marsh, Oakey, Ware, Wright) (3:43)

There's an up-and-down melody line that anticipates 'The Things That Dreams Are Made Of' – but not quite because there are knocking effects and electropunk distortions in the fade. The lyric is a surreal confusion that suggests that when 'a crow and a baby had an affair, the result was a landslide'. So does it represent an uneasy political alliance leading to electoral victory? But, 'the result was…' also a *Dare*! What this critique of interspecies relationship means, is less than obvious: 'With one wing on the town and a gleam in an eye of red'. The fierce miscegenation is a dark fusion in which 'my dream was the baby, the crow was your hair', with the implied threat that if she ventures from his side, she'll end up in a field as someone's manure – mushrooms growing from her back, feeding some damn carrion crow. *Crow: From The Life And Songs Of The Crow* was a 1970 book of poems by Ted Hughes. Is this a poetic metaphor, or just a clash of menacing images? 'Do you want to contribute to the corruption of the world?'. Listen, read, discuss. Analyse and evaluate. Answers in an email, please.

'The Touchables' (Marsh, Oakey, Ware, Wright) (3:21)

There was a trendy 1968 movie romp called *The Touchables*, described by a critic as 'A sort of fidgety mod pornography'. Written by Ian La Frenais, the film featured a theme by the original UK psychedelic band Nirvana. And then, of course, there was the prohibition-era *The Untouchables* from the classic TV series and the 1987 movie. To touch, or not to be touched? Frazzled synths are driven by a kick track to combine with pleasantly tuneful melodic contours that take Philip's range close to the edge. To be touchable is to need. To need is to be vulnerable. It's a primal drive that operates when the spirit is wilting, and the flesh is weak. The throwaway line 'eight days a week' may or may not reference as far back as *Beatles For Sale* in 1964.

'Gordon's Gin' (Jeff Wayne) (2:58)

Gordon's is the world's best-selling dry gin, produced in London since 1769. The company's Pearl & Dean movie screen adverts seem a curious source for a cover version, but the syncopated drum track and nimble synth figures adapt well in both dry, crisply fizzing and intoxicating ways, leaving a tangy and pungent aftertaste. Gordon's would've been wise to adopt this version, as it was a substantial improvement on the made-for-movies original. Allegedly, American-born naturalised Brit Jeff Wayne scored some 3,000 of these catchy ad themes (including the one for Fry's Turkish Delight) in the 1970s before he devised a spectacular theatrical presentation based on H. G. Wells' *The War Of The Worlds* novel.

'Being Boiled' (Marsh, Oakey, Ware) (4:21)

This is a spikier mix of the first song Martyn and Philip wrote together and the only track on the album not co-produced by Richard Manwaring. Recorded on 8-track in Sheffield in February 1980 with John Leckie – adding synthetic horns programmed by The Boys Of Buddha – this is harder, with sharp handclap-driven percussion, although there's a feeling that it loses the original single's organic cohesion.

In 2021, Heaven 17 presented a *Reproduction + Travelogue*: 40th Anniversary Celebration at Sheffield City Hall (on Saturday 4 September, then the London Roundhouse on Sunday 5 September) in which Glenn Gregory convincingly replicated the vocals.

'WXJL Tonight' (Marsh, Oakey, Ware, Wright) (4:40)

The album's ambitious closing track was played by John Peel on his late-night Radio 1 show of 29 May 1980, recalling a number of intriguing crossovers. Producer Trevor Horn based Buggles' number-1 single 'Video Killed The Radio Star' on J. G. Ballard's story 'The Sound-Sweep' – the song concerning the imminent obsolescence of radio in the face of more visual media: which almost became a self-fulfilling prophecy when the Buggles video got heavy MTV rotation. There are also possible links to Harry Chapin's touching 1973 story-song 'W.O.L.D', which tells the tale of a washed-up DJ in a song that also embodies radio call signs and jingles.

WXJL is also a fictitious radio station – 10,000 watts of power, news headlines on the hour, assailed by the technological innovation of automatic stations, into the science-fictional weirdness of being the Earth's last manned radio station. Philip's forceful voice tells of 'the way it was in the past', with a mild satiric nudge about the time when people would 'listen to the DJs talk about the songs they didn't know', only 'to fill in space between the songs that talk of love and other things, as if it really mattered', before 'automatic stations came and sent them all away'. Ian and Martyn add backup radio station clichés and harmony slogan chimes – 'hit pick or phone-in show' – while the narrative focus shifts to the last DJ's perspective; he addresses the listener directly: 'Now I'm left alone ... and you're the one who makes the choice to turn me on or turn me off'. With headphones clamped in tight, speaking alone into the studio microphone, it's a vivid and cleverly-contrived image that closes with the empty appeal, 'I don't want you to go tonight!'. 'Alexa, play Human League...!'.

Bonus tracks from the *Holiday 80* double-single were added for the 1988 CD, plus the 'Boys and Girls'. 'Tom Baker' single, extending the running time to 67:58. (see below)

'I Don't Depend On You' (Marsh, Oakey, Ware) (4:35)

A further bonus track produced with Colin Thurston and originally issued as being by The Men.

'Cruel' (Marsh, Oakey, Ware) (4:40)

The instrumental mix originally issued as the single B-side of 'I Don't Depend On You' by The Men and produced with Colin Thurston.

Related Releases
Holiday 80 (Double Single) (1980)

Producer: John Leckie
Studio: Devonshire Lane, Sheffield, February 1980

Release date: April 1980, Virgin SV105
Chart position: UK: 56

This collection, issued in multiple formats, is made up of four tracks. In the wake of a *Top Of The Pops* appearance (8 May) performing an edit of Gary Glitter's breakthrough hit 'Rock 'N' Roll', this double-single crawled up to a humble 56 in the UK. The Human League's clean-edged weirdness was starting to draw attention and make inroads into the post-punk consciousness.

The package was reissued in two forms on the back of the success of *Dare* – a normal double-pack and a limited edition double-pack with a gatefold sleeve, including a bonus photo spread. This time it went as high as number 46, in a five-week chart stay starting in February 1982. The song 'Rock 'N' Roll' itself was to return – all the way to a 1988 number 1, as part of the 'Doctorin' The Tardis' mash-up from KLF's Bill Drummond and Jimmy Cauty masquerading as The Timelords.

'Being Boiled' (Marsh, Oakey, Ware)
The newly recorded revision, with synthetic horns programmed by The Boys From Buddha.

'Marianne' (Marsh, Oakey, Ware) (3:18)
Strongly melodic, with The Human League in sentimental mode, recalling a childhood day spent 'Running 'round the garden in your mother's shoes, playing silly sisters', although, now 'I've got a life of my own'.

This was engineered and produced by The Human League with John Leckie in Sheffield on 8-track in February 1980, during the same sessions that resulted in 'Rock 'N' Roll/Nightclubbing'. An earlier demo of the song – called 'Stylopops You Broke My Heart' – is featured on the deluxe edition of *A Very British Synthesizer Group* (2016), with the same clinking intro sounds but a lyric about 'living on a bomb site', and Philip assuming a father's role, dropping into a talking tone to address his daughter. The later, more-forceful mix as 'Marianne' has stronger squelchy bottom-end bass pulses augmented with counter backing harmonies as Philip emotes 'I take one look at you/It leaves me breathless'.

Biographer Peter Nash complains that the track is 'overloaded with background noise that only a radar expert could unravel': which is his opinion, to which he is entitled. Philip suggested there was a further even-more-superior version of the song that Virgin sat on: 'They wouldn't put it out, because they didn't like it'.

'Rock 'N' Roll/Nightclubbing' (Glitter, Leander/Bowie, Osterberg) (6:23)
This takes the Gary Glitter hit, with faux handclaps slowing as it segues into Iggy Pop's composition from *The Idiot* (1977) – a song Iggy wrote with David Bowie, using a Roland drum machine for the rhythm track. Iggy himself

had headlined The Human League's first European tour. For this track, the band's early sullen obscurantism, ponderance and occasionally pretentious songs were buried by simple inanity. There was nothing on *Reproduction* or *Travelogue* to compare.

Paul Gadd has one of the strangest career profiles in the long, convoluted history of pop/rock. As a long-term wannabe star, he'd started out as a teenager playing Soho's 2i's coffee house. Then, at the very dawn of the 1960s, he was Paul Raven, with failed singles for Decca and two produced by George Martin for Parlophone. He worked as a warm-up act for TVs *Ready Steady Go*, recorded under the alias Rubber Bucket, and covered George Harrison's 'Here Comes The Sun' as Paul Monday: none of which caused nary a ripple. It was only by teaming up with producer Mike Leander that he got his break. Yet, his first genuine chart hit was ironic in the sense that 'Rock And Roll' also failed to find a responsive audience. It was only when radio programmers flipped the disc and began playing the largely instrumental B-side that it began picking up sales. Hence, as 'Rock And Roll Part 2' climbed into the top ten in June 1972, Gary Glitter appeared on *Top Of The Pops* in a virtually non-singing role! But once he was there, he ran the grotesquely exaggerated comic-absurdist persona through a series of ludicrously overblown hits – such as 'I'm The Leader Of The Gang (I Am)' – including three number 1s.

'We did Gary Glitter's 'Rock And Roll' at a time when he was considered a fool', said Philip. Of course, this was well before his spectacular fall from grace and imprisonment due to child-abuse allegations. For the BBC, and as far as most music histories are concerned, he has become an Orwellian unperson. Back then, he was simply another glam-and-glitter name competing alongside The Sweet and T. Rex, with The Human League drawn in particular to the Glitter Band's distinctive live double-drum of Pete Phipps with either Pete Gill or Tony Leonard: replicated here with precision-programmed rhythms. 'Do you still recall in the jukebox hall when the music played/And the world span around to a brand new sound'? – well, now it was spanning to an even newer sound.

It was Martyn Ware's idea to cover the song. In their B.E.F. guise, Ware and Marsh used Gary Glitter as a guest vocalist on their version of the Elvis Presley hit 'Suspicious Minds' (for their 1982 *Music Of Quality And Distinction Volume One* album), while The Human League would later cover The Glitter Band's 'Let's Get Together Again'.

'Dancevision' (Marsh, Ware) (2:22)

Recorded opposite Kelvin Flats in Sheffield on a budget Sony 2-track in November 1977, this is a remnant of The Future, when cheap one-finger synths and Casio noises beep and burble with a neat kinky clarity.

A short instrumental track originally recorded by Ian and Martyn as The Future, when Adi Newton was still a member. Adi released his own longer version of the piece in 2015 as part of his career-spanning *Horology 2* compilation, which also included several other tracks by The Future. The 2002 CD *The Golden Hour Of The Future* does not include 'Dancevision'.

'Only After Dark' (Richardson, Ronson) (3:51) b/w 'Toyota City' (Marsh, Oakey, Ware, Wright) (3:24) (German B-side was 'WXJL Tonight' written by Marsh, Oakey, Ware and Wright)

Label: Virgin VS 351
Release date: May 1980
Chart position: Did not chart

After the marginal success of 'Rock 'N' Roll', the group didn't want another cover song as a follow-up but were over-ruled by Virgin.

Outlining the changes that were happening within the band, The Human League were featured in venerable Rock journal *ZigZag* (number 105, September 1980) alongside Killing Joke and The Skids, and for *NME* The Human League provided a 'Consumer's Guide To Synths': about how they'd taken the punk ethic to Dixons, and Tamla to Top Shop. Philip confessed, 'I felt at a vast disadvantage until I conned the money out of my Dad to buy a synthesizer. I still can't play it'.

Machines (Compilation) (1980)

Label: Virgin V2177
Release date: August 1980

This is a vinyl celebration showcasing the label's finest synth-pop signings, including Orchestral Manoeuvres In The Dark ('Messages'), Tubeway Army ('Down In The Park'), Thomas Leer ('Private Plane'), John Foxx ('Underpass'), Public Image Limited ('Pied Piper') and The Human League's 'Being Boiled'.

Cash Cows (Compilation) (1980)

Label: Virgin MILK1
Release date: August 1980

A new wave compilation including XTC ('Respectable Street'), Japan ('Ain't That Peculiar'), Public Image Limited ('Attack'), Captain Beefheart And The Magic Band ('Dirty Blue Gene'), Kevin Coyne ('Taking On The World') and The Human League's 'The Black Hit Of Space'.

Album release – White Souls In Black Suits (1980) by Clock DVA

Personnel:
Adi Newton: vocals, synthesizer, clarinet, bowed guitar
Charlie Collins: soprano, alto, baritone and sopranino saxophones, flute, percussion, bells
David James Hammond: guitar
Roger Quail: percussion
Steven James 'Judd' Turner: bass

Production and additional mixing: Richard H Kirk, Stephen Mallinder, Chris
Watson
Engineer: Jon Mills at the DVAtion Studios in Sheffield
Label: Industrial Records IRC31
Release date: December 1980
Chart position: –
Running Time: 53:04

After leaving The Future, Adi formed the first lineup of Clock DVA, continuing
the extreme intensity and experimental nature of the work he'd done with
Ian and Martyn. While also utilising the more organic acoustic drums, it was
enhanced by the inspired free-jazz interjections of brilliant saxophonist Charlie
Collins, who played solos as brittle and dangerous as walking barefoot on
broken glass.

With production input from Cabaret Voltaire on two tracks, this package
initially emerged in a cassette-only edition on Throbbing Gristle's Industrial
label, which had already distributed incendiary material by American writer
William S. Burroughs. *White Souls In Black Suits* has subsequently been
repackaged in vinyl and CD formats. There are eight tracks, allegedly edited
down from some 15 hours of studio improvisation:

Side One: 1. 'Consent' (5:05) 2. 'Discontentment (1 & 2)' (6:03) 3. 'Still/Silent'
(7:22) 4. 'Non' (11:07)
Side Two: 1. 'Relentless' (5:27) 2. 'Contradict' (5:23) 3. 'Anti-Chance (Film
Soundtrack Keyboards Assemble Themselves At Dawn)' (14:08)

With Paul Widger replacing David James Hammond, Clock DVA then signed
to Fetish for *Thirst* (24 January 1981) – co-produced with Ken Thomas, and
a continuation of their uncompromising industrial-experimental extremism,
with powerful 'Sensorium', the dense martial assault of 'Four Hours', 'White
Cell' and 'Impressions Of African Winter'. DVA split shortly afterwards, with Adi
going on to form further lineups, while the remaining members joined singer
Peter Hope in a stunning new band named The Box.

The Human League Split – and Reform

'Boys And Girls' (Wright, Oakey) (3:11) b/w 'Tom Baker' (Wright, Oakey) (3:58) by The Human League

Personnel:
Philip Oakey: vocals, synthesizer
Adrian Wright, Ian Burden: synthesizer
Label: Virgin VS395
Release date: 20 February 1981
Chart position: UK: 48

'Tom Baker' (Oakey, Wright)

Also added as a *Travelogue* bonus track, this B-side is an instrumental that opens in glacial slowness before kicking into a percussive bridge to a stronger, denser, more up-tempo sequence. There are blasts from the Boys from Buddha horns and various sonic references recalling sounds from the BBC Radiophonic Workshop; weak on melody, but with roaring and zapping effects to provide grit between the smoothly evolving theme. Delia Derbyshire would be proud.

The Boys from Buddha horns unite The Human League's pre and post-split phases in that they are also credited on Heaven 17's *Penthouse And Pavement*. Martyn told me, 'That's just me and Ian playing synthetic horns. We like the idea of having different names for things'. Ian explained that the idea evolved from the automatic show they set up with Talking Heads:

> We were down in London setting up slides for that, and the engineer was listening to the tracks. He said he played in a jazz band and didn't like all the electronic stuff much, but he did like the one The Boys from Buddha. He just misinterpreted it ['Listen to the voice of Buddha'] and we thought, 'Great name!'. So when we did the electronic horns on *Travelogue,* we called them Boys from Buddha. Then, to emphasise the continuity, we thought we'd make them reappear again for 'Play To Win', to make sure people knew who was involved. And it wasn't Philip or Adrian: it was myself and Martyn.

Tom Baker, of course, was the fourth and possibly the finest incarnation of the Doctor in the BBC-TV *Doctor Who* series from 1974 to 1981.

'Boys And Girls' (Oakey, Wright)

There's an early mix of this song on the *A Very British Synthesizer Group* collection, although the catchy playground rhyme format provides evidence of a decisive shift away from the more experimental work that precedes it. Although it's a bonus track here, this is also a track that would constitute a significant development in The Human League's fortunes. We will meet it again shortly. A repetitive bass figure underpins the strong 'Boys and girls come out to play' chorus that invites sing-along participation: a nursery rhyme from Mars with backwash effects. Subsequent verses comment on the process of growth towards imagined maturity. 'Boys and girls, I love you dearly/But I hate to have you near me'.

Then The Human League split. 'WXTL Tonight' carried tantalising suggestions of an impending split – 'the way it was in the past, a long time ago, before staff levels dropped'. So staff levels dropped.

A lot of people thought The Human League project was over. But they'd only just begun. It seems the main point of contention was between Philip Oakey and Martyn Ware – over personal differences and aesthetics that sent their filters into wild oscillations. According to Philip: 'Myself and Martyn are both sort of quite pompous, and it was hard to fit us in the same group'. Times change, people alter. A band is not forever. 'The once clear artistic goals were now becoming more obscured by their inability to agree on a unified direction', as Virgin press tactfully phrased it. So, although the factions continued operating on different shifts in the same studio, the group acrimoniously bifurcated as exactly as cellular division, in October 1980. The split in the ranks meant that Martyn and Ian Craig Marsh went on to form B.E.F., abandoning what was left of The Human League (but retaining royalties from new Human League product in return for relinquishing their rights to the name). The Human League were already heavily in debt to Virgin, and contracted to start a European tour or else face severe legal penalties imposed by the promoters.

There was considerable bitchiness in the press and in a Radio 1 *Newsbeat* interview. There were recriminations and name-calling, with more than a whiff of post-divorce bitterness in the air. It would take a long time to heal while incidentally offering the bonus of feeding hungry journalists good copy. (Martyn conceded that 'It doesn't do us any harm', when I put this gossip slant to him!) Much later in an interview on the *Made In Sheffield* DVD, Philip admitted, 'I wish it had never stopped. I still miss it. I still miss Martyn and Ian very much'.

Meanwhile, how do you solve a problem like Phil Oakey? Philip had ideas the size of planets; Jupiter-sized planets; cyberphilia. And in the lull between the split and the first post-split recordings, he switched up from musing to motion. He began sketching songs that were more pretension-free, reduced down from generalised tales of dehumanisation to directly personal statements of loss, love and the things that hits are made of – colour, romance, style and fun – yet retaining the ideas and construction that made The Human League unique. Dragged back from the brink of disaster, the group's remaining members had to unlearn something of the past in order to locate the pure undiluted centre, and in the process, learn a new vocabulary.

Produced by John Leckie at Sheffield's Monumental Studios, the tracks that make up the fifth Human League single constitute the first evidence of life after the defections. To fill the musical gap – facing financial disaster and potential bankruptcy – Adrian turned his hand to keyboards and did so remarkably successfully. A one-time art student and former ice cream salesman who lived on Dobcroft Road close to Ecclesall Woods, he would also co-write some of the band's biggest hits with Philip Oakey. And just in time, brunette Joanne Catherall and blonde Susan Ann Sulley – hereafter known as Susanne Sulley – were being recruited with the tagline 'With your looks you could go far.' Philip pondered in retrospect, 'We thought, 'What do we need? We really badly need someone to play synthesizer', so we went out and got two people who couldn't do anything. At all. So they joined'. Susanne adds, 'It's different, nobody else had done it before ... he (Philip) wanted a tall black singer, and he got two short white girls who couldn't sing'. On such random quirks of chance is music history made.

The story of their first encounter has entered pop mythology. The two schoolgirls – aged just 17 and 18 and best friends since they were 13 – used to go out dancing four nights a week at a futurist Sheffield nightclub called The Crazy Daisy Disco. Philip and Adrian just happened to be there and noticed them, their attention drawn by the girl's immaculate makeup, unique dress style and idiosyncratic but distinctive dance moves. Philip approached Susanne – the elder of the two girls – and said, 'I'm from a band called The Human League. We were just watching you and your friend dancing. Would you like to do a tour of Europe with us?'. Naturally, the girls were initially wary. In Harry North's picture-strip history in *Smash Hits*, Susanne said, 'Get lost!', with Joanne adding a 'Get yer 'air cut!'. But they knew about Human League. They knew who Philip was. Although, predictably, their parents flat-out refused permission. Joanne and Susanne did concede far enough to go around to the studio the next morning when they tried out a few vocal lines that went down pretty well. The now-departed going-heavenwards Martyn Ware had previously supplied the band's upper-register vocals, so the collective needed a replacement voice.

The following Sunday, Philip – in full pop-star regalia of postbox-red Revlon lipstick, lopsided hair and high heels – clumped around to Joanne's parent's house for lunch. Their conversation won the doubters around, eroded parental reluctance, and grudging permission was extended. The same magic worked on Sulley's mum and dad in their house in the suburb of Gleadless: a few Supertram stops south-east of Sheffield city centre.

The new Human League lineup debuted live at Rotter's nightclub in Doncaster, with the girls – who obviously had no prior professional experience – initially considered as guest dancers who supplied only incidental vocals, for which they were remunerated on a £30-a-week basis. Doom was widely predicted when Sheffield's cult-industrial darlings ditched avant-garde pretensions and drafted in two scenic girls to sing and dance. Susanne remembers, 'I saw a photo of it recently, and we looked so young' (*Hot Press*, April 2011).

The ensuing European dates went ahead. To close the tour, The Human League played a high-profile concert at London's Hammersmith Odeon

(December 4). Susanne admitted, 'We'd been getting a lot of hostility from blokes on the tour who resented us', until the massively positive audience response at the Hammersmith Odeon turned that perception around. The girls had go-goed their way into the hearts of hard-core followers, and now, the world was ripe for conquest.

Susanne was – and is – striking, gushing, stroppy, radical, charming, and passionate about The Human League and Sheffield Wednesday football club. She'd been a Saturday girl at a hairdresser during the summer recess, but she never worked as a waitress in a cocktail bar: 'I was an usherette in a cinema for a while, and I loved that'. Joanne is less confrontational, but equally radical and striking. They share an aesthetic and a strong friendship. After taking time off school at the (now-demolished) Frecheville Comprehensive in order to do the tour, they returned to the classroom to complete their exams. They did fine, which left them clear to join The Human League on a full-time basis. It would be their career.

Although they appear on the cover of 'Boys And Girls' – issued in a limited-edition gatefold sleeve – they didn't actually participate in the track itself. The Human League performed the song as part of their European tour set, in which Ian Burden was also brought in to assist. He'd played in a Sheffield band called Graph, who'd also used films: because 'We didn't have anyone who was visually striking or who could dance'. But he was also an accomplished, trained musician in ways that neither Philip nor Adrian were. In a strangely prescient happenstance, Ian Burden's Graph had once supported Jo Callis' Shake at The Nashville.

Pete Frame created one of his meticulously-researched family trees, charting the interactions between The Human League and The Rezillos (*Sounds*, 25 June 1983). It documents how Ian Burden met Ian Craig Marsh and Martyn Ware 'at boarding school in Peterborough in the early-1970s and kept in touch'. After playing in a band called Ophiuchus, the first Graph lineup recorded a track called 'Drowning', which was issued on Fast's Earcom (Fast 9a), with Ian (bass), Ian Elliott (guitar, vocals), Martin Rootes (keyboards) and Nik Allday (drums, replaced by Rod Siddall). From April until December 1979, they became Salon Graph with the addition of vocalist Pam Young who also played melodica. From January to July 1980, they became Musical Janeens, who contributed a track co-written by Ian – called 'Glen Miller And His Contemporary Intimacies Meets The Musical Janeens Uptown With A Packet Of Jellies And A Caribbean Monolith' – to the Sheffield compilation *Bouquet Of Steel* (Aardvark STEAL2), alongside tracks by The Comsat Angels, Artery and I'm So Hollow, after which Ian graduated into The Human League. 'I was unemployed at the time, and being paid to travel around Europe for a few weeks, sounded like a good idea, even if I did have about two days to learn the set!'.

Virgin were quick to issue 'Boys And Girls' b/w 'Tom Baker' as a single. When it reached number 48, this lineup bore the distinction of producing The Human League's debut top 50 record, at a time when synth-based new-romantic bands were being talked about as the new movement in style: the new wave of the new vain; one lop-sided fringe and two girls, ready to set the politics of fashion to a metronomic rhythm.

Dare! - The Human League (1981)

Personnel:
Philip Oakey: vocals, synthesizer, cover design
Philip Adrian Wright: slides, occasional synthesizer, cover design
Ian Burden, Jo Callis: synthesizers
Joanne Catherall, Susanne Sulley: vocals
Martin Rushent: programming
Dave Allen: assistant programming and engineering
Ken Ansell: cover layout and coordination
Brain Aris: photography
Producers: The Human League, Martin Rushent, at Genetic Sound, Streatley,
Berkshire between March and September 1981
Label: UK: Virgin V2192, USA: A&M SP-6-4892
Release date: 16 October 1981
Chart positions: UK: 1, USA: 3, Canada: 1, Australia: 1
Running time: 40:46

Who dares, wins. If The Human League did not exist, no record label would've dared invent them.

When Martyn Ware and Ian Craig Marsh quit, it seemed to many observers that the great Human League adventure was over. After all, Ian and Martyn were the group's creative 50-per cent, weren't they? They were the musicians. They were the only group members who could actually play. Certainly, Virgin seemed of that opinion because they promptly re-signed the duo under their new guise. What was left? – Adrian Wright, who played slides and films. And Philip Oakey who had asymmetrical hair, manicured nails and a perfectly-pierced nipple. Of course, there was the story of how he'd met Joanne and Susanne when he saw them dancing at the Crazy Daisy: attracted by their stylish dance moves. Although perhaps he'd had the Mystery Girls in mind (Katie Kissoon and Lisa Strike from the failed The Men project), the way their voices blend into the single's more dance-floor-orientated sound.

Where Heaven 17 thought in terms of subversive strategies, Philip Oakey thought of quality control. Ian and Martyn had quit at a point when Human League were heavily indebted to Virgin, so the next move had to accelerate momentum by a process of redirection from obliqueness to something capable of mass appeal towards a market globalization, making the same essential message so compelling that the sales pitch would transcend frontiers and cultural differences. If it was to be a 'concept campaign', Philip Oakey was to be the product. The Human League would marry technology with the subtle textures of the times in a changing face of décor to reflect social shifts; an unlearning into colour, romance, style and fun – muted, but with strong character, retaining the ideas and structures that made them unique; coordination as a recurring theme, pattern and texture merged in perfect harmony, with nothing to degrade the image quality or modulate the pin-sharp sound signal; a high-risk/high-yield path. And, if expensive to make and valueless as culture, wasn't that the entire point of Andy Warhol's book *The Philosophy Of Andy Warhol (From A To Be & Back Again)*? For the first time, The Human League actually rehearsed their set.

The 'Boys And Girls' single had been the litmus test. It was a sound razored back through necessity, recorded with just Philip and Adrian, with session keyboard player Ian Burden: brought in as a *temporary* solution. Yet it *had* charted: if only modestly. So Ian was invited to join full-time. Because Marsh and Ware were using Monumental studio, the group took some Sheffield song demos down to new producer Martin Rushent at his Genetic Sound Studios in Reading, where the tracks were collectively elaborated into the new album. Rushent had proven his producer potential with the October 1978 album *Separates* (United Artists) – the second by punk group 999 – and he was skilled in the new music technology. His studio was fully equipped to take advantage of his sequencing and programming abilities in order to create adventures in words and sound, purring it out over a pulsing electric current. He proposed, 'It's almost impossible now for an artist to keep totally up to date with the new technology available. Some of the machines are really quite difficult to operate without several months of familiarisation if they are going to be used in any meaningful way … and I think there has to be somebody associated with the band who is on top of those things and knows what is possible with them'. Rushent was to be to The Human League what Trevor Horn became to Frankie Goes To Hollywood and ABC, or Daniel Miller was to Depeche Mode, or Martin Hannett was for New Order and other Factory Records acts.

A note about the instrumentation on folk supergroup Pentangle's *Basket Of Light* (1969) album states defiantly that 'All the instruments played on this album are acoustic'. But hey, the times they were a-changin'. The studio equipment listed for *Dare* is intimidatingly electric, there's nothing here that doesn't involve taking a massive hit from the national grid, with a time code generated by the Roland MC-8, bass sounds from Oakey's old Korg 770, the Korg Delta analogue semi-poly string synth, a Linn LM-1 drum machine, the Yamaha CS-15, Roland System 700, Roland Jupiter-4, Casio VL-1 and Casio M10. It was a manifesto. Philip claimed, 'The sounds were *theoretical*, inside a machine. Nothing was mic'ed up, so the first time you heard them was when they'd been to the tape recorder and come out the speakers'.

Dare became one of the most iconic albums of the decade and made The Human League synth-pop's first superstars. It's the album by which the group are most instantly recognised: the thing that hits are made of. A musically ambitious, driven and voracious album, with giddy grenades of shared invention; a triumph of content and considerable style, at once phenomenally commercial and gleefully avant-garde. Bliss it was, in that dawn, to be alive. Fans could sequence these tracks on their own home mixtapes, there were pin-ups in *Smash Hits* and *The Face*, and features in the music press. There was a 'Dare To Be Different' issue of *Jackie* (no. 931, 7 November 1981), a 'Special

Outrageous Edition' with Human League, Cabaret Voltaire and Leif Garrett! *Smash Hits* even published a four-page cartoon-strip group history: an artfully caricatured 'satirical special drawn by Harry North', retelling the story of the group's irresistible rise and rise.

'George Michael and Paul McCartney are pop stars – we're not', Joanne would claim emphatically. For Human League interviews had become bantering affairs that required multidirectional microphones, with Joanne and Susanne contradicting Philip, while Adrian contributed a third stream of opinion that frequently differed from the other two. Although they did respond to the interviewer's questions, they appeared to be debating among themselves, interrupting, questioning, deriding each other as they baffled their way towards some common ground of agreement.

When it comes to matters electronic, things were already approaching critical mass. Depeche Mode from Basildon made their first chart appearance, at number 57 in April 1981 with 'Dreaming Of Me', following it with their breakthrough 'New Life', which reached 11 in June. That was still on the chart when Leeds electro duo Soft Cell began their climb to number 1 (5 September 1981 for two weeks) with 'Tainted Love'. The first Depeche Mode album – *Speak And Spell* – with Vince Clarke as the primary writer arrived on 5 October 1981. When Depeche Mode first appeared on *Top Of The Pops* with their synths and big revolving Revox spools, Stephen Singleton, Mark White and Martin Fry were watching TV in Sheffield, thinking, 'That should've been Vice Versa'.

American music channel MTV launched on 1 August 1981, offering access to British acts with a flair for visual presentation – something Human League were uniquely qualified for, and the fact that 'Don't You Want Me' topped the American chart for three straight weeks, is in no small degree due to MTV's high rotation of the Steve Barron-directed video. It tells and spells out a drama of love and pro-feminist heartbreak on a film set, as the camera pans back to cunningly reveal that the opening sequence doesn't simply announce another stock video but relates a narrative of its own, with meaningful over-the-shoulder glances inch-perfect hairdos and inch-and-a-half perfect makeup. Susanne, in fur coat, prowls away as a pistol is aimed from a parked car, into Oakey's final unmoving face at the close. Angst-ridden. It creates four minutes of high-grade cinematic magic. The Human League were eye candy of an elevated order. Here were people who do things you wouldn't dare. Did they even have lives when they were not in videos?

Even the album art stands out – an image that perfectly evokes the spirit and mirrors the feel of the band: an upfront, no-nonsense, fashionable unit. Design is credited to Philip and Adrian, as interpreted by Ken Ansell. It's a concept lifted from an issue of *Vogue* – four closely-cropped Brian Aris close-ups of Philip, Joanne, Susanne and Adrian, framed by large areas of white space. It's a distinct shift from the depersonalised abstraction of the previous two album covers.

For the 16 July 2006 issue of *The Observer,* Neil Spencer nominated *Dare* as one of 'The Fifty Albums That Changed Music': 'Until *Dare*, synthesizers meant solemnity. Phil Oakey's reinvention of the group as chirpy popsters, complete with two flailing girl-next-door vocalists, feminised electronica. Without this – and Oakey's lopsided haircut – squads of new romantics and synth-pop acts would've been lost'.

'The Things That Dreams Are Made Of' (Oakey, Wright) (4:14)

Joy is not something that has figured strongly in The Human League discography thus far. This is a testosterone-fuelled song about joy, where the melody tumbles from an assembly of chords and notes processed by a dazzling harmonic arrangement that suggests the expanding of a near-limitless musical and imaginative world. This is a song people want to sing. Hear it on the radio first thing in the morning, and it replays in your head all day. There might just be a touch of Cold War irony in the invitation to 'march-march-march across Red Square', but this is the opening track of an album that captures exactly what people's 1982 dreams were made of – travel, adventure, cash to spend, ice cream, food and fun, sweet dreams and moist underwear. There's a suspicion that it's slightly more consumerist than the impossible dream of universal love, peace and harmony of an earlier pop tribe; less on the hippie trail headful of zombie, and more the gap-year romp through the global theme park into which the world was reshaping itself. Yet it's also wide enough to encompass Norman Wisdom, a lift to the top of the Empire State (Human), and 'Johnny, Joey, Dee Dee' – Adrian Wright's lyric reflecting his affection for punk rockers the Ramones. Maybe the lines 'Meet a girl on a boat/Meet a boy on a train' are not intentionally androgynous, but they do seem to imply that your potential lover's gender is more the result of a whim than of premeditation. In his book *Perfect Pop: The Human League* (Star Books, 1982), writer Peter Nash declares that *Dare* represents 'a pruning of intellectual surplus and the honing of fantasy fodder', which might be one point of view. Nevertheless, if this is the great lost single that never was, Richard X featuring Kelis heavily sampled it for their August 2003 top-20 hit 'Finest Dreams'.

'Open Your Heart' (Callis, Oakey) (3:53)

With an irresistibly catchy little earworm synth hook played on a Casio VL-Tone, and a pure pop melody, the new Human League distinctively mark out the clear blue water distancing from what had come before. And finding such an original group sound is as rare as finding a sachet of shampoo without 25 per cent extra, free.

Although he was born in Rotherham, Jo Callis was studying at Edinburgh College of Art when he became guitarist Luke Warm with lively punksters The Rezillos – for whom he wrote the contagiously singable 'Top Of The Pops' (number 17 in September 1978; 13 in *NME* on 9 September). The song was artfully slanted at scoring a slot on the TV show of the same name, and it worked like a charm, with hyperactive vocalist Fay Fife stealing the screen action by taunting, 'Sing song, then fade away, ding dong, what's the future in the pop

music industry?'. Jo's future also involved writing all the original songs on
the Rezillos LP *Can't Stand The Rezillos* (Sire Records SRK6057, July 1978):
including 'Flying Saucer Attack', '2000 A.D.' and the single '(My Baby Does)
Good Sculptures'. After The Rezillos split, and after a one-off EP as Shake (with
drummer Angel Patterson), and because they shared the same management, Jo
found himself travelling down to Sheffield in a loose workshop format in order
to help Human League out with songwriting: unpaid, except for expenses!
A shared affection for tacky 1960s TV and movie-related junk and ephemera
helped Jo bond with Adrian Wright. Ian Burden said, 'Jo came down and we
messed about, and it worked out'. Then Jo played on the songs he'd helped
write, went on *Top Of The Pops* with the group, and was initially employed by
them on a monthly basis. When the tour happened, he was invited to join as a
full member. He brought not only a degree of musical ability but a proven top-
20 pop sensibility into the reconfigured collective, asserting his influence on the
melodies and structures when he co-wrote 'Seconds', 'Darkness' and 'Open Your
Heart'. Jo plays nifty analogue synthesizer here, along with Adrian Wright and Ian
Burden. Martin Rushent sequences and programmes the drum machines.

The Rezillos' trashy comic-strip sci-fi flirtation formed a natural Human
League fit, to the extent that on 20 November 1981, at a 15-song Glasgow
Apollo concert, the group performed a cover of The Rezillos November-1978
single 'Destination Venus' (written by Jo Callis and produced by Martin
Rushent). It stayed in the set until around June 1982. Low-fi live bootleg
versions that sound raw and exciting can be found by scouring the internet.
The Human League also performed a live version of Lou Reed's 'Perfect Day',
which has never officially been released.

'The Sound Of The Crowd' (Burden, Oakey) (3:56)

Metronomic dance rhythms throb compulsively throughout, niggling
synths squiggle, and Catherall and Sulley answer Philip's lead vocal in shrill
harmonies that rise into an explosive crescendo. It's a ringing anthem and
a declaration. This is a working-class Sheffield night on the town; bright
moments in dark times. Never mind the bucolic dreams of getting back to
the countryside, this is a paean to the excitement of city living. But while the
chorus is direct – 'Get around town, where the people look good/Where the
music is loud' – the verses retain a surreal edge, though Ian Burden explains
away 'Make a shroud pulling combs through a backwash frame' as spontaneous
stream-of-consciousness placeholder words used simply to communicate the
tune to Philip, who nevertheless incorporated them intact into the finished
composition. It was remixed from the original single. In the video, Adrian
adopts a couldn't-care-less look, and the girls' dance moves are slick but
naturally and intuitively choreographed. To journalist Steve Sutherland, this
song is 'a giddy clarion call to arms; an urgent call for everyone to borrow their
sister's finest glad rags, whack on some eyeliner and flaunt it in the face of
austerity'. (*Melody Maker*, 29 October 1988).

'Darkness' (Callis, Wright) (3:56)

Dark matter comprises most of the mass of the universe. This song is not about that. One of Adrian's very rare excursions into writing lyrics it's simply about being scared when the lights go out, although he admits to having been unsettled by reading Stephen King's novel *Salem's Lot* (1975), and also lifted the line 'all the sounds of fear' from a 1973 Harlan Ellison short-story collection. It starts with Philip's freestyle 'la la la' scat before the strong verse kicks out, with a nervy paranoid edge running over a dirty growing analogue bass riff that works as precisely as a Swiss watch.

Four songs in, and there's not a weak track on this album. Philip explained, 'We don't play electronic music, we play pop music that happens to be done on synthesizers'.

'Do Or Die' (Burden, Oakey) (5:25)

This was performed live on the first edition of the more adult-themed sequel to TV's *Tiswas* – called *O.T.T.*: launched 2 January 1982 – with Adrian wearing a stylish Adam Ant 'Prince Charming' t-shirt. The brief set takes the show neatly to the close of the first part, as the voice-over intones, 'And so we leave Human League, still not knowing whether they're doing or dying, as we take one of Central's mega-fabbo commercial breaks' – in much the same way that the track takes the album neatly to the close of the first side of the vinyl edition.

'Get Carter' (Roy Budd) (1:02)

Opening side two of the vinyl version, a piercing Casio VL-1 outlines the haunting theme from Michael Caine's best early movie, set in the gritty Newcastle gangland: played manually with no computer sequencer involved. As an unusual cover, the track must be seen as following the tradition set by 'Gordon's Gin' from *Travelogue*. Melancholy and lonesome, it also functions as a scene-setter for 'I Am The Law'.

'I Am The Law' (Oakey, Wright) (4:09)

Judge Dredd is the future Mega-City One lawman of the comic *2000 AD*, and his steely and inflexible catchphrase is here used in a sensitively-wrought track taken at a more serious pace than the rest of the album, offering multiple levels of potential meaning. One of the first songs that Philip wrote with Adrian following the Human League Mark 1 split, there's a feeling that when he sings, 'You know I am no stranger/I know rules are a bore/But just to keep you from danger/I am the law', he's cautioning and policing the more hedonistic impulses of someone close – someone on the dangerous edge of indiscipline; protecting them from themselves; from their own darker impulses. In the transition from the purely experimental work produced with Ian and Martyn towards the more-pure pop to come, this must be considered a key track.

There were other cultural crossovers. By way of response, the anti-robot resistance movement in Mega-City One calls itself The Human League, chanting

in one lurid *2000 AD* panel, 'WE ARE THE HUMAN LEAGUE!'. For Irish group
The Undertones' 'My Perfect Cousin' – their chirpy number-9 hit from March
1980 – 'His mother bought him a synthesizer/Got The Human League in to
advise her/Now he's making lots of noise/Playing along with the art school boys'.
    Were The Human League still considered art school boys and girls?
Apparently, they were.

'Seconds' (Callis, Oakey, Wright) (4:58)
Unwavering and relentlessly powerful LinnDrum programming underscores
an introduction that nears a full minute of gradual instrumental build before
Philip delivers two verses without the benefit of a chorus. The song climaxes
midway with an explosion of white noise mirroring the Lee Harvey Oswald
gunshot of 22 November 1963 that echoed around the world; a line lifted
from a newspaper headline, taking the life of 'the golden one'. The full-media
assassination of JFK in Dallas is a moment burned into the 20th-century image
iconography with all the emotive power of Yuri Gagarin's first orbit; ricocheting
down through the years to the killing of Martin Luther King, and reflected in
Mark Chapman's gunning down of John Lennon. The song rams the message
home until the second half: another two minutes and 30 seconds of chorus
repetition: 'It took seconds of your time to take his life/It took seconds'.
Selected as the B-side of the 'Don't You Want Me' single, there are some who
would argue that 'Seconds' is the vastly superior track.

'Love Action (I Believe In Love)' (Burden, Oakey) (4:58)
'This is Phil talking...', and he addresses his advice directly to the listener.
Opening with a deep baritone voice, the melody line is matched to a
propulsive tension between voice and rhythm, with unforced organic ease,
leading into a cracking middle-eight section crammed with a delicious lyric. If
Phil Oakey ever wrote better lines than these, I have yet to encounter them:

> I believe, I believe what the old man says
> Though I know that there's no Lord above
> I believe in me, I believe in you
> And you know I believe in love

It's followed by 'I believe in truth, though I lie a lot': a beautifully-constructed
lie delivered with concise precision. Technically speaking, Martin Rushent
provides the synth sequencing and drum-machine programming with his then-
programmer and engineer David M. Allen. The Roland System 700 modular
synth makes use of the pitch-to-voltage converter and envelope shaper to
create the distinctive synth sounds, while Jo Callis' guitar was fed into the synth
and used to shape and trigger the sounds: its kinetic energy producing the
unusual choppy synth part. Recording 'Love Action' was the first time Jo Callis
was in the studio with The Human League.

There's a theory that 'This is Phil talking' deliberately copies the Iggy Pop line 'Jesus, this is Iggy' (from 'Turn Blue'), while Philip admits that the 'old man' who dispenses words of wisdom is Lou Reed – neither of which are a detraction, but act as igniting ingredients in one of Human League Mark 2's most accomplished tracks.

George Michael's 2002 politico-dance 'Shoot The Dog' single heavily samples 'Love Action'. It trailered George's *Patience* album and effectively attacks both British Prime Minister Tony Blair and American President George W. Bush.

'Don't You Want Me' (Callis, Oakey, Wright) (3:56)

This is, above all others, the track that people associate The Human League with most. This is their record that genuinely got to number 1, then went into 'minus figures'! It's a glistening four minutes of glamour, poise and promise, fantasy and escapism. It's the story's intrigue that draws the listener in; conjecturing to what degree it reflects the state of relationships within the band. Philip had been married: 'A husband and lover too' according to 'Love Action'. But they'd divorced. It was no secret he was now emotionally involved with Joanne. She might never have worked as a waitress in a cocktail bar, but it could be argued that he'd picked her out, shook her up, turned her around and turned her into someone new. Although, she'd probably have found a much better place, either with or without him.

Did the back-and-forth dialogue lyric reflect a real-life conversation between them? No. According to Philip, the characters are based on the 1954 Judy Garland and James Mason version of the much-remade *A Star Is Born* movie. It's an explanation that actually makes perfect sense unless it's a sleight of hand deliberately used as a diversionary tactic because elsewhere, he attributes the idea to a story filched from a four-page spread in the trashy American magazine *Intimate Confessions*.

To accompany Oakey's photo-love picture-strip lyric, Callis and Wright crafted a much harsher synth score than the eventual album version. When Rushent was initially unable to generate the sound they required, he eventually rigged up a complex triggered patch. Jo told *Melody Maker:* 'The MC8 was programming the chords through the System 700, but the whole thing was triggered by a guitar-strumming pattern ... as I played the strumming pattern, it didn't matter what I played on guitar, the same chords would be coming out of the synthesizer, but to the rhythm, I played' (18 December 1982). Rushent was still unhappy with what they'd created, so Martin and Callis carried out extensive remixes of the track, giving it a softer, more-acceptable – and in Oakey's opinion, more 'poppy' – sound. Hence it was relegated as the album's final track.

The degree of cultural assimilation was such that dialogue from 'Don't You Want Me' formed the TV ad for Fiat's 2002 Spiritu di Punto campaign, with the petrol-station cashpoint picking out the synth figures.

Above: Now We Are Six. The Human League..

Below: Heaven 17. Music Of Quality And Distinction.

Left: Where it all began, *The Golden Hour Of The Future*. (*Black Melody Records*)

Right: The three-piece Cabaret Voltaire began with 'Extended Play'. (*Rough Trade*)

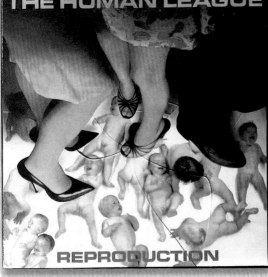

Left: *Reproduction* established The Human League at the epicentre of synthcore. (*Virgin*)

Right: 'March, March, March across Red Square', the controversial *The Dignity Of Labour* E.P. (*Fast Records*)

Left: Originally issued as an Industrial Records cassette, Clock DVA's debut album would later emerge in vinyl and CD formats. (*Industrial Records*)

Right: *Travelogue*, the second Human League album. (*Virgin*)

Left: The first Human League line-up play 'live' for BBC television as if they were in a sound laboratory.

Right: 'The Path Of Least Resistance, it seems the only way,' a refutation of taking the easy path.

Below: 'The Path Of Least Resistance' from the BBC-TV programme *Mainstream*, 6 November 1979.

Right: Philip and Joanne sing 'Don't You Want Me' on Dutch TV show *TopPop*.

Above: She might not have worked as a waitress in a cocktail bar, but Susanne sings 'Don't You Want Me'.

Right: With 'Don't You Want Me' at number one, they perform the hit on *Top Of The Pops*.

THE HUMAN LEAGUE
DARE!

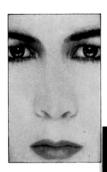

Left: 'The Things That Dreams Are Made Of'... *Dare*. (*Virgin*)

THE LEAGUE unlimited orchestra

Right: There never was a League Unlimited Orchestra, but the fiction resulted in a very fine album. (*Virgin*)

...AND DANCING

THE HUMAN LEAGUE
FASCINATION!

Left: 'Looking for a new direction, in an old familiar way,' the American edition of '(Keep Feeling) Fascination'. (*Virgin*)

Right: ABC styled themselves 'The Radical Dance Faction' for the iconic album *The Lexicon Of Love*. (*Neutron Records/ Mercury*)

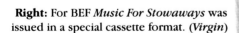

Left: 'Someone, Somewhere, Cracks Down', Cabaret Voltaire at their finest. (*Virgin/ Some Bizzare*)

Right: For BEF *Music For Stowaways* was issued in a special cassette format. (*Virgin*)

Left: The Corporate Handshake that introduced 'Penthouse And Pavement'.

Right: Live 'Temptation' on *Top Of The Pops* with Carol Kenyon.

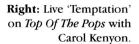

Left: Martyn and Ian play 'Temptation' on *Top Of The Pops*.

Right: A sequence from the 'Come Live With Me' video.

Left: Heaven 17 perform on *The Tube*.

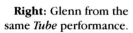

Right: Glenn from the same *Tube* performance.

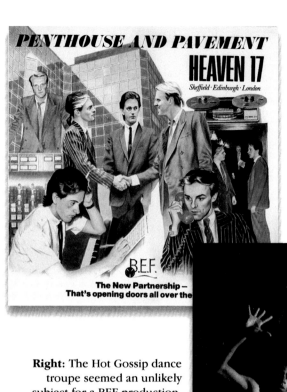

Left: For Heaven 17, side one is 'Pavement', side two is the 'Penthouse'. (*Virgin*)

Right: The Hot Gossip dance troupe seemed an unlikely subject for a BEF production. (*Atlantic*)

Left: The British Electric Foundation was always more than just Heaven 17. (*Virgin*)

Right: Maybe no album could follow *Dare*. But *Hysteria* has a lot to recommend it. (*Virgin*)

MAN
GUE

HYSTERIA

ELECTRIC DREAMS

ORIGINAL SOUNDTRACK FROM THE FILM

CULTURE CLUB · GIORGIO MO
GIORGIO MORODER WITH PHIL
JEFF LYNNE · HEAVEN 17 · HEL
P.P. ARNOLD

Left: Perhaps *Electric Dreams* was not a classic movie, but the soundtrack more than compensates. (*Virgin*)

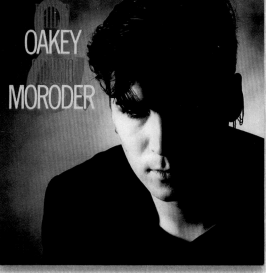

OAKEY
MORODER

Right: Oakey meets Moroder, and both come out of the meeting with dignity intact. (*Virgin*)

Left: Philip Oakey sings 'before he leaves the camp he stops,' on 'The Lebanon'.

Right: 'Pop people with their serious hats on'. The Human League perform 'The Lebanon'.

Left: Jo Callis delivers the distinctive and controversial Rock guitar on 'The Lebanon'.

Right: Joanne Catherall sings during 'The Lebanon' video.

Left: Adrian Wright claims 'The Lebanon' was inspired by the Sabra and Shatila massacres.

Right: Susanne Sulley sings 'before the soldiers came' on 'The Lebanon' video.

Left: The third Heaven 17 album includes 'This Is Mine', their final top twenty single. (*Virgin*)

Right: *Crash* includes 'Human', the second Human League *Billboard* number one hit single. (*Virgin*)

Left: *Romantic?* was the last Human League album for Virgin. (*Virgin*)

Right: *Octopus* spawned major hit singles in a time of guitar-based BritPop. (*East West Records*)

Left: Proving that electro was still a force to be reckoned with, *Secrets* from 2001. (*Papillon Records*)

Right: Filmed in December 2003, *Live At The Dome* includes all the hits and more. (*Secret Films*)

Left: Philip Oakey guests on one track on this Victoria Hesketh album. (*679 Recordings, Atlantic*)

LITTLE BOOTS
HANDS
10TH ANNIVERSARY EDITION

Made In Sheffield. The birth of electronic pop.

The Human League. Heaven 17. ABC. Cabaret Voltaire. Pulp.
The birth of electronic pop.

★★★★★
Uncut
'Excellent' ★★★★
Q
'A must buy' ★★★★
Record Collector
'Fascinating' ★★★★
Mojo

Made In Sheffield.

DVD
SV001

Right: Subtitled 'The Birth Of Electronic Pop 1977-1982', *Made In Sheffield* tells the full story. (*Sheffield Vision*)

THE HUMAN LEAGUE CREDO

Left: *Credo* was the ninth studio album which came ten years after *Secrets*. (*Papillon Records*)

In November, *Dare* was issued as a picture disc in a black sleeve. The picture disc was reissued in a white sleeve soon after. And on a purely personal note, my short story 'Dare' was published in *Knave* magazine (vol.19 no.2, February 1987): it quotes The Human League.

The following bonus tracks were added for the 2012 'Dare/Fascination' 2-CD set (Virgin CDVD 2192):
'The Sound Of The Crowd' (12" version) (6:28), 'Don't You Want Me' (Extended dance mix) (7:31), 'The Sound Of The Crowd' (Instrumental) (4:12), 'Open Your Heart'/'Non-Stop' (Instrumental) (8:41), 'Don't You Want Me' (Alternative version) (3:57)

Bonus tracks featured on the 1997 USA CD edition, Caroline Records CAROL 1114-2:
'Hard Times' (Oakey, Wright, Callis) (5:42) (Originally issued as the B-side of 'Love Action (I Believe In Love)') 'Non-Stop' (Callis, Wright) (4:15) (Originally issued as the B-side of 'Open Your Heart')

Contemporary Singles
'The Sound Of The Crowd' (Oakey, Burden) (3:55) b/w **'The Sound Of The Crowd (Add Your Own Voice)'** (Oakey, Burden) (3:05)
Personnel:
Philip Oakey: vocals, synthesizer, cover design
Adrian Wright: slides, occasional synthesizer, cover design
Ian Burden: synthesizers
Joanne Catherall, Susanne Sulley: vocals
Label: Virgin Records VS 416
Release date: 20 April 1981
Chart position: 12

First issued as a single, Mike Nicholls reviewed this in *Record Mirror*: 'The familiar synthesized clacking renders this unmistakably Human, but it also highlights what has always been an essential League failing: the germ of a great melodic or rhythmic idea being spread so thinly that the impetus of the original riff all but evaporates'. He also commented on the record's red 'colour coding', to denote its dance intentions. Beginning with a simple establishing rhythm joined by deeper bass notes, the song swirls with rhythmic propulsion as the girls' voices track Oakey to the chorus, buttressing his major lines. The melody peaks with little screams before returning to the opening. To writer Peter Nash, 'It was admittedly trite compared to their former work, but at the same time was imbued with a lively quality that made it addictive'. Pop, yet existing outside of pop, this is the track that provided the group's major breakthrough in that it rose to number 12 on the chart (30 May), and opened ears that had previously been closed: the week that Adam and the Ant's 'Stand And Deliver' was number 1.

Joanne recalled in *Melody Maker* in October 1988:

We were still at school, and me Mum came and knocked on the window of this lesson I was in. I think it was A-level communication studies. I went over, and she said that Philip had just phoned and we had to do *Top Of The Pops* that night. I had to ask the teacher to leave in order to go to London ... Philip was living in a real dump at the time and had to use the payphone across the road to check on our chart position.

They were a group made up of amateurs and misshapes, on the punk principle, with success now assured. The single's success determined that the track was remixed and included on *Dare*. The track was recorded at Genetic Sound in March 1981 with Martin Rushent producing The Human League for the first time and was also the first track to feature Joanne and Susanne.

The initial batch of 7" singles had laminated picture sleeves, while the 12" edition carried a sleeve sticker, expanding the original track from 3:55 to 6:32, b/w an alternate 'The Sound Of The Crowd (Instrumental)' running to 4:11 (Virgin VS41612). The original 3:01 instrumental-edit 'Add Your Voice' mix would later be included as the closing track on the 1982 *Love And Dancing* album by The League Unlimited Orchestra.

A Canadian 12"-vinyl/cassette EP, Virgin VEP 304, includes the following:

'The Sound Of The Crowd' (6:25), 'Tom Baker' (4:02), 'Boys And Girls' (3:15), 'Dancevision' (2:22), 'The Sound Of The Crowd (Add Your Voice)' (4:10)

'Love Action (I Believe In Love)' (Oakey, Burden) (3:50) b/w 'Hard Times' (Oakey, Wright, Callis) (4:53) by **The Human League** (Red)

Personnel:
Philip Oakey: vocals, synthesizer, cover design
Adrian Wright: slides, occasional synthesizer, cover design
Ian Burden, Jo Callis: synthesizers
Joanne Catherall, Susanne Sulley: vocals
Label: UK: Virgin VS 435, USA: A&M SP-12049
Release date: 27 July 1981
Chart position: UK: 3

Produced by Martin Rushent, this was the second single issued prior to the album itself, and was more positively reviewed by Sunie in *Record Mirror*: 'This is tasteful, tuneful, witty and danceable, and you can't ask for much more than that from a single' (1 August). 'We were an arty bunch of people looking at pop music from the outside' recalled Philip. The song premiered on TV's *Multi-Coloured Swap Shop,* with Philip androgynously in kissproof lip gloss: jacket slung loose across his shoulders, Susanne and Joanne in striking black Kohl eye makeup and red lipstick, against laboratory banks of electronic equipment. It continued their inevitable progression up the charts, peaking at number 3 on the official BBC chart. It entered the *NME* chart at 21 on 15 August, leapt to 4, then took the number-2 spot below Shakin' Stevens' 'Green Door'. After it slumped to 6, it returned to second place on 12 September, beneath 'Tainted Love' by Soft Cell.

Powerfully percussive and overlaid with tinkling synths, 'Hard Times' is largely an instrumental overseen by Martin Rushent, with Philip, Joanne and Susanne interjecting 'Hard times' at intervals in variously expressive tones. It of course quotes the first verse of 'Love Action', with which this track is subsequently sequenced, utilizing the filtering intro synth riff as an immaculate linking device, and reusing it. Omitted from *Dare*, the track nevertheless opens the *Love And Dancing* remix album and was later salvaged onto the 2005 *Original Remixes And Rarities* collection. Human League would perform 'Hard Times' live as the lead-in to 'Love Action' on the *Live At The Dome* 2005 DVD.

An effortlessly danceable repetition that revolves as sparkly as a disco mirrorball, this was more than just a throwaway B-side. It was a sound that was being picked up by black New York radio stations and fed into their own radical electrofunk montages – a two-way interaction that in turn, inspired Martin Rushent to attempt a replication of what hip hop DJs such as Grandmaster Flash were doing with synth bass and LinnDrum.

The Australian band Severed Heads sample the first LinnDrum beats off 'Hard Times', and loop it, using it as the rhythm track for 'Exploring The Secrets Of Treating Deaf Mutes' on their 1983 album *Since The Accident* (Ink Records; Virgin 206 176 for Europe).

The 12" edition of the Human League single (VS435-12), expanded the 3:50 single edit and the 4:53 'Hard Times' into 'Hard Times'/'Love Action (I Believe In Love)' (10:09), with an 11:10 instrumental flip. Much later, there was a 1988 CD single (CDT6) made up of the following: 'Hard Times' (4:53), 'Love Action (I Believe In Love)' (5:06), 'Hard Times (Instrumental) (5:44), 'Love Action (Instrumental) (5:23)

'Open Your Heart' (Oakey, Callis) (3:53) b/w **'Non-Stop'** (Callis, Wright) (4:15) by **The Human League** (Blue)
Label: Virgin VS453, Canada VS1145
Release date: 28 September 1981
Chart position: 6
This was the first single to feature Jo as one of the six band faces on the sleeve, and was issued immediately prior to the launch of the album itself. It appeared at number 17 (NME, 17 October) the week Adam and the Ants' 'Prince Charming' was number 1, and climbed to 7 the following week. On the rival BBC chart, it was number 6 (17 October), followed by a screening of the band's first specifically-filmed video (directed by Brian Grant) on the 22 October episode of *Top Of The Pops*.

The 12" edition (VS453-12) again sequences 'Open Your Heart'/'Non-Stop' – from their 3:53 and 4:15 single edits – into an 8:15 A-side b/w an 8:41 instrumental mix.

'Don't You Want Me' (Callis, Oakey, Wright) (3:57) b/w 'Seconds' (Callis, Oakey, Wright) (4:59) by **The Human League** 100
Label: UK: Virgin Records VS466, USA: A&M SP-17184
Release date: 27 November 1981
Chart positions: UK: 1, USA: 1
Now, five years later on, they've got the world at their feet. They even won the Best Newcomers Award at the 1982 BRIT awards.

At 7:30 pm on Thursday, 26 November 1981, The Human League played a sold-out concert at The Lyceum Theatre on Tudor Way in their hometown of Sheffield. Admission was just £3.

There had already been three successful singles lifted from *Dare*, and Philip considered that to be quite sufficient. But Virgin's chief executive Simon Draper thought differently and pressed for a fourth single, against the band's wishes. But once he got his way, not only did it become the UK Christmas number-1, but the year's biggest-selling single too. 1981 had not been a good year for single sales, and 'Don't You Want Me' was the only release to qualify as a domestic million-seller. Everyone knows the opening line, 'You were working as a waitress in a cocktail bar – it's woven into the generational mythology that defines the decade. The technique of alternating male and female vocal lines – with Susanne Sulley giving barbed love/hate responses to Oakey's narrative urging – seems to add the magic. It had worked for Sonny & Cher, Nancy Sinatra & Lee Hazlewood and Esther & Abi Ofarim, as it would for Chrissie Hynde with UB40. The contrasting gender dialogue gives the unfolding storyline an irresistible momentum.

The single repeated its spectacular sales performance in the USA, where it hit number 1 in *Billboard* for three straight weeks from 3 July 1982. Its American success – accelerated by the high-gloss movie-quality video exploiting the band's extreme visual appeal – heralded what was soon termed the second British invasion, with Duran Duran, Culture Club and, oddly, A Flock Of Seagulls forming a new wave of sophisticated Brit-glam. Philip initially identified a potential target of The Human League as getting as big as Kim Wilde. They'd exceeded that. As on 'Empire State Human', they'd grown tall, tall, tall, to become the biggest humans in the land.

Taken up by the metrosexual metropolitan/cosmopolitan southern gilded youth, there were some who saw The Human League as nothing more than glitzy and superficial; a magpie of styles; a bright and brittle look posing as advanced modernity. Kohl, not dole. Pat Sweeney wrote, 'Everything The Human League – and pop in general – meant in 1981, was encapsulated in that video – the foregrounding of artifice; it's self-conscious play with images;

the anxious neurotic quality of a pop aesthetic which had grown too clever for its own good and was desperately trying to feign innocence'. (*NME*, 21 January 1984).

But with the album and single simultaneously hogging their number-1 positions and being played through every media device known to humankind, it seemed that the synthesizer had eclipsed the guitar as pop's main instrument of choice; while the drum-machine – originally conceived as a novelty click track built into home organs – was becoming the percussive base of just about every record that got a sniff at the UK top 30. A startled Musicians' Union even kick-started a 'Keep It Live' campaign, fearing that the new push-button technology spelt unemployment for musicians' time-served and obsolescence for traditional instrumentation.

There was a limited edition single with poster insert. The 12"EP (VS466-12) simply includes the 3:57 and 4:59 single edits, but adds the 'Don't You Want Me' extended dance mix (7:30) on the B-side. The German maxi-single 12" included the bonus track 'Do Or Die'.

'Don't You Want Me' returned to the top 20 in October 1995 when Virgin issued a new remix to coincide with the release of the group's second *Greatest Hits* album, and the single did so again in March 2014 when it climbed to 19. (Video director Steve Barron later went on to do 'Crushed By The Wheels Of Industry' and 'Come Live With Me' for Heaven 17.)

'Being Boiled' (Oakey, Marsh, Ware) (3:45) b/w 'Circus Of Death' (Oakey, Marsh, Ware) (4:47)

Label: Fast Product 4; Australia EMI-657
Release date: August 1980
Chart position: UK: 6

The Human League's massive commercial breakthrough with *Dare* and 'Don't You Want Me' had some unexpected side effects – that a reissue of Kraftwerk's formative-electronica 'The Model' b/w 'Computer Love' deposed Shakin' Stevens from the number-1 spot, is surely no coincidence, bringing some deserved recognition to the German electro pioneers. Then, cover-blurbed as 'Electronically yours', there was a stereo remix of the original mono Fast Product 'Being Boiled': an early peak along the rising graph of tension. It failed to chart at the time, but this stereo remix was reissued in January 1982 in light of The Human League's new pop-star visibility. It entered the chart at number 19 (16 January), climbed to 9 and peaked at six on 30 January. This stereo mix is the version later included on the 1988 *Greatest Hits* compilation and has also been included on subsequent greatest-hits albums.

But there was more to come. 'Being Boiled' was heavily sampled by Liberty X in March 2003 for their cover of the Chaka Khan song 'Ain't Nobody': as 'Being Nobody' by Richard X vs Liberty X.

Methods Of Dance (Compilation)
Label: Virgin OVED5
Release date: November 1981
A compilation that unites B.E.F. ('Groove Thang'), Heaven 17 ('Soul Warfare'), The Human League ('Do Or Die Dub' (Special Edit)), Devo ('Going Under'), Magazine ('The Great Man's Secrets'), Japan ('The Art Of Parties') and the Conny Plank-produced 'Der Mussolini' by D.A.F.

The Human League in 1982 and 1983

Love And Dancing (1982) by The League Unlimited Orchestra

Released: July 1982
Virgin OVED6, USA A&M SP-3209
Produced by Martin Rushent and The Human League
Label: UK: Virgin OVED6, USA: A&M SP-3209
Release date: July 1982
Chart positions: UK: 3, USA: 135
Running time: 35:40

This is a companion volume to *Dare*, remixed through hours of sonic surgery, cutting and splicing by Martin Rushent, extended and resequenced, and titled as a nod to Barry White's Love Unlimited Orchestra. Riding the tsunami set up by the success wave of *Dare* and its singles – a game element that's racked up enough sales to make a pocket calculator with a nervous disposition, short-circuit – *Love And Dancing* climbed to number 3 on the album chart, where it operated as an effective stopgap release during the band's struggle to write new material. As Martin Rushent's deconstruction/reconstruction mixing-board project – the first to use the tapes of a full album as source material – it established a presence and a precedent that others would follow, with Soft Cell's mini-album EP *Non Stop Ecstatic Dancing* – and later Pet Shop Boys – utilising an identical strategy.

Side One: 1. 'Hard Times' (5:40) 2. 'Love Action (I Believe In Love)' (5:12) 3. 'Don't You Want Me' (7:18)
Side Two: 1. 'Things That Dreams Are Made Of' (5:10) 2. 'Do Or Die' (4:36) 3. 'Seconds' (2:25) 4. 'Open Your Heart' (2:35) 5. 'The Sound Of The Crowd' (2:55), 'Mirror Man' (Oakey, Callis, Burden) (3:48) b/w 'You Remind Me Of Gold' (Oakey) (3:36)
Label: UK: Virgin VS522, US: A&M AM-2587
Release date: 8 November 1982
Chart position: UK: 2

'A change of mind, another start, a brand new day'. Produced by Martin Rushent at Genetic Studios, Oakey later playfully suggested that Adam Ant was the mirror man in question. With Human League having repositioned themselves from the darlings of the progressive faction of the music press, to sharing pinup space with Adam in *Smash Hits*, maybe there were other more-personal considerations too. 'You know I'll change, if change is what you require'.

On tour, the group packed little Casiotone keyboards in order to capture fleeting musical ideas. Susanne recalls: 'We toured with it ('Mirror Man') on the *Dare* tour, and it was called something different – 'I Can't Get To Sleep At Night' – but Philip used to make up the words as we went along. We only had one verse and used to repeat it twice. One night in L.A., these men were being really obnoxious, and he started singing about 'the martini-swigging crowd' or something. 'Mirror Man' was a much better title'. (*Melody Maker*, 29 October 1988).

Ten mixes and eight months later, there was a sharp, snappy Motown rhythm track – a glance back at Northern Soul – with Jo Callis playing a Roland polyphonic guitar synth: 'You can hear the guitar synth on the on-beat, going chang-chang-chang. It sounds quite piano-ish on that. It's also on that sort of descending line too, but it's buried under a lot of things there. It just helps to build it up'. (*Melody Maker*, 18 December 1982). A well-groomed shorthaired Oakey sings into a theatre dressing-room mirror in the video; the lopsided peekaboo fringe had served its purpose and been superseded. In Harry North's satirical comic-strip retelling of The Human League story in *Smash Hits,* Philip says, 'With platinum-selling records, now I can afford to get *both* sides of me 'air cut!'. His video introspections are interspersed with black-and-white clips of speed-ace Donald Campbell's fatal record-attempt crash at 528 km/h on Coniston Water in his famous Bluebird craft.

This was the first new material to be issued since *Dare*. According to Joanne, 'When we started work with Martin, 'Mirror Man' and 'Fascination' were the beginning of the new LP. But we took so long, we decided to put them out as singles. It wasn't a progression, but it was a big change'. The hotly-anticipated single entered the chart at number 9 (20 November) and climbed to 2 for the following three weeks: just below 'Beat Surrender' by The Jam. Over at *NME*, the story was even more extreme. From an entry at 29 (20 November) it rocketed to three, before taking the number one spot for one week before surrendering to The Jam.

'You Remind Me Of Gold' has woozy synths over compulsive bass lines, with some unexpected melody changes illuminated by the girls' dreamily delightful harmony interjections.

There was a limited-edition 7" picture disc and an extended 'Mirror Man' (4:21) on the 12" (VS522-12), along with the 3:36 single edit of 'You Remind Me Of Gold', and an instrumental dub version at 3:53 in length. Later, there was a unique first-ever video single made up of the official videos for 'Mirror Man', 'Love Action' and 'Don't You Want Me' (from Virgin Video in conjunction with Maxell tapes): a format that never really made commercial inroads.

'(Keep Feeling) Fascination' (Oakey, Callis) (3:39) b/w 'Total Panic' (Oakey, Callis, Burden) (3:23)

Personnel:
Philip Oakey: vocals, synthesizer
Philip Adrian Wright: slides, synthesizer

Ian Burden: synthesizers, bass
Jo Callis: synthesizers, guitar
Joanne Catherall, Susanne Sulley: vocals
Label: UK: Virgin VS 569, US: A&M AM-2547
Release date: 11 April 1983
Chart positions: UK: 2, US: 8

With an abrupt, soaring and slightly discordant synth burst, Philip opens before Jo Callis adds the first of his rare vocal lines: 'Decisions to be made'. The girls' voices – first Susanne then Joanne – set up a dialogue, and so the conversation turns. In the video the girls sing the title hook, sharing Phil's taste in ruby lipstick, while Jo wears a black leather jacket and plays electric lead guitar out of his skin, while Ian adds determined bass. Maybe it's 'Looking for a new direction/In an old familiar way', though this truth may need some rearranging.

The track was produced at Genetic Studios, and remixed by Chris Thomas. This would constitute Martin Rushent's final Human League production for seven years.

The single entered the chart at 16 (23 April), climbed to 4, then 3, before finally peaking at 2, just beneath Spandau Ballet's 'True' (14 May), to be replaced at second place the following week by Heaven 17's 'Temptation'! The 1980s generation was now on full gush, with other top-3 singles including David Bowie's 'Let's Dance', Duran Duran's 'Is There Something I Should Know?' and Culture Club's 'Church Of The Poison Mind'. Yet, as one of only three singles in two years, '(Keep Feeling) Fascination' was *Melody Maker*'s Single Of The Year!

The B-side 'Total Panic' is a bass-heavy instrumental with strong dub echo effects and stabbing synth horns – a mélange of teasing half-familiar flourishes that remind you of this and that, though it has its own independent identity.

There was a 12" edition (VS 569-12) with an extended version at 5:00 in length, plus an improvisational mix (6:15), and the original 'Total Panic' (3:23) was added to the 1988 mini-CD single (CDT24).

Fascination (1983, US and Canada vinyl EP)

Label: USA: A&M SP-12501
Running time: 32:37
Chart position: US: 22

'Fascination'? 'It's about us', admitted Philip. ''Keep looking for a new direction/In an old familiar way'. That's The Human League in two lines', taking the band from its synth-only trademark to a synthesizer-sounding group into a button-pushing electronic definition.

Somewhat frustratingly, A&M Records refused to release the 'Mirror Man' single in America, 'unless there was to be an album hot on its heels'. So it remained unreleased in the US until 1983 when it was issued with the alternate B-side 'Non-Stop'. It peaked at number 30 in the autumn of that year. It was also incorporated into this stopgap EP.

Side One: 1. '(Keep Feeling) Fascination' (Extended) (4:56) 2. 'Mirror Man' (3:48)
3. 'Hard Times' (4:54) (Originally the B-side of the 1981 single 'Love Action', and
also featured on the 1982 remix album Love And Dancing.)
Side Two: 1. 'I Love You Too Much' (3:18) (An early Martin Rushent-produced
version of the song that would be reworked as part of the 1984 album Hysteria –
'It's like The Glitter Band', Philip told Smash Hits.) 2. 'You Remind Me Of Gold'
(3:35) 3. '(Keep Feeling) Fascination' (Improvisation) (6:12)

'I Love You Too Much' (Dub) (Burden, Callis, Wright) (5:54) (2008
digital download bonus track.)

Dare/Fascination! (Special CD) (2012)/Japan-only Fascination!
limited edition single CD (2015)
1. 'Hard Times'/'Love Action (I Believe In Love)' (Instrumental) (11:08) 2. 'Mirror
Man' (3:51) 3. 'You Remind Me Of Gold' (3:38) 4. '(Keep Feeling) Fascination'
(Extended) (4:59) 5. 'I Love You Too Much' (3:20) 6. 'Mirror Man' (Extended)
(4:23) 7. 'You Remind Me Of Gold' (Instrumental) (3:54) 8. '(Keep Feeling)
Fascination' (Improvisational) (6:15) 9. 'I Love You Too Much' (Dub) (5:53) 10.
'Total Panic' (3:29)

Amor Secreto (Nick Fury) (3:20) b/w **Por Fin, Esto Es** (5:51) (Nick
Fury, Laurie Heath) **by Nick Fury**
Release date: 1983 (Spain only, DRO DRO-034)
Produced by Philip Oakey – who also took credit for synthesizer, with Ian
Burden's bass and Jo Callis on resounding guitar – this one-off project
represents a rare excursion into EuroPop sung in Spanish. Plus, there was an
English version, for which the song became 'Secret Love'. The motivation for
The Human League involvement is not immediately obvious.

Releases from ABC and Cabaret Voltaire

The Lexicon Of Love (1982) by ABC
Personnel:
Martin Fry: lead vocals
Mark White: guitars, keyboards, backing vocals
Stephen Singleton: alto and tenor saxophones
David Palmer: drums, percussion, Linn LM-1 programming
Mark Lickley: bass (on singles 'Tears Are Not Enough', 'Poison Arrow' and 'The Look Of Love')
David Robinson: drums (on single 'Tears Are Not Enough')
Label: UK: Neutron NTRS1, USA: Mercury SRM-1-4059
Release date: 21 June 1982
Chart positions: UK: 1, USA: 24, Canada: 3, Australia: 9

The world is full of strange arrangements. Meanwhile, back in Sheffield, promptly after issuing a final electro single called 'Stilyagi' b/w 'Eyes Of Christ' (1980, Dutch Backstreet Backlash Records BBR003), Vice Versa assumed the newly-minted identity of ABC, and linked up with producer Trevor Horn to create another decade-defining album that took them all the way to number 1, spawning an impressive run of high-concept hit singles. From out of the same volatile crucible of sound as Cabaret Voltaire, Clock DVA and The Human League, Sheffield was already being branded as the new Liverpool of the electro beat-style boom.

The Crackdown (1983) by Cabaret Voltaire
Personnel:
Stephen Mallinder: vocals, bass, trumpet, piano
Richard H Kirk: synthesizer, guitar, clarinet, saxophone, Japanese bamboo flute
Alan Fish: drums, percussion
David Ball: keyboards, drum programming, tape operation
Producer/engineer/mixer: Flood, with Stevo Pearce as executive producer and single's remix
Executive producer: Stevo Pearce
Singles' remix: John Luongo
Label: Virgin/Some Bizzare CV1 CVDV1
Release date: 18 August 1983
Chart position: -

Was it just a coincidence that Cabaret Voltaire released their 'Just Fascination' b/w 'Crackdown' double A-side 12" single in July 1983? Issued through a Some Bizzare-Virgin hook-up, it was probably their most concerted assault on the electronic dance-funk market, a massively powerful release, intense enough to suck your eyes back into your head.

The Cab's fifth studio album followed *Mix-Ups* (October 1979), *The Voice Of America* (July 1980), *Red Mecca* (September 1981) and *2X45* (May 1982), which had all scored highly on the indie chart. *The Crackdown* probably received more media coverage than all of its predecessors laid groove-to-groove. But that fact said more about the non-recognition afforded their earlier work than it did about any radical new departures evident on *The Crackdown*. Inevitably there were developments, a greater sense of discipline and maturity. But what they lost in risk, they gained in certainty, and largely, everyone was a winner.

There's a higher vocal profile than on previous work, with distortion and effects kept to a minimum. There's some voice phone-in distancing on '24-24', odd found-sound tape dialogue in the eerie instrumental 'Haiti' and in the fade of the compulsive 'Talking Time'. But to compensate, there's a corresponding intensifying of dense storming cross-rhythms and percussion: particularly on 'In The Shadows'. There are some frills added by ex-Soft Cell member Dave Ball, and some creative ideas from engineer Flood: another name known to those familiar with Soft Cell liner notes. But ultimately, any judgement of loss or gain came down to context.

Viewed as the latest instalment of the Cab's saga, there were key techniques, logical evolutions, and familiar reference points sufficient to satisfy the most discriminating of purist devotees. Yet sucked into the new chart company that the marketing strategy invites, there had to be comparisons with the Blancmanges and Passages of this world, setting up the Cab's hypnotic repetition, density, accumulative intensity and dynamic tension, against electropop's more immediate hooks and melodic bribes. On repeat-play at high volume, *The Crackdown* condenses out favourably, head and shoulders above all such ephemeral analogies, but it's odd that such comparisons had to be made in the first place. As electro-pioneers, the album's lineage predates the entire genre! But this is entertainment. This is fun. 'Talking Time' instructs, 'Lesson one, you clap your hands', and the suggestion is hard to resist as they dance blipping jabs of fizzy electric washes over fast-popping mechanical percussion augmented by Alan Fish's planished sheet-metal drumming. This is state-of-the-art 1983 electric music for the mind and body. And any slight recidivist preferences on my part for the vintage violence of *Red Mecca* or *2 X 45*, should be politely ignored.

Two nodes of a diffuse molecular machine, Cabaret Voltaire, were barely on nodding terms with the charts. As an art project, they had the respect of their peers, which extended down to subsequent generations of electro-experimentalists. They were an example of what could be achieved with a drum machine, synths and a radical manifesto ripped from William Burroughs and Tristan Tzara. But Mark E. Smith of The Fall once confided to me that, 'It's a bit art school. It's very Sheffield in'it, let's face it. The Cab's are real uptight about the fact that they shared a studio with The Human League, but will never admit to themselves that basically they never really got over The Human League becoming pop stars'

Heaven 17 – Back to The Future

It had all started with Martyn Ware and Ian Craig Marsh. First with Adi Newton and then with Philip Oakey. Now it had simply reverted to that original protean duo all over again. So was it a reset to factory settings, back to the harsh experimental extremism of *The Golden Hour Of The Future*? No, they'd crossed over from industrial basement tape manipulations into high-gloss laminated productions. They moved south down the M1 to London and became B.E.F. in order to undertake a new series of amusing and innovative projects. Ian told *NME*: 'Human League were really an early British Electric Foundation project. We selected Phil and Adrian, and now we're letting them carry on, and we'll still get money from the third album!!!'. Working on the Rene Magritte principle that to be effectively subversive, one must assume a façade of reassuring convention, they assumed a financier-chic in order to destabilise 'mega-pop' by infiltration and mystification. Caught up in a satiric/ironic replication of the new breed of *big-bang* Thatcher-era entrepreneurialism complete with smart threads, red braces, briefcases and Glenn Gregory's ponytail, they succeeded in vexing and confusing the music press with a series of idiosyncratic projects.

Melody Maker's Lynder Barber saw through the scam on 3 October 1981.

This is 1981, not the soppy, liberal '60s. Time to toughen up and take sides, trample on a few souls and destroy a few careers: it's all in a day's work. Things are getting dangerous out there, haven't you noticed? Pesky rioters ... what's needed now is a bit of hardheaded business acumen and dollar machismo'.

As in, not! This is 'The New Partnership: That's opening doors all over the world'.

Music For Stowaways (1981) by B.E.F. (British Electric Foundation)

Label: Virgin (Cassette edition VCV2888)
Release date: 31 March 1981
Running time: 32:11
Side One: Uptown
1. 'The Optimum Chant' (4:10) 2. 'Uptown Apocalypse' (3:12) 3. 'Wipe The Board Clean' (3:46) 4. 'Groove Thang' (4:06)
Side Two: Downtown
1. 'Music To Kill Your Parents By' (1:26) 2. 'The Old At Rest' (5:37) 3. 'Rise Of The East' (2:50) 4. 'Decline Of The West' (7:05)

'Stowaways' was an early term for the Walkman portable cassette player, which liberated music from the front-room sound system, and took a walk with the listener, relinquishing the present to embrace a future scan of mobility.

Reviewed as a 'weld of innovation and intelligence that stuck its neck above the sound of the crowd without even having to try' (*Melody Maker*, 3 October 1981), the album was reformatted as the vinyl LP *Music For Listening To* later in the year, with a different track list and cover art, aiming its release at export markets.

Side One: Penthouse side
1. 'Groove Thang' (4:06) 2. 'Optimum Chant' (4:12) 3. 'Uptown Apocalypse' (3:12) 4. 'BEF Ident' (0:37)
Side Two: Pavement side
1. 'A Baby Called Billy' (4:00) 2. 'Rise Of The East' (2:50) 3. 'Music To Kill Your Parents By' (1:27)

Reissued as *Music For Listening To* (CD BEF 1):
1. 'Groove Thang' (4:06) 2. 'Optimum Chant' (4:12) 3. 'Uptown Apocalypse' (3:12) 4. 'BEF Ident' (0:37) 5. 'A Baby Called Billy' (4:00) 6. 'Rise Of The East' (2:50) 7. 'Music To Kill Your Parents By' (1:24)
Bonus tracks: 'Wipe The Board Clean' (3:46), 'The Old At Rest' (5:37), 'Decline Of The West' (7:15)

Penthouse And Pavement (1981) by Heaven 17

Personnel:

Glenn Gregory: lead and background vocals

Martyn Ware: synthesizers, Linn LM-1 drum machine, piano, percussion, backing vocals

Ian Craig Marsh: synthesizers, saxophone, percussion

Malcolm Veale: synthesizers, saxophone

Josie James: backing vocals (Crusaders Royal Jam singer on 'Penthouse And Pavement')

Steve Travell: piano ('Soul Warfare')

John Wilson: credited as 'And Introducing' seventeen-year-old genius, bass, guitar, guitar synthesizer ('Pavement' side)

Ray Smith: cover painting

Producers: B.E.F, Peter Walsh, at Maison Rouge (Sheffield)

Engineers: Peter Walsh, Steve Rance

Label: Virgin V2208; Canada: Virgin VL2225

Release date: September 1981

Chart position: UK: 14

Running time: 38:12 (Expanded edition 50:32)

In the raw Darwinian struggle that is free-market capitalism, there are some who get the penthouse while others stay at pavement level.

The album branding claims 'Sheffield, Edinburgh, London', with Ray Smith's cover painting setting the tone for the sales campaign of Heaven 17's debut full-length album. In smart suits and ties, the three men shake hands in a satisfied deal-done way – Ian wears the ponytail and pinstripe suit, taking the red-telephone call in the lower right; Martyn adds notation to sheet music in the lower left, while Glenn loosens his red tie in order to address the meeting of the board in the upper left. For more musical reference, there's a mixing desk where the art overlaps onto the reverse of the sleeve, and there are reel-to-reel tapes just below the album logo.

Side One - Pavement
'(We Don't Need This) Fascist Groove Thang' (Ware, Marsh, Gregory) (4:20)

Developed from the hard, fast instrumental 'Groove Thang' on *Music For Stowaways* and banned by the politically-sensitive Radio 1, this storming agitprop dance track (b/w 'The Decline Of The West') became the debut Heaven 17 single, released on 6 March 1981, reaching 45 on the UK chart on 28 March 1981. A fierce denunciation of racism and fascism – utilising funk as its vehicle, whipped into a compulsive climax propelled by jumpy bass and dirty horns – it attacks US President Ronald Reagan and UK Prime Minister Margaret Thatcher. Brothers, Sisters... this is committed dance on the radical edge; the things that different dreams are made of – because, no, we don't need that fascist thing here, and if kids were dancing to this and chanting along with the chorus, that was a positive subliminal message as part of what were then known as the Rock Against Racism and Anti-Nazi League movements.

'Penthouse And Pavement' (Ware, Marsh, Gregory) (6:23)
A journey deep into a shiny world of compulsive adventure, hedonism and wonder, with choppy funk bass rhythms to contrast the high life with the low life. Issued in November 1981 as the album's fourth single, it shows Glenn's voice melding integrally into the mix contours, emphasized by Josie James' chirping girl chorus. For the video – set at the B.E.F. conceptual headquarters – there's a sense that the track forms a cyberspace anticipation of some red-braces Wall Street free-market merger in the discord and anomaly of a deal opening – a taste of a window that needs to be filled, with shapes that stroke the beauty of a secure transaction, to be joined again into that final satisfying consummation: a very ironic take on the 'greed is good' mantra.

'Play To Win' (Ware, Marsh, Gregory) (3:37)
There's an exotic festival-like vibe with strong clattering percussion, horns and a catchy synth whistle. Issued in August 1981 as the album's third single, Ian and Martyn do the callback responses to Glenn's vocal lines and the insinuated spoken repetition 'and then he said'. From city clubland to theatre to sex in fairyland, it's necessary to 'step on the heels of chance', to dare to play for high stakes in the great roulette of life, with Heaven 17 assuming that same Gordon Gekko pretence of a 'break the bank' master plan.

'Soul Warfare' (Ware, Marsh, Gregory) (5:04)
'There is no place to run/Until the fighting's done/More bloodshed every day/ The soul war's here to stay'. If the meaning is not exactly clear, the album's default setting is busy funk rhythms with keywords relating to conflict, fighting, social discord and struggle. With hard electro handclaps and Steve Travell on atmospheric piano, Glenn's forceful vocals take the lead, with precise, punchy lines feeding into harmony passages and cross-phrases and an uncharacteristically lengthy exercise in guitar-bends around the midpoint. This track closes the first side of the vinyl edition in pristine style.

Side Two - Penthouse
'Geisha Boys And Temple Girls' (Ware, Marsh, Gregory) (4:33)
This opens with a spattered calligraphy of sounds with just a hint of exoticism. Then there's a softer close-harmony departure, with a greater subtlety than previously in evidence, contrasting the perfect creatures on-screen with the messier misunderstandings and breakdowns of everyday reality – prompted by Peter Mayle's book *Will I Like It?* (1977), which contrasts idealised and actual sexual encounters, as if to show that Heaven 17 can exist in other dimensions.

'Let's All Make A Bomb' (Ware, Marsh, Gregory) (4:03)

The line 'Take the M out of MAD' refers to the Cold War balance of nuclear terror encapsulated by the policy of mutually-assured destruction. The gift of one hundred scientists is the shiny new techno-pornography of megadeath: a brand new militaristic toy to idolize. What is the correct response to lethal political absurdity? 'Ignore the sirens, let's have fun ... Let's celebrate and vaporize'. There is another parallel meaning – 'Let's all make a bomb' is also a term used to describe making a lot of money. The darkest of dark humour, set to whistles, energy pulses and sonic detonations. A nihilistic joy.

'The Height Of The Fighting (He-La-Hu)' (Ware, Marsh, Gregory) (3:01)

This has sparse instrumentation over whiplash LinnDrum, with the repetitive, barked keywords 'Heat, War, Sweat, Law', as sirens rip from the left to the right channel and back again. It's either a satire on the military mindset or maybe it's just giving a radical frisson to the dance floor rhythms.

It was remixed with more aggressive drums and the Beggar & Co horns and issued in 1982 as the album's fifth single. Though it failed to chart in the UK, it did hit number 20 in New Zealand. The B-side 'Honeymoon In New York' is a minimalist electro-dance instrumental with B.E.F. writing credits, later collected onto the lavish *Play To Win: The Virgin Years* (Edsel Records, March 2019).

'Song With No Name' (Ware, Marsh, Gregory) (3:36)

Sharp stabbing synths build into the hectic 'can't sleep' repetition, 'Trying hard to find a rhyme'. Glenn calms the dynamic for the verses, articulating his sleeplessness 'Sold on a need to be famous', before it hits back into the frantic synth riff with border-jumping effrontery, skewing back and forth with heavy percussion and dramatic synth effects. A 'New version' of the track (4:41) was included on the 12" 'Come Live With Me' single.

'We're Going To Live For A Very Long Time' (Ware, Marsh, Gregory) (3:15)

There are growling, snarling synths as Glenn sings about about living the good life – 'Come and talk to God on the party line'. Ian and Martyn confirm God's views in complementary harmony – 'Come and join the fun on the way to Heaven': surely a tongue-in-cheek salvation. This is the Heaven 17 track that most closely approximates a *Dare* outtake, using an identical drum track to The Human League's 'Marianne', with the repetitive loop 'for a very long time' ramming the message home as it ends the track.

Bonus tracks included on the 1997 American edition:

'I'm Your Money' (Extended mix) (Ware, Marsh, Gregory) (5:10) (Single VS 417)

Release date: May 1981

The provocative idea of total chemical love possession or self-exploitation, integrating spoken vocal samples ('Sign here'; Buy this'), built around a raw rotating beatbox loop, syndrum, and Kraftwerk's chugging 'Trans-Europa Express' riff.

'Play To Win' (Extended mix) (Ware, Marsh, Gregory) (7:29)
See main track entry

Bonus tracks included on the 2006 remaster:
'Groove Thang' (by **B.E.F.**) (Ware, Marsh, Gregory) (4:07)
See main track entry

'Are Everything' (12") (Pete Shelley) (4:28)
A song first done by The Buzzcocks in 1980, issued as the 'Special Fortified Dance Mix' B-side of 'I'm Your Money', with acoustic guitar by David Lockwood, and more than a passing nod to The Kinks' 'All Day And All Of The Night'; glamorous quirky futuristic punk.

'I'm Your Money' (12" version) (Ware, Marsh, Gregory) (5:10)
Included on the Canadian edition of the album.

'Decline Of The West' (by **B.E.F.**) (Ware, Marsh) (7:17)
This was the part of *Music For Stowaways* that became the B-side of '(We Don't Need This) Fascist Groove Thing'.

'Honeymoon In New York'/'B.E.F Ident' (by **B.E.F.**) (Ware, Marsh, Veale) (2:52)

Geisha Boys And Temple Girls (1981) by **Arlene Phillips' Hot Gossip**
Personnel:
Alison Hierlehy, Kim Leeson, Roy Gale, Richard Lloyd King, Floyd Pearce: vocals
Simon Phillips: drums
Steve Travell: piano
John Wilson: guitar, bass
Ian Craig Marsh, Martyn Ware, B.E.F.: synthesizers, Roland Jupiter 4, Roland System 100, synclavier, LinnDrum
Producer: Martyn Ware
Label: Dindisc DID13
Release date: 1981
Running time: (42:28)
The dance troupe formed by American choreographer Arlene Phillips were picked up for *The Kenny Everett Video Show* during its Thames TV period

when their routines and costumes were considered risqué. When they graduated to accompanying Sarah Brightman on her hit single '(I Lost My Heart To A) Starship Trooper' (number 6 in 1978), an album seemed the next logical step, with B.E.F. stepping in to mastermind the project as an opportunity to recycle some old Human League songs.

Side One: 1. 'Soul Warfare' (B.E.F., Glenn Gregory) 2. 'Houses In Motion' (Eno, Byrne, Harrison) (No B.E.F. connection) 3. 'I Don't Depend On You' (Marsh, Ware, Oakey) (The song from the The Men single) 4. 'Burn For You' (Sting)
Side Two: 1. 'Geisha Boys And Temple Girls' (B.E.F., Gregory) (Done by Heaven 17 on Penthouse And Pavement) 2. 'Morale' (Marsh, Ware, Oakey) 3. 'Word Before Last' (Marsh, Ware, Oakey) 4. 'Circus Of Death' (Marsh, Ware, Oakey).

Music Of Quality And Distinction Volume 1 (1982) by Various Artists (B.E.F. with various guests)

Label: Virgin V2219
Release date: 1982

Using the decayed institutions of the music industry while simultaneously avoiding them, Glenn Gregory was signed to B.E.F., not Virgin. And with Heaven 17 up and running, the brand continued at a playful tangent, with a host of guest vocalists reviving a series of vintage hits through new B.E.F. arrangements and productions. In addition to Gregory performing 'Witchita Lineman', there's Sandie Shaw covering 'Anyone Who Had A Heart', Gary Glitter ('Suspicious Minds'), former Manfred Mann vocalist Paul Jones ('There's A Ghost In My House') and Billy Mackenzie of The Associates ('The Secret Life Of Arabia' and 'It's Over'). But the most successful track was Tina Turner doing the Norman Whitfield and Barrett Strong Motown classic 'Ball Of Confusion', which, it could be argued, single-handedly resurrected her becalmed career.

A second volume – *Music Of Quality And Distinction Volume 2* (DIXCD 108) – was issued in September 1991 by Ten Records through Virgin, with Tina Turner returning for 'A Change Is Gonna Come', while B.E.F. with Lalah Hathaway covered Sly and the Family Stone's 'Family Affair' as a spin-off single (Ten TEN369) which reached number 37. Other highlights include a returning Billy Mackenzie ('Free') and Scritti Politti's Green Gartside ('I Don't Know Why I Love You'). Martyn Ware and Ian Craig Marsh also take producer credits for Scritti Politti's chart single 'She's A Woman', with Shabba Ranks joining them for the revival of that Beatles song – their version taking them into the top 20 for the last time (March 1991 (Virgin VS 1333)).

A third instalment – *Music Of Quality And Distinction Volume 3* (Wall Of Sound WOS 120CDX0) – didn't appear until 2013, but retained the same formula of using guest vocalists to revive classic songs – including Sandie Shaw ('Just Walk In My Shoes'), Green Gartside ('Didn't I (Blow Your Mind This Time)'), Glenn Gregory ('It Was A Very Good Year') and Boy George ('I Wanna Be Your Dog' and 'Make Up'). It was issued as a CD and on iTunes.

The Luxury Gap (1983) by **Heaven 17**

Personnel:
Glenn Gregory: lead and background vocals
Martyn Ware: synthesizer programming, Linn LM-1 drum machine, backing vocals, arrangement
Ian Craig Marsh: synthesizer programming, arrangement
Greg Walsh: piano, synthesizer programming, arrangement
John Wilson, Ray Russell: guitar, guitar synthesizer
Nick Plytas: grand piano
Simon Phillips: drums, percussion
Don Myrick: saxophone
Michael Harris, Rahmlee Michael Davis: trumpet
Louis Satterfield: trombone
Carol Kenyon: backing vocals
Sarah Gregory: screams
John Barker: orchestra, conducting and arranging
Ray Smith: cover concept and painting
Producers/Engineers: B.E.F., Greg Walsh, Martyn Ware, Ian Craig Marsh, at AIR Studios and The Town House (London)
Label: UK: Virgin 2253, USA: Arista AL 8-8020
Release date: 8 April 1983
Chart position: UK: 4
Running time: 37:39

On 4 September 1983, Miles Copeland told *The Daily Mail*: 'The secret of longevity lies not in reacting to the market, but in determining it. Reacting to it means you have lost faith in what you are doing'. Heaven 17's faith was about to be vindicated. They were aiming for the overground and wouldn't take no for an answer. *Penthouse And Pavement* had reaped critical praise in the style-sensitive press, and established Heaven 17 as an ultra-credible name in the electro dance-funk wave, with image and ethos perfectly in place. *The Luxury Gap* took all of that and ratcheted it up into lavish commercial success, spawning a series of lush high-profile hits that still sound impressive today. 'Heaven 17 have always looked forward rather than back. Respect them for it.', urged Dave Rimmer in *Smash Hits*.

The cover art has Glenn in the centre, flanked by Ian and Martyn, standing against a tropical backdrop with a yacht glimpsed between the palms in the golden sunset glow: a symbol of the gap between opulence and street life.

'Temptation' – an electrifying collaboration with the amazingly soulful Carol Kenyon – entered the *NME* chart at number 19 on 23 April): the same week The Human League's '(Keep Feeling) Fascination' entered, two rungs lower. Both singles reached the top 3, and though Spandau Ballet's 'True' blocked out the top slot, first the Human League, then Heaven 17 took turns to stake out the number-2 position for two weeks apiece. New Order ('Blue Monday'),

David Bowie ('Let's Dance'), Tears For Fears ('Pale Shelter') and Blancmange ('Blind Vision') also showed on the same listing.

'Crushed By The Wheels Of Industry' (Gregory, Marsh, Ware) (5:54)

In a continuity carryover of the left-wing socialist realism of the previous album, 'Some drive tankers, some are bankers', and 'Some are nurses, some steal purses/Some are workers, some are not'. The rhythms are deliberately mechanical, with machine regularity overlaid by industrial sounds, yet with a strong melodic line and jazzy keyboard as they chant 'Work work work' by way of counterpoint. Heaven 17 here found the balance between manifesto and jive. If it's time for a party, there's a double edge to the 'liberation for the nation now'.

Remixed by Greg Walsh, it was issued in August 1983 as the album's fifth and final 7" single (VS628), with parts I and II spread across both sides and an extended dance mix on the 12". It entered the *NME* chart at number 24 on 10 September), climbed to 19 the following week, and peaked at 10, starting its decline just as Culture Club's 'Karma Chameleon' took over the number-1 spot. Nevertheless, for an album's final single, that's a pretty impressive achievement.

'Who'll Stop The Rain' (Gregory, Marsh, Ware) (3:04)

Again there's a kind of terminal dance vibe, borne on funky bass and female harmony voices, with a minimal keyboard hook. There might be 'flame in the streets and tension uncharted', but 'Let's be happy, let's be famous whatever the weather'. The rain is the deluge of events carrying the world remorselessly towards meltdown, but with the solace of love, they can still be the golden boy and golden girl. The 12" extended version (Arista CP723) effectively allows greater time for the contagious interplay to develop, while an American 12" Chris Nelson dub remix emphasises the rhythm track as snatches of voices rise through the dense mesh of instrumentation.

'Let Me Go' (Gregory, Marsh, Ware) (4:23)

A vibrating masterpiece; the properties of synths pushed where they'd seldom ventured before. No politics, no global crisis, just the numbing pain of broken romance; of walking alone haunted by memories that won't let go. It was the album's first single (pre-album issue) released on 30 October 1982 (VS532), and was spelt with an exclamation mark! – it had already appeared on the USA-only *Heaven 17* album. It also became the band's debut top-40 entry (issued as a 4:19 edit b/w a 4:59 instrumental). Again, the 12" features a lushly sophisticated extended version (6:14) that reaches the full arrangement potential, with backing vocals from The Hereafter, and yes, they just might've been 'The best years of our lives'. From a technical standpoint, it was also the first hit record to use the Roland TB-303 bass synthesizer, which later formed a defining feature of the acid house movement. 'Found guilty of no crime', in an evolution into greater maturity.

'Key To The World' (Gregory, Marsh, Ware) (3:42)
There's a real sense that this album is living on the pulse of modernity. 'Trying to fill the luxury gap/Has pushed me to the brink' – with a flourish of synth brass to announce an urgent vocal condemnation of selling his soul for charge-plate gold, with high horn bursts blasting through the mix. Maybe financial liquidity can be eased by a credit-card purchase of all those tempting consumer items on your wish list – the key to a venal acquisitive materialist world, but to the credit agencies, he's already Mr. Obsolete. Delete! 'S-H-O-P-P-I-N-G...!' (as The Pet Shop Boys put it), yes. 'Pop-Pop-Pop-Pop Muzik' (as M put it) can be witty, ironic, wry, perceptive, subversive, and yet, still danceable.

'Temptation' (Gregory, Marsh, Ware) (3:34)
Here Glenn is at his most demonically lascivious – a preacher on the pulpit of love, tormented by the sensual lures of his seductive amanuensis, erupting into a compulsive power-chorus driven by handclaps and complex programmed rhythms, urged on by the gorgeous gospel-infused vocals of the stunning Carol Kenyon employed in spine-shivering answering response. If Donna Summer and Giorgio Moroder first made electro sexy – with just girl and synthesizer – this is the consummation of all that promise. This is not only the quintessential Heaven 17 track, but a key track of the decade. Believe me, I was and still am tempted!

Released as a single in the UK/Europe on 8 April 1983 (VS570, b/w 'We Live So Fast'), it climbed to number 2 in the charts. In 1992, Brothers In Rhythm remixed the track, and it returned to the chart, peaking at number 4. An alternate version was recorded for the 2008 Heaven 17 remake on *Naked As Advertised* with Billie Godfrey as guest vocalist. 'Temptation' featured on the soundtrack of the iconic *Trainspotting* movie and was included on *Trainspotting 2: Music From The Motion Picture, Vol. 2* (October 1997).

'Come Live With Me' (Gregory, Marsh, Ware) (4:18)
Sumptuously slow and dramatic, heaven only knows the way it should've been – an aching need, regret and yearning; a cross-generational affair: 'I was 37, you were 17/You were half my age'. Performed on *Top Of The Pops*, Glenn winces at the lines 'At least there's no submission to heart's treason' and 'The strong are sometimes wrong, but the weak are never free' as though he fears their cheesiness. Yet they work with glittering precision within the song's context. Personally, I love this track.

It was released on 24 June 1983 as the album's fourth single (VS607), in a 3:35 remix (b/w a new version of 'Let's All Make A Bomb'. The 12" EP adds a new version of 'Song With No Name'. Both this track and the hit 'Temptation' feature orchestration scored and conducted by John Wesley Barker working with a full 60-piece ensemble.

'Lady Ice And Mr Hex' (Gregory, Marsh, Ware) (3:46)

This has a slow movie theme-like segue from the previous track, with meandering free-form piano and sweet close-harmony passages that frame Glenn's lead narrative into a 'do do do' midpoint break. It's intelligent grown-up electro for sure, although the lyrics are vague and open to interpretation – who Lady Ice and Mr Hex are or represent is left deliberately ambiguous: 'She'll trip you out and trap you in/Strain every nerve to make you spin'. Theories range from narcotic references to Superhero graphic novels, to characters from obscure cult celluloid of yesteryear. Sometimes precision is overrated.

'We Live So Fast' (Gregory, Marsh, Ware) (3:49)

Here there are jerky high-energy synths and echoed voices, driven on frantic rhythms set to catch the accelerating pace of life. The lyric catches the precarious confidence of thriving and surviving on wits; the instant response and instinct that separate the winners from the losers, the penthouse from the pavement, but 'Those who think young, will still survive'. An alternate 6:01-length 12" mix released as the US 'Temptation' B-side on 8 April 1983 allows even greater scope for vigorous high-octane syncopation.

'The Best Kept Secret' (Gregory, Marsh, Ware) (5:09)

Synths arc, like falling stars. A slow dreaminess closes the vinyl album with sensitive harmony lines, percussion from British drummer Simon Phillips, and softly-muted trumpet from Michael Harris. John Barker contributes to the orchestral scoring, but this track is never less than Glenn Gregory flaunting an impressive vocal range, with B.E.F. fine-tuning. Themes tie into some kind of continuity – 'The power of voice is the key to the world' – closing into the repeated refrain 'Falling hard, falling hard', and synths that spiral down to brightly burn like falling stars.

Bonus tracks on the 2006 remaster

'Let Me Go' (Extended mix) (6:22), 'Who'll Stop The Rain (Dub)' (6:15), 'Crushed By The Wheels Of Industry (Parts I and II)' (6:59), 'Come Live With Me' (12") (4:34) The American edition issued on Arista includes the re-recorded former B-sides 'Let's Make A Bomb' and 'Song With No Name' but omits 'Let Me Go' and 'Who'll Stop The Rain', which had already been included on the US *Heaven 17* album, with other tracks lifted from *Penthouse And Pavement*.

'Let's Stay Together' (Al Green) (3:33) b/w 'I Wrote A Letter' (Inga Rumpf) (3:34)
by Tina Turner

Label: Capitol (CL 316)
Release date: 7 November 1983
Tina Turner's second collaboration with B.E.F. following 'Ball Of Confusion', was this revival of the Al Green song, which not only took Turner up to number

6 in the UK but, in doing so, resurrected her career. At the time, she was far from the iconic 'Simply The Best' megastar. Following her acrimonious split from her former husband Ike Turner, she was at a career nadir, prematurely considered an unfashionable burned-out has-been. Martyn and Ian rescued her in order to open 1982's *Music Of Quality And Distinction Volume 1* with her cover of The Temptations' 'Ball Of Confusion'. Its success as a single (especially in Norway, where it reached number 5) led to Capitol Records taking an interest. Giving 'Let's Stay Together' a stylish slow-soul groove, placing Turner's power vocals in a setting that worked around Martyn's arrangement and programming with a dexterous studio team – including Glenn Gregory (backing vocals), Frank Rocotti and Rupert Hine (percussion), Ray Russell (guitar) and fluid saxophonist Gary Barnacle – the single's success on both sides of the Atlantic was vital in re-establishing her presence, and enabling the mega-selling *Private Dancer* album (May 1984), which included a further B.E.F. production: Turner's cover of David Bowie's '1984'.

Hysteria by The Human League (1984)

Personnel:
Philip Oakey: vocals, programming, keyboards
Philip Adrian Wright: occasional keyboards
Ian C. Burden: bass, keyboards, guitar
Jo Callis: guitar, keyboards, vocals
Joanne Catherall, Susanne Sulley: vocals
Martin Rushent: drum programming (2, 8 and 10); Jim Russell: (7)
Producers: The Human League, Chris Thomas, Hugh Padgham, at Air and The
Town House, London.
Engineers: Bill Price, Renate Blauel
Label: UK: Virgin V2315, USA: A&M SP4923
Artwork: Simon Fowler (Photography), Ken Ansell (Layout)
Release date: 7 May 1984
Chart positions: UK: 3, USA: 62
Running time: 39:59

There's no success like failure, and failure is no success at all, according to
Bob Dylan. Success can be as problematic as failure, bringing its own stress
and expectations. The meaning may still not be exactly clear, but The Human
League navigated the tricky extremes of both as they attempted to follow up
the unexpected hugeness of *Dare*, which was already far back in 1981. On
the face of it, they appeared as a solid, clever and commercially-constructed
contrivance with pure pop plans and a corporate identity that could conquer
the world. They *had* conquered the world, hadn't they? Their logo was strong,
bold, sure.

Dare had established the concept of high-end/high-art disco-pop for mind
and body, complete with sing-along hit singles – an off-kilter thing of art-
damaged Euro-futurism; a self-assembled plasticised aesthetic continuum.
Susanne and Joanne brought a more chart-friendly get-thee-to-the-dance-
floor attitude with a wraparound sound of elation: an image that first fit
casually into the pop matrix, then smashed it to smithereens. *Dare* was, and
remains, their defining statement of the decade. But, a prescient Oscar Wilde
warned, 'Nothing is so dangerous as being too modern – one is apt to grow
old-fashioned quite suddenly'. You don't stay ahead by standing still. So the
immediate fallout was not easy, with only a couple of singles ('Mirror Man' and
'(Keep Feeling) Fascination') where maybe there should've been an album.

King Kong was the album's working title; they reduced it down to *Right* – the
regular single-word trademark – before it became *Hysteria*. Susanne said: 'We
went to America, came back in September and started working then'. Jo added,
'We had two weeks off, then we went straight down to Martin (Rushent) with
two numbers we'd written just prior to the tour. But by the time we'd started
working with Chris (Thomas) in summer 1983, we had nine or ten of the 11
tracks that are on the album, in various stages of backing'.

Perhaps there was too much self-conscious contemplation on the meaning of their mission statement. It was no longer enough to simply go into the studio and make music. There had to be deliberation before, during and after – a conceit that undermined the refreshing simplicity of what had been sparkling supermarket pop. The result was over two years spent in different studios, gathering a mountain of unfinished tapes: Oakey said, 'We were in Air studios every day, at £1,000 a day, for over a year', and the band saw off two producers – Martin Rushent and Chris Thomas (who was simultaneously producing The Pretenders) – before Hugh Padgham nursed the project through to completion, while trends turned against the group and funds ran low.

Where Heaven 17 had ramped up and expanded the scope of *their* music when *Hysteria* eventually emerged, there was little of the sweeping playful confidence of *Dare*, and in many ways, it seemed to be a more cautiously hesitant project. If disorganisation was the key, *Hysteria* was the result. At worst, '*Hysteria* is *Dare* after the thrill has gone', accused reviewer Biba Kopf (*NME*, 12 May 1984). '*Hysteria* isn't electricity – rather the sound of batteries running down', taunted Bill Graham (*Hot Press*, May 1984). I suggest that they're both wrong. Their judgements were based on expectations of another *Dare*, and *Hysteria* was never intended to be that. Imagination and change had to be the guiding forces.

To Philip, *Hysteria* was premeditated to be a 'quiet bedsit album', to the extent that reviewer Bill Graham claimed that it 'sounds like a demo. With few exceptions, it is bereft of the secondary melodies, dynamic effects and all the other production and arrangement sleight-of-hand that can transform useful songs into *bona fide* hit records' – intimating that simplicity is the hardest of all musical aspects to achieve effectively.

The cover art was also reduced down to simple block lettering in alternating red, violet, yellow, orange and pink spread across the gatefold spelling out HUMAN LEAGUE, although it shows MAN GUE with the italicised *Hysteria* in the bottom-right when closed. Inside there's a Simon Fowler photo-assemblage of the group strewn around a bare room, marquetry floor, Adrian watching Norman Wisdom on TV, to which Oakey turns his back. Biba Kopf's savaging of the album, extended to what he termed 'the giant, insipidly-coloured *Mr Men* sleeve lettering' – a case of armed snobbery, as though, through a love affair with the media, it presented the shadow rather than the substance of achievement.

Meanwhile, during the group's conspicuous absence – with the Islas Malvinas lost and reclaimed, and Mrs. Thatcher returned for another term in office – the scene had developed other hearts and pulses. Electronics was by now less an innovation in itself and more a mainstream thing. Synths were out in force, and fickle audiences moved on to poseurs anew. Some bands were filching some of the enticing elements and putting them into a new more-complex music ecology, where others were too specialized to adapt or were quick to unlearn and readapt. Duran Duran were becoming huge – their second number one 'The Reflex' topping the chart the week *Hysteria* was released. Orchestral

Manoeuvres In The Dark were a few places below them, ahead of Blancmange, Cocteau Twins and Depeche Mode. Thompson Twins – also with South Yorkshire connections – were making major top-10 inroads. Even Queen had issued *The Works* (February 1984), which veered heavily away from the straight rock they'd previously excelled in, into electronics. For a while, it seemed that real flesh-and-blood drummers were on the endangered-species list.

In Sheffield, there were newer, more-extreme bands who'd taken from what The Human League and Cabaret Voltaire had achieved and pushed the ideas further. Concert promoter Ron Wright who'd booked early Human League and Vice Versa university gigs, formed Hula, who signed to Red Rhino for the cult indie albums *Cut From Inside* (1983) and *Murmur* (1984). After the breakup of the first Clock DVA lineup, members Paul Widger, Roger Quail and Charlie Collins, with Terry Todd and vocalist Peter Hope, reformed as Box, who signed to Go! Discs for the albums *Secrets Out* (1983) and *Great Moments In Big Slam* (1984). Adi Newton activated The Anti-Group (T.A.G.C.) for new adventures before forming a new Clock DVA lineup in 1987. Chakk issued 'Out Of The Flesh' produced by Richard H Kirk. Mark Brydon of that band later formed Moloko, and figured briefly in The Human League story. There was also the classically strange In The Nursery, formed by twin brothers Klive and Nigel Humberstone. Cabaret Voltaire continued their Some Bizzare/Virgin hookup with the stunning *Micro-Phonies* (1984). In another part of town, *Hysteria* (3 August 1987) was also the title of the fourth studio album by Sheffield hard-rockers Def Leppard. It proved to be Def Leppard's best-selling album to date.

But to some ears, The Human League was still music for future generations.

'I'm Coming Back' (Oakey, Wright) (4:07)

With the sound stripped back to its bare electro basics – programmed drums surrounded by a vibrating dance of synths, with a simple relationship lyric delivered by Philip with strong vocal support from Joanne and Susanne – it shows all the plain-spoken strengths of the band's essential blueprint. 'The Human League always tried hard to avoid obviousness', stressed Philip, as if in a deliberate reaction against the popular post-*Dare* synth mechanics, disputing the need for ever-denser undergrowths of arrangement to operate in absolute isolation from New York beatbox pyrotechnics. Colin Irwin's more sympathetic review stated the track 'is also exhilarating and celebratory, with Callis coming up trumps again with a seething guitar underlay that contrasts spectacularly with the synth lead and the girl's fresh-throated vocals' (*Melody Maker*, 12 May 1984). The track rises into a catchy and distinctive chorus – 'I don't care what you do/ I'm coming back' – although there's a slight feeling of riding on cruise control.

'I Love You Too Much' (Burden, Callis, Wright) (3:26)

This has a pulsing rhythm track with all the requisite core synth-pop elements, topped off with a repetitive and hummable chorus, and Philip's talk-singing narrative limned by a high wordless female voice. The lyrics are by Adrian

Wright, who also co-wrote the lyrics on 'I'm Coming Back' and 'Life On Your Own' with Philip. All the other lyrics on the album are courtesy of a solo Oakey. Originally intended as the single to follow '(Keep Feeling) Fascination', and already trailered as one of the B-sides on the American mini-album, this is a version remixed without Martin Rushent, but it nevertheless preserves something of its rough-demo freshness and spontaneity.

'Rock Me Again And Again And Again And Again And Again And Again (Six Times)' (Austin, Brown) (3:32)

The Human League have a curious track record where cover versions are concerned. But when it comes to the ferocious persistence of dance beats, they don't come much more primal than the Godfather of Soul himself. James Brown cajoled Lyn Collins into this raw R&B shouter in 1974, with repetitions built into the structure of the song as a basis for unabated funk improvisations.

Produced without Chris Thomas' involvement, The Human League effectively transpose the song, giving it a shiny new-age disco setting – an elision of cultures that frug and gyrate all over the Sheffield dance floor. It could be seen as part of a revivalist ripple in which The Residents recorded Brown's 'It's A Man's Man's Man's World', and the Flying Lizards covered 'Sex Machine' – though, in truth, the much-sampled James Brown had never quite gone away.

'Louise' (Callis, Oakey, Wright) (4:55)

Produced with Hugh Padgham and Chris Thomas, this was the third and final single to be lifted from the album, b/w a radical remix of 'The Sign' (VS723), and it was a moderate success, reaching number 13 in a ten-week chart run. It's a charmingly sparse and minimal keyboard production that relies on the strengths of the wistful brief-encounter story narrative rather than any production tricks or an ambitious arrangement. To journalist Steve Sutherland, it was a masterpiece of humility, in which Oakey's former robotic voice 'has been softened and enriched by experience to battered and resigned lover's croon' (*Melody Maker*, 29 October 1988). It resembles the kind of love-story-in-pictures tale found in such forgotten magazines as *Mirabelle* and *Valentine*, as it tells frame-by-perfectly executed-frame about how he accidentally meets his ex. The singer is sitting in the café drinking coffee. Looking up, he sees his former squeeze getting off the bus, and he hurries out before she has a chance to walk away. Tellingly, it takes her a moment to recognize who he is. It's a reassuringly normal story with no pretence of glamour – an image that could have been snatched from a 1960s realist movie shot in monochrome, such as *A Kind Of Loving* (1962) or Alan Sillitoe's *Saturday Night And Sunday Morning* (1960). It's easy to slot the scenario into the Sheffield Interchange on Pond Street or further along at Arundel Gate, although there could be other factors at play. Subsequent interviews have suggested the former lovers are the same couple that feature in 'Don't You Want Me'; that this is a kind of sequel set a few years down the line, carrying the trace of some unrecognised hurt. While that would certainly figure, it still works as a stand-alone story in its own right.

It might be possible to be unmoved by the spoken verse that follows the bittersweet instrumental break – where Philip says, 'There are wounds that you don't wanna heal' – but it would take a cold heart to manage it. There's no closure; he's holding onto a fantasy he doesn't want to let go of. There is tenderness, yet she still hops onto the next bus, carrying her suitcase, with just enough trace of lingering affection for him in her smile and her wave, to believe, 'as if we were still lovers'. It's evident that he's been carrying a torch for her for so long, he's burned a hole in his heart. But the fact that she's carrying a suitcase indicates she has other destinations in mind than reconciliation.

Humane but never humourless, 'Louise' was rated highly enough for it to later be revived by Tony Christie for inclusion on the *Made In Sheffield* album (2008, Decca/Autonomy), and by Robbie Williams (with producer William Orbit) on both his electro-themed *Rudebox* album (2006), and referenced as a lyric response in his 'Ghosts' (*Intensive Care*, 2005).

'The Lebanon' (Callis, Oakey) (5:03)

Issued as a single just prior to the album release, this was something of a radical departure, and what *Select* magazine called 'a previously taboo chattering guitar sound' – which Callis defended with 'The Human League aren't to me now a synthesizery-sounding group. I'd say it's still an *electronic* group'. 'The Lebanon' became the highest charting of the album's three singles, yet the fact that it stalled no higher than a respectable 11, meant that *Hysteria* was to be a kind of new normal after the stratospheric breakthrough-highs achieved by *Dare*; a holding operation for synth-pop freaks, rather than one step beyond.

It began with a Jo Callis backing track created simply on cassette, and a comment from Chris Thomas. 'It was a mistake when I let people play guitars on our records', admitted Philip in retrospect. 'It would've been very hard not to, because, without Ian Burden and Jo Callis, I'd have been nowhere. I'd be back on the hospitals. But we were wrong ... that was when we started losing our identity. That won't happen now. The Human League will remain pure'. (Interview with Jim Shelley: *NME*, 5 November 1988).

One way to achieve that purity was the group's rigorous attempt to control the use of promotional images. They refused to do photo sessions to accompany press interviews, insisting instead on providing their own publicity shots, for which the magazine in question was obliged to sign a special release. This is why their band images from this era have the formal, posed quality of term-end school team photos. That kind of media manipulation was prone to backfire when they were deemed uncooperative and standoffish.

'Betrayed' (Oakey, Wright) (4:02)

This began side two of the vinyl edition: where the pop is purer and the magic is constant. It opens with something of a flip back to 'The Lebanon' in its visions of the 'Ruins of another country' ... 'Blown by the desert breeze'. But this time, it was the north of England in the wake of the 'Tory holocaust'. As dry and weary as that breeze, there are echoed synth drums programmed to a slow, remorseless slyness, with complex instrumental changes to frame the lyric and Philip's strident enunciation. It's taken at an agonizingly slow pace – broody and intense with a startling bass run from Ian Burden. The girls are absent, and the understatement feeds the drama.

'The Sign' (Burden, Callis, Oakey) (3:46)

A kind of calling-out-around-the-world anthem, as Philip asks 'if you want to know what's going on', while the girls chant back, 'Everything will be fine' – their reassuring message punched home with blares of synth horns. Jim Russell gets a programming credit on this track that lies somewhere between play-by-numbers Casio future-world pop and trash-aesthetic soul. There's an extended remix (5:12) on the B-side of the 'Louise' 12".

'So Hurt' (Burden, Oakey) (3:53)

Regret. Broken memories. Shouting and tears. Again there's the reiterated motif of loss, although here it's disguised behind a catchy melody line and a recurring synth hook. Joanne and Susanne provide supportive and sympathetic harmonies. Lines such as 'Set your face against the tide' and 'Soul deceiver' offer themselves as useful alternate titles, while 'Just like the clock went back ten years/To make a new beginning' would backdate events to before even The Future. Given that chance, would we do things differently? No – 'Your memories mean nothing now/You're just a little older'.

'Life On Your Own' (Callis, Oakey, Wright) (4:06)

This is razored down to the basic vital ingredients that make up the unique Human League equation, with no exaggerated frills or flourishes. There's a strong – if downbeat – narrative, riddled with melancholy isolation. 'It was Al Stewart brought up to date', joked Philip, even if he states that his solitary lifestyle is self-imposed. There's a distinctive programmed LinnDrum rhythm track and a catchy chorus, with Philip's voice blending smoothly with Joanne and Susanne's. Colin Irwin claimed, 'The sensitivity of the lyric is matched by the tenderness of Oakey's vocal, a haunting tune, an inspired arrangement and a lovely mellow guitar run from Callis'.

Recorded at AIR Studios with Chris Thomas and Hugh Padgham producing, it was lifted as the second of three *Hysteria* singles – b/w 'The World Tonight' (VS688) – and despite being promoted by a *Top Of The Pops* appearance, it climbed no higher than 16 (7 July 1984). The video interprets the lyric literally, and shows Philip wandering post-apocalyptic streets while the other band members fade in and out like phantoms. Inevitably, the single was aided and abetted by a harder extended 5:48-length remix on the 12", which was collected onto the *Original Mixes And Rarities* album (November 2005), which has added samples, laughter and strings snippets.

'Don't You Know I Want You' (Burden, Callis, Oakey) (3:09)
The hallmark bass synth, establishes the bottom line. 'Got the keys to my car/But I don't want to go nowhere', admits Philip. Because I'm your friend and you're my friend, but tell me where does friendship end? It's a light, inconsequential flyaway joy, with Joanne and Susanne answering Philip's vocal over a jaunty electro soundtrack that pops like popcorn. 'You can act like a monarch/Or a pillar of the bourgeoisie', or you can work as a waitress in a cocktail bar. This song was worked up from the instrumental track 'Total Panic' from the '(Keep Feeling) Fascination' EP.

Bonus tracks for the 2005 CD edition
'Thirteen' (Burden, Calllis, Wright, Oakey) (B-side of 'The Lebanon twelve-inch and single) (4:10)
A slow instrumental with a ripple of guitar and sharp-snap drums led on a spiralling synth retuned to resemble an old Farfisa keyboard. It's a smooth, reflective musical phrase that builds and intensifies most effectively through repetition.

'The World Tonight' (Burden, Oakey) (B-side of the 'Life On Your Own' 12" and single) (4:08)
Catherall and Sulley take the verses strongly – 'Calling all the other nations/ Bring alive the world tonight' – while Philip joins simply for the chorus. Produced and mixed with Chris Thomas and Hugh Padgham, the bright, snappy synth riff craftily filches from 'Life On Your Own', although this is a distinctively original Burden/Oakey composition in its own right and easily rivals its more dour flipside.

'The Lebanon' (Extended), **'Life On Your Own'** (Extended), **'The Sign'** (Extended)

Related Releases
'The Lebanon' (Callis, Oakey) (3:45) b/w **'Thirteen'** (Burden, Callis, Oakey, Wright) (4:10)
Label: UK: Virgin VS 672, USA: A&M AM-2641
Release date: 23 April 1984
Chart positions: UK: 11, USA: 64
Recorded at London's AIR Studios with Chris Thomas and Hugh Padgham (the latter who'd worked with The Police) producing, this was in many ways a radical departure from the band's blueprint manifesto, raising many a plucked and painted eyebrow. It strongly features Jo's heavily up-front riffing rock guitar and delves into the complex politics that were then ripping Lebanon apart in the wake of Israeli incursions intended to counter Palestinian militancy in the border refugee camps. Adrian Wright later claimed the uncharacteristically-committed lyric was provoked by TV news footage covering the Sabra and Shatila massacres.

The music press was less than sympathetic, considering the message to be little more than an attempt at credibility from a band they more associated with flash and glamour: which is unfair. Weren't they the people's capitalists? Philip said, 'We're dogmatically leftist, but it's complicated. Our manager would say everything you do is political'. The single accordingly charted lower than might've been expected – 11 in the UK and 64 in the USA.

When what was needed was a single with maximum effect at this most critical career juncture, for some critics, what was delivered offered little comfort to the soul or any other part of the anatomy. In a skittish *NME* review, Gavin Martin called The Human League 'more pop people with their serious hats on. From the singles bar to the problem page to a glossy magazine romance, Phil and the girls explored every avenue of true love ways ... this is a propulsive streamlined slab of modern rock that bares its teeth and stamps its feet, hopelessly immobile and incapable of agitation' (28 April 1984).

The track opens with a nagging bass guitar figure that erupts into Jo's explosive guitar riff. Philip sets the stage with 'She dreams of 1969', with Susanne and Joanne adding 'before the soldiers came'. Alternating their lines, they continue, 'Before he leaves the camp, he stops', as the girls complete with 'He scans the world outside', and where there used to be some shops 'is where the snipers sometimes hide'.

Can't dance music also carry serious social issues? – Heaven 17 were unequivocally nailing their colours with '(We Don't Need That) Fascist Groove Thang'; The Specials topped the chart for three weeks with their dour essay on urban decay, violence and the kind of deindustrialisation with which Sheffield was only too familiar: 'Ghost Town' (June 1981). Why couldn't Human League do the same? Because he wore dangly earrings, and the girls were dressed for a night out at the Crazy Daisy? Had people forgotten 'Dreams Of Leaving' on *Travelogue*?

Philip was invited to participate in the Band Aid 'Do They Know It's Christmas?' charity single (which raised funds for victims of African famine), but he turned it down, reportedly because he thought he'd been asked to record a duet with Bob Geldof, little anticipating what an event the record would turn out to be. Philip later regretted declining that opportunity. Instead, The Human League played their own benefit gig for the Ethiopia famine-relief fund at Sheffield City Hall on 11 December 1984 – a five-song 30-minute set on a bill with Alvin Stardust, Howcher, Dave Berry and Snatch – not quite Live Aid, maybe, but it was the band's first live work in two years, with former Comsat Angels Steve Fellowes and Andy Peake on guitar and keyboards (replacing Adrian Wright and Jo Callis), with drummer Jim Russell: Martin Rushent's one-time engineer. They did one new song, called 'Millions'. Philip told *NME*: '1984 was such a horrible year. But you are glad to be one of the loony left, and proud to live on the Yorkshire coalfields, where there are still ordinary people who can't easily be bought' (22 December 1984).

Meanwhile, the 3:45 single edition was flipped with a 4:10 'Thirteen'. There was a 12" (VS 672-12) with an extended 'The Lebanon' (5:52) and instrumental version (5:07), and an extended 'Thirteen' (5:00).

Oakey Collaborates with Giorgio Moroder

Electric Dreams (Soundtrack) (1984) by **Various Artists**
Label: UK: Virgin V2318, USA: Epic SE 39600
Release date: July 1984
Chart position: 46
Running time: 34:25 (USA and Europe CD, cassette and LP edited version); 50:28
(Europe CD, cassette and LP extended edition)

The Science Fiction had always been there. The high-profile visuals were an obvious add-on, so involvement with a movie was inevitable. Released 20 July 1984 by Virgin Films, *Electric Dreams* was a light fluffy romantic sci-fi comedy featuring the bespectacled Lenny Von Dohlen as young work-obsessed architect 'Miles', Virginia Madsen as cello player 'Madeline' who moved into the upstairs flat, Maxwell Caulfield (as Bill) and a computer called Edgar, voiced by Bud Cort. Bip-bip-bip-PRINT – it develops into a fairy-tale love triangle between man, woman and computer. After all, computers were new, weren't they? They were what was happening, albeit two years after William Gibson had coined the term 'cyberspace' in his 1982 short story 'Burning Chrome'. 'Back in the old days before computers roamed the Earth, people used to learn things by reading words on a page', recalled an Apple Macintosh Performa advert from 1994.

As the first feature film by pop-promo director Steve Barron, it was not a great movie, but it has goodies on offer (the video effects that reveal Edgar's cybernetic thought processes, the champagne poured into Edgar when he overloads, and the fascinating visual effects that ensue as the bubbly soaks into his printed circuits and chips), and the film was rescued by the way the strong soundtrack was woven into the story. It performed even better when it transferred to VHS home video, aided by public familiarity with the songs! Steve Barron went on to direct *Teenage Mutant Ninja Turtles* (1990).

'Together In Electric Dreams' (Oakey, Giorgio Moroder) (3:52 on US edition, 5:18 European edition) by **Giorgio Moroder with Philip Oakcy**
Written primarily by German disco-supremo Moroder, with no particular vocalist in mind, it was film director Steve Barron – who'd shot the high-gloss video for 'Don't You Want Me' – who suggested Oakey. And who refuses a collaboration invitation from the man who'd masterminded Donna Summer's 'Love To Love You Baby'? Not Oakey, that's for sure: 'All we ever wanted was to sound like Donna Summer – she was our ideal', he told *Sounds* (10 August 1985).

After the first recording, Moroder told Philip that the first take was 'good enough, as first time is always best'. However, Oakey – who'd considered the take as just a rehearsal – insisted on doing a second take. Though Moroder agreed, Oakey subsequently said he believes Moroder still used the first take. Synths fall like silver around a perfect dance-pop confection, with Philip's voice matched to Moroder's song construction in a marriage made in electric heaven. Philip even wears a *You Have Been Judged* Judge Dredd *2000 AD* t-shirt in the promo video, as if further proof of the Science fiction connection were needed.

Issued as a spin-off single following the perceived failure of The Human League's 'Life On Your Own', 'Together In Electric Dreams' peaked at number 3 in the UK on 27 October 1984 (Virgin VS 713) – though it got no higher than four on the rival *NME* chart, beneath Wham!'s definitive anthem 'Freedom'. The success of 'Together In Electric Dreams' encouraged Virgin to chance a third single from *Hysteria*: hence 'Louise'.

'Chase Runner' (Marsh, Ware, Gregory) (3:00, 4:53 for extended edition) by Heaven 17

This movie inadvertently reunites the two separate feuding strands of The Human League Mark I onto the same soundtrack album, although the Heaven 17 contingent contribute a high-energy track that's restyled as 'Counterforce II' on the B-side of their 'Sunset Now' single. It's an instrumental that actually sounds like the theme for an action movie, and incorporates high-speed car-chase samples, with the thinly-pitched whistle-able tune gliding and curling over choppy percussive rhythms.

Philip Oakey And Giorgio Moroder (1985)

Personnel:
Philip Oakey: vocals
Giorgio Moroder: synthesizer
Arthur Barrow: synthesizer, drum programming, bass
Richie Zito: guitar
Joe Esposito, Elizabeth Daily: background vocals
Producer: Giorgio Moroder, at Musicland Studios, Munich; Powerplay Studios, Zurich.
Engineer/mixer: Brian Reeves
Label: UK: Virgin V2351, USA: A&M SP-5080
Release date: 19 July 1985
Chart position: 52
Running time: 32:44

In 1974 when Italian-born composer/producer Giorgio Moroder co-created 'Love To Love You Baby' with Pete Bellotte and Donna Summer as an album-length soft-core erotica stretching out to 16:49 in length, he was opening up disco music as never before. The infectiously contagious 'I Feel Love' from the same team (issued 1 May 1977) – with just girl and synthesizer – not only took dance music in an entirely new direction that made techno, Hi-NRG and house music possible, but it brought it global number-1 status too. It all started here.

With Moroder born 26 April 1940 – hence 15 years older than The Human League singer – how could Philip Oakey not be flattered by the invitation to collaborate?

'Why Must The Show Go On' (Oakey, Moroder) (4:10)
This has hard pile-driver programmed drums, as Philip takes the tuneful pop vocal with an assured confidence that was frequently missing from *Hysteria*. Moroder provides his regular fast-electro swooshes and squiggles in and around. Noël Coward might've posed the title's theatrical aphorism before Moroder, and Leo Sayer provided a refutation with his 'I won't let the show go on', but for Philip and Giorgio's intoxicating electro-glide, each line is shaped as a question: 'After the race is run/After the victor's song/Why must the show go on?'.

'In Transit' (Moroder) (0:56)
At a toe-tapping 142 bpm, and with the classic simplicity of evolving chimes, this brief instrumental strips the Moroder technique down to its most basic elements, and it works like a charm. Oakey is nowhere to be seen or heard, but for this interlude, no vocal is necessary. There was a 12" mix (1985, VS772-12) that segued 'In Transit' into the next track 'Goodbye Bad Times' (b/w a Moroder 'Goodbye Bad Times (Instrumental)' (5:20).

100

'Goodbye Bad Times' (Oakey, Moroder) (3:51)

Continuing the thumping 'In Transit' rhythm track, Oakey's terpsichorean tunefulness is jacked into one-two-three-four-five senses working overtime around Moroder's sonic drills and neural spikes. Yet, it's simultaneously as light and gauzy as summer UV rays. The basic track was recorded and mixed by Brian Reeves in the spring at Moroder's Musicland studio in Munich. Philip explained: 'They gave me eight lyrics to write in a week, and that's what you got. There's two rotten ones ... one of them's the single. It's got a rotten middle eight: a real Barry Manilow. But I think sometimes doing it fast is very good'. The single actually charted as high as 44 in July 1985.

'Brand New Love (Take A Chance)' (Oakey, Moroder) (3:59)

Just because there's a certain sameness about the template (programmed drums interfaced with dancing electronica), that factor is never allowed to become predictable. There are cooing background voices behind Philip's urgings to take a chance on a brand new love, sequenced into what sounds suspiciously like a midpoint guitar solo. There's even a catchy la-la fade. As easy as Pi r-squared.

'Valerie' (Oakey, Moroder) (3:24)

Cut loose from the Human League family but not straying too far from its essential core values – as if to form an equation that emphasises roots and continuity – this slight, flimsy pop sound with its squelchy bass line might've formed a Human League B-side in some alternate time stream – as though 'Valerie' is in some way a gene-related meme to 'Louise'.

'Now' (Oakey, Moroder) (4:26)

A walloping drum track galvanises a stirring anthemic chant with a positive-future message that looks beyond divisions and national borders, because 'at this point in history' – Now, right now! – there's a chance for better tomorrows. The whole world is on TV. 'We can prove we are not alone'. It will be a struggle, but if we all unite, everyone can live like kings. Vocal effects feed into the extended fade. These are also the things that dreams are made of.

'Together In Electric Dreams' (Oakey, Moroder) (3:52)

The original nu-electro take of '(Together In) Electric Dreams' also formed the second track on the *Now That's What I Call Music: 4* compilation (26 November 1984). On the tracklisting it followed Paul McCartney's 'No More Lonely Nights'. And though it's not a Human League track, it found itself creeping into Human League concert setlists, and onto their various greatest-hits collections.

'Be My Lover Now' (Oakey, Moroder) (3:51)

With a strong, uncomplicated straight-ahead rhythm with no pretensions beyond the dance floor, and issued in August 1985 as the album's third single

(VS800, b/w an instrumental Steve Bates remix), this made a solitary showing on the chart at number 74. Moroder knew how to programme drum tracks that fire neurons in the bloodstream, interfaced with Philip's direct line 'Let's forget the future, and live today' – suffice it to say that he'd moved well beyond The Future!

'Shake It Up' (Oakey, Moroder) (4:16)

Set to subsonic synths, Philip's baritone voice intersects, overlaps and duets with itself, providing the minimalist lyric repetition urging the listener to 'shake it up', rocking them again and again and again and again and again and again (way more than six times!). Sometimes simplicity can be all that's required – it's not always necessary to taste the gravity, feel the movement of the planet beneath your feet and inaugurate new arrangements every ten seconds. Sometimes recurrence can be all that's necessary.

The album could've been more, but it could've been considerably less too. Both participants vindicate themselves with dignity. The partnership would not be repeated, but the opportunity of working with the legendary Moroder was surely a career high point for Philip, and an experience he'd never regret.

Bonus tracks on the 2003 CD reissue

'Together In Electric Dreams' (Extended) (6:26), 'Together In Electric Dreams' (Instrumental) (5:10), 'In Transit' (Extended) (0:50), 'Goodbye Bad Times' (12" remix) (5:40), 'Goodbye Bad Times' (Instrumental) (5:20), 'Be My Lover Now' (12" remix) (6:14), 'Be My Lover Now' (Instrumental) (4:58)

How Men Are by Heaven 17 (1984)

Personnel:
Glenn Gregory: lead and background vocals
Martyn Ware: Roland System 100 bass, LinnDrum programming, backing voices
Ian Craig Marsh: Roland System 100, Fairlight CMI programming, backing voices
Greg Walsh: Roland System 100 bass, Fairlight CMI programming
Nick Plytas: Roland System 100 simulated classical guitar, piano
Ray Russell, John Wilson: guitars
Mo Foster: fretless bass
Michael Harris: flugelhorn
Phoenix Horns Esquire (from Earth, Wind & Fire): horns
Afrodiziak: backing vocals
David Cullen: orchestral arrangements
Producers: B.E.F., Greg Walsh
Engineer: Jeremy Allom
Ray Smith: cover art and photography
Label: UK: Virgin CDV 2326, USA: Arista AL8-8259
Release date: September 1984
Chart position: UK: 12

In the terminology of global brands, you get lowest-common-denominator advertising – a kind of global bland – or you get successful brand loyalty but which might be inappropriate at a different time. The high-concept Heaven 17 irony operated through a deliberate imitation of a global brand that spells hype rather than hope, and irony is a difficult tool to decipher.

From the urgent hard-line impatience of *Penthouse And Pavement*, through to the blossoming pop-soul richness of *The Luxury Gap* – when Heaven 17 were momentarily rated the coolest band on the planet – they'd acquired a glacial sheen of near-invulnerable perfection. They knew the tricks involved in assembling studio-perfect tracks, and they performed that function flawlessly – something lost and something gained.

There's a story that Heaven 17 were taking advantage of new Fairlight sounds that provided clearer and brighter samples, while Human League were caught up in a learning curve with the Synclavier II, which could resynthesize acoustic sounds with its own oscillators for very precise sonic changes, and that was a reason for the delayed release of *Hysteria*. That, too, was a difficult tool to use. By way of contrast, a Casio VL-Tone used on one *Dare* track was later auctioned at Christie's (29 August 1986), starting off from a retainer of just £60-£80.

Spizz of Spizz Energy joined Heaven 17 on guitar for a tour of European TV stations in early 1984.

'Five Minutes To Midnight' (Gregory, Ware, Marsh) (3:46)

This opens the album like some soundtrack for a workout video with grunts and heavy-exercise breathing. 'To break, or be broken' – led by Glenn's strong, powerful lead voice wrapped in orchestration with tight vocal backup. There are odd aspects – 'yeah-yeah-yeah''s jeered like a mocking chant, and phased voices that indistinctly mumble 'Waiting for the heat to come'. The title is taken from the Cold War code for the Doomsday Clock's countdown to nuclear annihilation: although knowing that is not essential for full enjoyment. This lyric is also where the album title comes from: 'You know how men are'. All royalties from UK sales were donated to CND (The Campaign for Nuclear Disarmament).

'Sunset Now' (Gregory, Ware, Marsh) (3:35)
British vocal group Afrodiziak sing the title frame and take the choruses in sunshine-light harmony, while Glenn adds scat vocals direct from 'here in Action Town', in a streamlined and blemish-free Greg Walsh co-production. The *Melody Maker* review enthused, 'They've moved still radically onward, experimenting intriguingly with subtle shifting rhythm on the one hand, while refining an even sharper pop edge on the other' (1 September 1984). Caron Wheeler – who would soon front Soul II Soul with Jazzie B – was part of the immaculate session trio Afrodiziak, with Claudia Fontaine and Naomi Thompson. B.E.F. had a knack for sourcing talent.

When this was issued as the album's first single (20 August 1984 (VS 708)) b/w 'Counterforce', it reached 24 in the UK. The extended 12" remix ratcheted up the percussive dance potential with dramatic Fairlight orchestration and voice echoes, taking it into the 'Bang bang, you're dead' phrase that hits the long fade-out groove.

'This Is Mine' (Gregory, Ware, Marsh) (3:51)
With a video that shows the trio acting out a bank robbery ('You can have it all/I don't need it'), this track was issued in October 1984 as the album's second single (VS 722) with B-side 'Skin'. But despite its strengths, it became Heaven 17's final chart entry (23) until the 'Temptation' remix in 1992. It's multilayered – 'Another BEF Production' – with voices interacting with The Phoenix Horns, and a high, clear trumpet solo, with additional horn for the extended mix (5:42). There is also a radio edit, a Filmix (7:18) and a Cinemix (8:55).

'The Fuse' (Gregory, Ware, Marsh) (3:05)
In a similar slow zone to 'Come Live With Me', this has Glenn confidently taking the vocal with an oozing slickness, as Martyn and Ian – with Afrodiziak on hand – provide answering voices. 'No time for might have been/You're on the winning team/No time to choose/It's time to light the fuse'. Heaven 17 were still a winning team, and although the meaning is less than clear, to me, it recalls Ian Dury's 'What A Waste' line, 'I could be the catalyst that sparks the revolution'.

'Shame Is On The Rocks' (Gregory, Ware, Marsh) (3:59)
This lyric may describe retribution arriving 'slower than the second coming', but the song itself rides a loose choppy techno-funk arrangement, with a

variety of background vocals and high-pitched voice effects, as Glenn struggles with the stigma of guilt. It's less than classic Heaven 17, but they are never less than smooth, competent and compulsive.

'The Skin I'm In' (Gregory, Ware, Marsh) (3:46)

'People say I need a new direction/People say I won't last'. Lavished in swirling, shimmering strings, this big self-belief power ballad seems specifically designed to showcase the strength of Glenn's stentorian tones, ornamented with Spanish guitar (a System 100 simulation) in a dream of endless time; a gradual sonic erosion that reveals the contours of the sculpture hidden inside the block of marble; a statement of certainty in the salvation-potential of love, until the track dissolves into a long dipping fade-out curve.

'Flamedown' (Gregory, Ware, Marsh) (2:59)

With synth horns blaring, this track was part of the various 'Sunset Now' formats, on the 12" cassette. Within what must now be considered the hallmark Heaven 17 sound, the overall mood is highlighted by soft three-part harmonies, but there's a fast-edit construction to provide depth. The lyrics to 'this curious song' concern a vaguely unsettling reunion on 'the glowing streets' that 'light up the heavy sky' beneath the bridge, with a suggestion that there's an unspecified backstory that must be resolved through 'the flame within'.

'Reputation' (John Wilson, Gregory, Ware, Marsh) (3:03)

A swaggering, vaguely retro-swing groove interacts infectiously with the voices of Afrodiziak: 'I can change my clothes/But I don't think I'll change my mind'. There are jazzy little keyboard snippets jabbing like frozen Morse code messages, and sophisticated guitar runs, all merging smoothly into the close-harmony chorus. It oozes so much style that it invites a Vaudeville dance routine until it seems to end way too soon. The full album was collected onto the *Play To Win: The Virgin Years* five-LP box set in 2019.

'And That's No Lie' (Gregory, Ware, Marsh) (10:02)

A long eerie intro recalls the Ligeti *2001: A Space Odyssey* voices, followed by synth waves over a rubbery funk bottom line, with girl soul voices urging Glenn's vocal on. 'But when the fire goes out/The dark starts moving in'. There's a jazz piano break with complex changes, and *a cappella* girl voices chant the verse lines into the fade. Make no mistake; this is the end! This is the new cool – a stunning showcase for Martyn and Greg Walsh's slick production values. On an album that sounds predominantly calculated and preconceived, there's little allowance for spontaneity or the kind of passion that fired 'Temptation', but this track is as good as and better than anything else Heaven 17 ever did.

Carried over into January 1985, it became the album's third single (VS 740) b/w 'The Fuse', though it charted no higher than 52. The 'Heaven 17 Megamix' by Sanny X – included on the 12" (VS 74013) – samples extracts from 'This

Is Me', 'Crushed By The Wheels Of Industry', 'Height Of The Fighting (He La Hu)', 'Penthouse And Pavement', 'Temptation', 'I'm Your Money' and 'Play To Win', and was later included on the 1986 remix CD *Endless* (CDV2383).

A 9:01-length mix appears on Virgin's 1993 compilation *Higher And Higher: The Best Of Heaven 17*.

Bonus tracks on the 2006 remaster
'This Is Mine' (Cinemix) (8:43), **'...(And That's No Lie)'** (6:17)

'Counterforce II' (3:08)
Originally the B-side of the 'Sunset Now' 12", this is a variant of the track that appeared on the *Electric Dreams* soundtrack under the alternate title 'Chase Runner', but here it's shorn of the police-siren traffic samples.

'Sunset Now' (Extended version) (5:21)

Contemporary Singles
'The Foolish Thing To Do' (Gregory, Marsh, Ware, Plytas) (3:38)
b/w **'My Sensitivity (Gets In The Way)'** (Luther Vandross) (3:33)
by **Heaven 17 featuring Jimmy Ruffin**
Label: Virgin VS859
Release date: April 1986
Commissioned for a movie that never happened, one-time Motown star Jimmy Ruffin was invited to provide a guide vocal intended to be re-recorded for the soundtrack, but this take was too good to not issue as a special one-off single. Ruffin's slow, conversational vocal, percolates through the arrangement with a cool soul sophistication, while Heaven 17 stand in as a backup trio. Now we know what becomes of the brokenhearted: they are here. Nick Plytas plays piano (and emulator on the B-side), and the track was produced under the B.E.F. name, with impressive session musicians – Camelle Hinds (bass), Preston Heyman (drums), Tim Cansfield (guitar), Carol Kenyon (vocals) and The Richard Niles Strings – though it failed to chart significantly. A new version of the song with Glenn taking the vocal appeared on the 1988 Heaven 17 album *Teddy Bear, Duke & Psycho*.

The B-side has Jimmy Ruffin performing the Luther Vandross song, with Carol Kenyon on backing vocals.

'Steel City (Move On Up)' (Extra Time Version) (Reddington, Jerry Knight, Ware, Ollie Brown. Steven Van Zandt) (4:59)
b/w **'Move On Up'** (3:42), **'Move On Up'** (Bonus beats) (2:49)
by **The Hillsboro' Crew**
Label: Virgin VS908-12
Release date: December 1986
This is a unique blipping electro-dance one-off benefit track for Sheffield Wednesday FC, with an 'Extra time' 12" mix produced by Martyn Ware, with

rapping vocals and a Heaven 17-style chorus from Martyn and Glenn Gregory. It's not the Curtis Mayfield song but does use a tune extracted from 'Sun City' by Artists United Against Apartheid (hence the Steven Van Zandt writer credit!), with a quote from Funkadelic's 'One Nation Under A Groove' dropped in. Martyn also played a production role on the tracks 'Oh Yes' and 'If It's Wednesday It Must Be Wembley', issued in May 1993 (Blue Wave SWFC1).

Crash by **The Human League** (1986)

Personnel:
Philip Oakey: vocals, synthesizers, keyboards
Philip Adrian Wright: synthesizers
Ian Burden: bass, keyboards, vocals
Jim Russell: guitar, drums, percussion, programming
Joanne Catherall, Susan Ann Sulley (reverted from Susanne): vocals
Paul Rabiger: keyboards, arrangements
Jimmy Jam: keyboards, synthesizers, programming
Terry Lewis: bass, drums, percussion, backing vocals
Lisa Keith: backing vocals
Steve Hodge: engineer
Artwork: Gavin Cochrane (Photography); Ken Ansell (Cover design, layout)
Producers: Jimmy Jam and Terry Lewis at Flyte Tyme Studios, Minneapolis
Label: UK: Virgin V2391, USA: A&M SP-5129
Release date: 8 September 1986
Chart positions: UK: 7, USA: 24
Running time: 44:40

In 1986 there were no more fashionable names than Jimmy Jam and Terry Lewis. The fleet-fingered Minneapolis-based console maestros ruled the dance floor. They started out as Flyte Tyme, which became The Time, in time to be adopted by Minneapolis' most famous son – his royal purpleness – Prince, playing a brand of R&B funk strongly in the Sly Stone/Parliament/James Brown vein. Striking out as a writing/producing team in their own right, Jam and Lewis quickly hit it big by masterminding the much-sampled S.O.S. Band's 'Just Be Good To Me', featuring their hallmark imposing-yet-impersonal Roland TR-808 drum machine.

Terry Steven Lewis (born 24 November 1956) and James Samuel 'Jimmy Jam' Harris III (born 6 June 1959) went from critical to commercial success with productions for smooth soulster Alexander O'Neal, The Force MDs, Cherrelle's debut album *Fragile* (1984) which launched her R&B hit 'I Didn't Mean To Turn You On', and ultimately Janet Jackson's massive Grammy-winning *Control* album from February 1986, for which Jam and Lewis co-wrote many of the titles, including 'When I Think Of You': Janet's first *Billboard* number-1.

Meanwhile, work on The Human League's fifth studio album was progressing fitfully in Philip Oakey's 24-track Sheffield home studio. Since they'd worked together on *Reproduction*, producer Colin Thurston had grown an impressive CV, taking in Magazine, Duran Duran and Kajagoogoo. But, 'We used to go over hi-hats that were too loud in bar 39 again and again', Philip complained. The diverse *Hysteria* was generally considered to have underperformed, but by anyone else's standards, it had done remarkably well. But The Human League had fallen into the Michael Jackson syndrome – no matter how many albums the king of pop sold with *Bad* (1987) or *Dangerous* (1991) (which were eye-watering amounts by the standards of just about every other act on the planet), they were deemed to have failed against the mega-success established by *Thriller* (1982). The same principle applied – to a lesser degree – to The Human League with *Dare*. They were competing with their own back catalogue! The confidence and clarity of vision behind *Dare* had become dissipated by success and critical analysis.

Crash was a J. G. Ballard novel that borrowed from computer terminology as well as discussing auto-eroticism.

On 26 January 1985, *Melody Maker* carried a story that Jo Callis had stepped back from live work with The Human League. He had quit, sort of. Joanne said, 'We were going to tour with *Hysteria*, but Jo Callis left and we felt we couldn't go on tour with his songs without him. Looking back on it, it was a silly decision'. But as their concert schedule was already infrequent, Virgin declined to issue an official announcement. But by then, Callis had left for real to record a glam rock-style EP as S.W.A.L.K., and to work with Feargal Sharkey: co-writing both sides of his single 'Loving You' b/w 'Is This An Explanation?' (June 1985, Zarjazz Records). So, drummer Jim Russell (who had played on Pete Shelley's Man & Machines tour promoting his excellent Martin Rushent-produced 1982 album *Homosapien*) and members of Comsat Angels were drafted in instead. But the sessions foundered and were ditched while the release deadline came and went.

It was decided that what was required was an outside perspective: hence, Jam and Lewis. In February, The Human League flew to Minneapolis and commenced four months of work at Flyte Tyme Studios. But despite a promising start, there were distinct differences in working procedures, which quickly created acrimony between the band and the producers. Their two approaches were antithetical – at best, they collided; at worst, The Human League were defeated. Adrian Wright and Ian Burden were sidelined in favour of the regular Jam and Lewis studio-musician mafia. In admirably candid interviews, The Human League explained how there were conflicts of interest and methodology that resulted in the band virtually abandoning the project after a 'disagreement over us wanting to play on things where Jimmy and Terry didn't want us to'. Susan explained: 'Jimmy and Terry took over far more than anyone else we've ever worked with, and they put their stamp on it. In the end, we just came away from Minneapolis and let them mix it as they wanted to'. (*Melody Maker*, 11 October 1986). Philip claimed, 'We didn't lose control, we let it go. We've had an interesting journey through the music industry, and that was one of the stops along the way: being a puppet in the normal American black music way of doing things'. Philip claimed to Jim Shelley, 'Basically, on *Crash* we were just an Action Man and two Cindy dolls'. (*NME*, 5 November 1988).

In a remarkably frank interview with journalist John McCready, Philip admitted, 'I would love to go out and do another LP that was as far ahead of everything else as *Dare* was, but doing that twice in a career is going to be very

very hard. I can't think of what to do about it, so in the meantime, there's a bit of treading water going on'. And was *Crash* a treading water LP? 'Yes', he responded (*NME*, 20 September 1986). Elsewhere he reiterated, 'We were lucky that we had *Crash* made for us by Jam and Lewis, so it looked like we were still living and breathing, but we weren't – we were in suspended animation somewhere'.

But the massive success of the album's first single, 'Human', returned The Human League to number one in America and back to relevance, in no uncertain terms.

'Money' (Burden, Wright, Russell, Oakey) (3:54)
For Motown's Barrett Strong, 'Money, that's what I want'; for Pink Floyd, 'Money, it's a gas/Grab that cash with both hands and make a stash'; for The Human League, 'You can have my money/I don't need it anymore'. Different strokes for different folks. The album's opening track sets the tone for what's to come, with the deep funk bass and riffing horns that will recur throughout. Joanne and Susan lead the vocals in tight harmony, while Philip's answering statements are mixed into the smooth arrangement. The Human League had always camped knowingly close to cliché and flirted perilously with formula, but they'd never before surrendered to the rhythm. They'd travelled a long way from Psalter Lane Art College. It's not yet certain if *this* was the intended destination.

'Swang' (David Eiland) (4:36)
A dance craze! A line-dancing craze! Mock-pop with tongues very much in multiple cheeks; a bizarre elision of strange elements; rap vocals in collision with hard dance rhythms, allied to a mutant swing. 'C'mon people, everybody swang!'. Ever since The Human League first unscrewed reality and filled it with brightly-coloured machine parts, there had been dance within the subversive components that made up the band's assembly – but cerebral dance, not gut dance – it had never been quite like this before. Philip insisted, ''Swang' is funny. Imagine Benny Hill, and then listen to it. It's a very weird song'. It's jerky and robotic in the way that Devo had once devised, and judging by Philip's energetic exhortations, he does seem to be well into it! 'Hey you/Let's do it, SWANG!'.

'Human' (James Harris III, Terry Lewis) (4:25)
Written and produced by Jimmy Jam and Terry Lewis specifically for the album, before the band had even arrived in Minneapolis, 'Human' deliberately takes advantage of the gender-mix dialogue that had powered 'Don't You Want Me', but to greater effect. Philip recalled: 'They played the backing track, which I thought was one of the best things I'd heard in my life, and then one day Terry sung the words to me, and I couldn't believe he'd managed to get a vocal tune that was right up to the backing track'. (*Melody Maker*, 29 October 1988).

For the male voice, Oakey tries to explain in reconciliation that infidelity is simply being 'human'; that we are all 'born to make mistakes'. In the final verse, the female voice (Joanne) turns the logic around in a spoken-word confession that she'd been human too. Philip stressed: 'We don't approve of the lyrics – two wrongs don't make a right, do they? In adultery. I think Jam and Lewis thought it was alright because the woman had done it too'. Or perhaps this track is simply an eavesdropping musical soap opera in miniature. The *Melody Maker* review commends a tale to 'bring a tear to the eye ... the perfect habitat for the everyday saga of broken vows, self-pity and sobbing regret'. (December 1986).

'Jam' (Burden, Wright, Russell and Oakey) (4:19)

With a throbbing bass sample and tense synth strings, the urging 'Jam, gotta get some jam' refrain sounds just a little incongruous. But the lyric insists this is starting 'oh-oh-over' – new experiences; new sensations for the heart; a wide-lens Americanised Human League with Philip's lead vocal ascending close to an uncomfortable falsetto, gyrating for the reason that if all our life is dancing, then let's just let the music play. 'Wooo-oo-oo-JAM!'. This might've worked had the track been blasted over the speakers at Manhattan's Studio 54', but the 54 had been closed down on tax evasion charges.

Back in Sheffield, The Leadmill was becoming the music venue of choice, and this track was not high on their playlist. 'Looking for a new direction' maybe, but perhaps not sufficiently 'in an old familiar way'.

'Are You Ever Coming Back?' (Burden, Wright, Russell, Oakey) (4:53)

The heat and wind that sigh through the 'pueblos', gust around the song arrangement. There's a strong rhythm track, and though the dusty locations that define the drone of the car engine towards the journey's-end village that rises in the distance seem to be American, the familiar Human League sound is reassuringly intact on this wistful song of romantic loss and remorse. The melody slides as cool as cream as the driver eases his foot off the gas pedal. The pulsing dance stance is played down, the haunting human element is increased, and the song works all the better because of it.

'I Need Your Loving' (Anna-Lynne Williams, David Eiland, Randy Davis, Langston Richey, Harris, Lewis) (3:43)

This is so much more Jam and Lewis than it is Human League, to the extent that it has the same rhythm as Janet Jackson's 'What Have You Done For Me Lately', and that's a fact! Does 'That's where I'm at' sound like something Philip Oakey might say?

This was the follow-up single to the immense success of 'Human'. Where Martin Rushent's production work had enhanced and brought out the best in The Human League, Jam and Lewis ruthlessly imposed their own preconceived vision on this project. That was the cause of studio tension. Nevertheless, Susan and Joanne – shamefully under-utilised on the last couple of tracks – are back limning the repetitive chorus most effectively.

'Party' (Burden, Wright, Russell, Oakey) (4:29)

More hedonistic fun, at a party where everyone is welcome, where you can swang to your heart's content. There'so trace of ABC's 'Radical Dance Faction', or of the '(We Don't Need This) Fascist Groove Thang' – no hard edges at all, not even the saving grace of deliberate pastiche or the escape clause of irony. There's just a mindless incitement to 'Come on, everyone is going to party party party', like a cut-up mix-and-match collage of lyrics shredded from every trash-pop party record of the past – it spins you right 'round like a record, baby, it's gonna use it up, gonna wear it out, it's a trip to boogie wonderland, 'cause boogie nights are always the best in town! According to Philip, it's 'our KC and The Sunshine Band song', which is less ironic than it seemed because he'd nominated KC as best single of last year (to *Melody Maker*). And yes, Philip, Joanne and Susan are all there, and are having a jolly good time.

The track is more filler than it is thriller. To Steve Sutherland of *Melody Maker*, 'It's as if they've completely given up the ghost, and in the absence of any real ideas, relinquished all responsibility and personality to a bundle of voguish funk manoeuvres and slick soul sheen'.

'Love On The Run' (Burden, Wright, Russell, Oakey) (3:53)

There's a demo version collected onto the *A Very British Synthesizer Group* compilation, which is *Dare*-clear and metronomically precise. The *Crash mix* is a little heavier and more textured, but don't 'look back in anger'. It's another story song – 'The page turned/Someone there to read my history' – with a strong forward-thrust, a high-gloss AOR radio sheen, ripples of treated vocal, and soul voices in the fade – lessons in balance, in wearing a different skin, in first-thought-is-best-thought, and to always 'write your own story'. For reviewer Steve Sutherland, this track was an exception to the album's 'unrelenting awfulness'- sounding 'like the League of old, a Motown pastiche instead of an imitation, galloping down a smart Four Tops sing-along boasting a brisk and triumphant chorus topped off with a cheeky steal from Argent's 'Hold Your Head Up''. (13 September 1986).

'The Real Thing' (Burden, Wright, Russell, Oakey, Steven Fellows) (4:17)

Of course, the song title started out as an advertising tagline for a brand of sugary cola – adopted here for one of Philip's ordinary tales of everyday romance. She works in an office, but can't wait for her latest assignation with her new lover. There's a single-line hint that just maybe he's already married because, as they drive away, 'There's someone left behind'. But, 'When you feel your chance has come/Who's going to throw it all away?'. The usual Human League accoutrements are augmented by unidentified sugary-high falsetto backing vocals and denser arrangement: both chic and Chic. The voices drop into a brief *a cappella* interplay as the track closes into the fade.

'Love Is All That Matters' (Harris, Lewis) (6:09)

'I know that there's no Lord above', Oakey had sung defiantly on 'Love Action'. But this song imposed on the group by Jam and Lewis seems almost devotional in tone, with Joanne and Susan cooing and carolling – 'Love forgiving, love for good/Love to keep us faithful' – before Philip enters to emphasise that, just maybe, the love he's hymning is more secular; more corporeal in nature. After all, music can draw upon gospel/spiritual impulses even when it's being deep-down dirty: 'Sexual Healing' anyone? This track is immaculately suffused with a production sheen as glowing as salvation; even more lavish on the extended mixes, with submerged voice samples, pauses and clink-clank breaks. It's a high for the album to go out on, epic in scale, even though it's more Jam and Lewis than it is Human League – looking forward more to Janet Jackson's Herb Alpert collaboration 'Diamonds' than it does to the Human League album *Romantic?*. It's a track suspended between the sublime and Christmas-tinsel sparkles. 'I believe in truth, though I lie a lot', said Oakey defiantly on 'Love Action'.

Bonus tracks added to the 2005 CD reissue

'Human' (Extended) (Harris, Lewis) (5:04), 'I Need Your Loving' (Extended) (Anna-Lynne Williams, David Eiland, Randy Davis, Langston Richey, Harris, Lewis) (7:15), 'Love Is All That Matters' (Extended) (Harris, Lewis) (7:47)

Related Releases

'Human' (Harris, Lewis) (3:45) b/w **'Human'** (Instrumental) (3:45)

Label: UK: Virgin VS880, USA: A&M 2861

Release date: 11 August 1986

This is the classy smoocher single that turned The Human League's career decline around, brought them back to number 1 in America, and made them hot as a pistol all over again! It's a near-eponymous title, recorded in February 1986 in Minneapolis' Flyte Tyme Studios, using sampled-drum technology. It was issued in a number of formats – the album version (4:24), extended version (5:03), a further version included on the 2005 *Original Remixes & Rarities* album (5:05), and this single edit with fade (3:48). The UK 12" includes an *a cappella* B-side (2:00) and an instrumental mix (5:00).

The single's release was glowingly welcomed by reviewer Barry McIlheney, who said it was 'elevated to the giddiest of heights by a beautifully-paced arrangement and the long-awaited arrival of the ladies halfway through the seduction. It's only when yesterday's giants like the League come back to wipe the contemporary floor, that you really comprehend just how much cack we've had to put up with over the last couple of years'. (*Melody Maker*, 16 August

1986). Elsewhere in *Melody Maker,* the single was equivocally reviewed as a place where 'song has never come closer to soap opera'.

The single smooched its way to number 8 on the UK chart.

'I Need Your Loving' (Harris, Lewis, Eiland, Richey, Williams, Davis) (3:43) b/w **'I Need Your Loving (Dub)'** (3:40)
Label: UK: Virgin VS900, USA: A&M SP-12213
Release date: 10 November 1986
'Human' was number 1 in America the week of 22 November 1986. But instead of playing high-profile promotional dates across the States, the group announced a new British tour – their first full tour for five years – starting with a series of small venues 'with room to dance', priced at a modest £5 and supported by Drum Theatre. Tied in with the live dates, this second single was lifted from *Crash* (with a reversion to the old Red designation), with mixes from the Flyte Tyme duo. But it logged the band's poorest-ever UK chart position, crawling only to 72. In the US, it peaked at 44.

'Love Is All That Matters (Edit)' (Jam and Lewis) (4:06) b/w **'I Love You Too Much'** (Burden, Callis, Wright) (3:22)
Label: UK: Virgin VS1025, USA: A&M SP-12227
Release date: 3 October 1988
This third single taken from *Crash* was only issued much later as a promotional vehicle for the Christmastime TV-advertised *Greatest Hits* album. Backed with a dub remix of 'I Love You Too Much' from the Rushent-era *Hysteria*, it reached number 41 in a five-week chart run. Philip commented: 'Good songs have to be pretty vague. You have to keep them guessing'.

Inevitably it was issued in multiple formats with a variety of track listings, including a 12" available in a limited-edition gatefold sleeve.

1986 US 12"
'Love Is All That Matters' (Extended) (7:45), 'Love Is All That Matters' (7" edit) (4:06), 'Love Is All That Matters' (A cappella) (2:45), 'Love Is All That Matters' (Instrumental) (4:09)

1988 international 12" release
'Love Is All That Matters' (Extended) (7:45), 'Love Is All That Matters' (Dub) (5:54), 'Love Is All That Matters' (Edit) (4:06)

1988 CD single (Virgin VSCD 1025)
'Love Is All That Matters' (Edit) (4:06), 'Love Is All That Matters' (Dub) (5:54), 'Love Is All That Matters' (Extended) (7:45)

'Hellhouse (Feel The Heat)' (Wright, Russell) (7:37) b/w **'Wow!'** (Wright, Russell) by **Wow!**

Label: Immaculate Records IMMAC6
Release date: April 1988
This is the garage/house/techno-acid brainchild of Adrian Wright and Jim
Russell, who'd played on *Hysteria*, *Crash* and Heaven 17's *The Luxury Gap*.
The single was issued through an indie label previously associated with the
Sheffield-based group One Thousand Violins. Written and produced by Adrian
and Jim, with female vocals courtesy of Virge, the track has loads of squiggly
acidic bits over a monster drum rhythm – a dance floor collision between
the contemporary sounds of Factory Records, London clubs and Sheffield's
industrial funk.

Adrian told *Melody Maker*: 'Writing scripts and making videos is my main
preoccupation, really. I never saw myself as a pop musician; I just became one
by accident! But I've realised that I can write good songs, so it seems natural to
do it' (22 April 1989).

Since the Mark I Human League lineup, Adrian had remained a member
until 1986, when – despondent with where the band were heading – he quit to
concentrate on film work and graphic design. He explained: 'That was always
my way of seeing it anyway. I want to make feature films, and I never saw this
group as something for life. There is going to come a time when it all seems
pointless'.

Romantic? by **The Human League** (1990)

Personnel:
Philip Oakey: vocals, synthesizers, percussion
Joanne Catherall, Susan Ann Sulley: vocals
Neil Sutton: synthesizer, percussion, keyboards
Russell Dennett: guitar, synthesizer, percussion, vocal
Jo Callis: percussion, synthesizer, programming
Mark Brydon, Robert Gordon, Martin Rushent: percussion, synthesizer
Producers: Timm Baldwin, Bob Kraushaar, Martin Rushent
Recorded at Genetic Sound Studios, Streatley, Berkshire; Mixed at Sarm West, William Orbit's Guerilla Studio, and The Human League Studios in Sheffield.
Engineers: David Dodd, Mike 'Spike' Drake, Timm Baldwin
Label: UK: Virgin CDV 2624, USA: A&M 75021-5316-2
Release date: 17 September 1990
Chart position: UK: 24
Running time: 43:37

It was 'romantic' with a question mark. There had been glamour – of course, there had been glamour – but The Human League had never been fully paid-up members of the flashy New Romantic continuum – although, central on the CD-insert photo, Philip had reverted to the asymmetrical side-styled one-curtain-drawn/one-curtain-open hair.

Crash had been a make-or-break project; a commercial success. But now, Adrian had gone, having felt marginalised during the album's recording. The band simply refocused on the core members, with whoever, and continued together for new electric dreams.

Though born in Sunderland, Mark Brydon had become a central player on the Sheffield music scene as a member of the highly-rated Chakk. When the industrial-funk band signed to MCA Records, Mark used the advance to design and construct FON Studios. Following Chakk's disintegration, he was the motivating force behind the 1987 hit single 'House Arrest' by Krush, and – with Chakk colleague Sim Lister – 'Hustle! (To The Music)' by The Funky Worm. But Mark achieved his greatest partnership break as Moloko with singer Róisín Murphy, taking the band name from the same source as Heaven 17 – the 1962 Anthony Burgess novel that was turned into Stanley Kubrick's dystopian 1971 movie *A Clockwork Orange*. The Human League always exercised sharp perception when choosing collaborators, and Sheffield was still a schizy megalopolis.

Philip said: 'Strangely, we seem to be part of the Sheffield underground again. The only thing the new people have in common is that they look weird – just like we used to. It stretches from where Bomb The Bass, Tackhead, The Beastie Boys and metal all come together. It's mostly comics people now. Comics are the only place nowadays where intellectual art is going on' (*Melody Maker*, 29 October 1988).

Meanwhile, Martin Rushent was back, reconciled after a seven-year absence.

For much of the 1980s, The Human League had been an adornment to life, zapping lyrical structures on high-speed rhythmic data lines. But being a popular beat combo is a rough old trade. By 1990 they were beginning to look be*league*red. Their lunar glitter had paled to that of a prehistoric Flying Saucer wreck entombed in a polar ice flow – an object of wonder and speculation but with little relevance to life as she was lived. Instead, there'd been the ephemeral challenge of trad-metal outlaw rock bands and a succession of teenage boy bands like brats out of hell, with all the risible sex appeal of Zippy, Bungle and George (characters from Thames Television's *Rainbow* (1972-1997).

The sixth studio album's release coincided with the launch of IPC's glossy monthly *Vox* magazine, which carried Ian McCann's downbeat review: 'Relationships, little stories, metaphors using bits of buildings, a jolly chorus, some fairly rudimentary programming and a somewhat leaden set of rhythms do not set up a massive comeback' (October 1990). On the evidence of *Romantic?*, it seems not. Read my lips – no, read my *words!* It was the perceived failure of *Romantic?* – which peaked at 24 on the album chart – that led to The Human League quitting Virgin in favour of East West for their next long-playing venture.

'Kiss The Future' (Oakey, Neil Sutton) (4:13)

Maybe an ironic title, under the circumstances. But hadn't The Human League always been futurists? Having learned from their adventures in Minneapolis, there's a strong wall of funk rhythms, but this time delivered on the group's own terms! Carried on what journalist Nick Griffiths described as 'Oakey's characteristic strained voice competing with funky, bubbling bass lines, fake brass and a trashy heap of programmed rhythms' (*Select*, October 1990), there are stray cut-up phrases fed into the mix, urging 'Go ahead', 'Uproot you', 'Take my hand', 'My consciousness exploded'. There are moments where it encroaches on radical Heaven 17 dance territory.

It was produced by Mark Brydon for the Fon Force (Fon stands for Fuck Off Nazis), along with Robert Gordon (co-founder of Warp Records), and was mixed by The Human League. This track marks a determined new start: 'Take the plunge and wipe the slate ... Your past life don't suit you'.

'A Doorway?' (Oakey, Sutton, Russell Dennett) (4:21)

This doorway is a vocal showcase for the harmonising Joanne and Susan to declare 'When you gave your love to me, I never gave you chains', with Philip adding supportive confirmation. They commendably advocate a love that is free from possessiveness, resting on mutuality and consent, expressed through honking bass and clattering sounds, with a squelchy, fluid instrumental break contrived by the same creative team behind 'Kiss The Future'. New love and adventure – this is a song that respects your territory, for 'Love is not a prison cell'.

'Heart Like A Wheel' (Jo Callis, Eugene Reynolds) (4:30)

In retrospect, it's always easy to determine why a certain song or record was a hit – a catchy hook, an opportunistic TV slot, maybe it's just the time of year, or maybe it's the time of man. Why a record was *not* a hit poses a more problematic question. This song was written by ex-Rezillos member Eugene Reynolds and Jo Callis, formerly of The Human League: 'I can always see myself as wanting to write songs for The Human League, but I might not necessarily always want to play with them', he'd tactfully explained to Joe Hosken in *Soundmaker* (11 December 1982).

The track was produced and mixed by Martin Rushent at Genetic Sound Studio, engineered by Timm Baldwin, and up went the beats-per-minute for a mix engineered by Neil O'Connor. Punchy, shimmering and wonderfully immediate, the track seemed to have all the necessary requirements to at least reach the top 10. And if this song had struck it big, the subsequent story and alternate history would've been different. Virgin would've been reassured about the market potential of The Human League; the contractual alliance would not have severed. For better or worse?

Neil Sutton plays the twittering, perambulating synth intro, breaking into a sparkling constellation before the intense three-way vocals recall something of the 'Dancing In The Street' message by saying 'Calling up the promised land' and 'Pass the message around the world'. The Johnny Seven, who gets a name-check, was a kind of a multifunction Action Man toy with armour-piercing accessories that have become something of a collector's item. Cultural esoterica has always been part of the Human League vocabulary, and this is The Human League at the top of their game.

'Men Are Dreamers' (Dennett, Oakey) (3:54)

Infidelity can be excused because we are human – flesh and blood – but also because men are repentful dreamers, in this slow debate on the gender politics of relationships, which shifts back and forth, as in some confessional daytime TV talk show. Can't we move on? 'Think about the future', he pleads. 'How can you say, forget yesterday?'. 'It's all over now', the girls argue back. Maybe he's a dreamer. With a slightly-phased edge – produced by Timm Baldwin, with mixes by Bob Kraushaar and Danton Supple – this is a subtle and nuanced track.

'Mister Moon And Mister Sun' (Oakey, Sutton) (4:42)

This is a plea to the cosmic heavenly bodies to hold their places within the constellations – to freeze time, to stop the clock – in order to make this moment of love eternal. 'In an age where you can make a synthesizer sound like anything from a tractor to an orchestra, The Human League still make theirs sound like synthesizers', said Mike Soutar (*Smash Hits*, 19 September 1990). As with the ticking intro and faux horns, this three-way vocal paean to love almost includes a Russell Dennett guitar solo! It was mixed by William Orbit – the name behind Bassomatic – who was the producer/remixer *du jour* who would go on to work his familiar washes of keyboard magic with Madonna, All Saints and Blur.

'Soundtrack To A Generation' (Oakey, Sutton) (4:35)

Opening side two of the vinyl edition, this was recorded at The Human League's Sheffield Studio, produced by Bob Kraushaar, assisted by David Dodd, and mixed by Danton Supple. There's an instrumental demo called 'FM' on the *A Very British Synthesizer Group* compilation, with a walloping drum track and jittery synths, building into a pleasing variety of near-repetitions. 'Years have gone on in between/But all I knew at 17, is all I know now', Philip confesses reflectively. Joanne and Susan's mischievous cries of 'Oh wow' and 'Holy cow' provide evidence that when your cranial control centre needs a little stimulation and trip hop fails you, The Human League still glitter before you in menace and allure within the city limits, but beyond the boundaries of desire. It's high-calibre electropop for sure. The only question that remains is which generation is this music a soundtrack to?

'Rebound' (Oakey, Sutton) (3:54)

This is slow enough to hardwire your neurons. A ponderous intro recalls the way 'I Am The Law' was ponderous, for they who hesitate are toast, with Joanne and Susan at their most beguiling as they warn 'Don't come any closer', followed by receding voice echoes. Nick Griffiths said it's 'a bloody good song, featuring only a couple of catchy synth lines, overlaid by one brassy electronic riff, and with a great reverberating chorus'. Sometimes, simple can be the best course to follow, even when 'The chronicle hasn't changed for 15 years'. After all, it's possible to overthink an idea.

'The Stars Are Going Out' (Oakey, Sutton) (4:05)

Some interpret this song as a reflection on the dimming of the group's career. Others refer to the Arthur C. Clarke short story 'The Nine Billion Names Of God' – first published in *Star Science Fiction Stories: Number 1* in 1953 – in which a computer system is installed in a remote Tibetan monastery in order to encode all the names of God: a task that would otherwise have taken the monks 15,000 years. With the task digitally completed, 'Overhead, without any fuss, the stars were going out'. Though the lyric is couched more in the terminology of the sad fading of love's energies, some critics have interpreted it as a self-aware reflection of the group's own inexorable decline towards a state of entropy – 'We used to be so tough/But just not tough enough', 'We used to be so bad/But that was just a fad'. If so, the metaphor is delivered in melancholy splendour with considerable confessional grace: 'We used to be so hot/A million kilowatt or more'.

There's a nuanced performance video of this song from a 1995 episode of *Later... With Jools Holland*, which is the version included on the 2003 DVD *The Very Best Of The Human League*.

'Let's Get Together Again' (John Rossall, Gerry Shephard) (5:01)
The first *bona fide* Human League chart entry had included a cover of the Gary
Glitter breakthrough hit 'Rock And Roll', so there would be a satisfying full-
circle aspect to covering this number-8 Glitter Band hit from October 1974
and to it being included on perhaps The Human League's final chart shot. As it
happened, there was more to come. The programmed rhythm track replicates
the original Glitter Band double-drumming remarkably well, and the melody
is contagiously tuneful, quality pop, with a confident Oakey lead vocal and
shared harmonies on the choruses. Joanne and Susan join towards the final
repetitions on what was obviously a fun track to record.

'Get It Right This Time' (Jo Callis, Jesse Rae) 4:12
There are trace elements that glance back to the Motown-esque 'Mirror Man'
rhythm track, but with quite advanced forward-looking chord changes that
hint at melodic prog rock. 'Smacked on my chin' maybe, but The Human
League are 'back with a grin'. This track is a strong assertion of confidence
in tomorrows yet to come – one that growls as it winds down to close the
album on an up rhythm. And yes, they got it more right this time than anyone
could've predicted.

Contemporary Singles
'Heart Like A Wheel' (Callis, Reynolds) (4:30) b/w **'Rebound'**
(Oakey, Sutton) (3:54)
Label: UK: Virgin VS 1262, USA: A&M 75021-2336-1
Release date: 6 August 1990
Highest chart positions: UK: 29, USA: 32
Issued in two CD-single formats, VSCDT 1262:
'Heart Like A Wheel' (4:30), 'Heart Like A Wheel' (Extended) (6:55), 'Rebound'
(3:58), 'Heart Like A Wheel' (Remix) (4:37)
The second edition (VSCDX 1262) substitutes the remix for 'A Doorway' (Dub)
(4:29). There was also a cassette single edition (VSC1262).

'Soundtrack To A Generation' (Oakey, Sutton) (4:21) b/w
'Soundtrack To A Generation' (Instrumental)
Label: Virgin VS1303
Release date: 12 November 1990
Chart position: UK: 77
There were two CD-single formats.
VSCDT 1303:
'Soundtrack To A Generation' (Edit) (4:01), 'Soundtrack To A Generation' (William
Orbit mix) (6:03), 'Soundtrack To A Generation' (Instrumental) (4:32), 'Soundtrack
To A Generation' (Pan Belgian mix) (4:40)
VSCDX 1303:
'Soundtrack To A Generation' (Pan Belgian dub) (5:55), 'Soundtrack To A

Generation' (808 mix instrumental) (4:44), 'Soundtrack To A Generation' (Dave Dodd's mix) (6:07), 'Soundtrack To A Generation' (A cappella) (2:47)

Related releases
'What Comes After Goodbye' (Walmsley, Robson, Hartley, Oakey) (4:03) b/w **'The Ghost In Me'** (Walmsley, Robson, Hartley) (3:55) by **Respect**
Label: Chrysalis CHSCD 3640
Release date: December 1990
As a Philip side-project performed with the Sheffield-based Respect, he provides distinctive vocals alongside the trio's powerful regular singer Josephine Robson. Above the basic electro-dance soundtrack, her clear vocal projection invests the track with near-classical overtones, while a trumpet solo adds class. In addition to the basic 7" single, on the maxi-CD edition, there was a seven-minute remix by Phil Harding and Ian Curnow, along with 'The Girl Needs Respect' and 'Ghost Dance'. The track was included on Respect's only album: *The Kissing Game* (1991, Chrysalis CCD1755). Chris Heaton produced, in league with Mark Stent, who would go on to production work for The Human League album *Octopus*.

'Black Night' (Glover, Blackmore, Gillian, Lord, Paice) (4:03) b/w **'Abide With Me'** (Monk, Lyte) (2:23 edited down from album-length 5:18) by **Vic Reeves**
Label: Island SIGH 7-13DJ
Release date: 1991
Vic Reeves: is he funny? With Bob Mortimer, the Leeds-born Vic (James Moir) formed the Morecambe and Wise of alternative comedy, substituting gags for surreal non-sequiturs, like 'What's on the end of the stick, Vic?' and the 'Dove from above', which became cult in-quotes from *Vic Reeves Big Night Out*, in order to baffle those not in on the joke. Maybe The Human League were fans. Inevitably, there was an album (*I Will Cure You* (September 1991, Island)), which spawned a hit version of the old Tommy Roe song 'Dizzy', while Vic's subsequent reworking of the old Christian hymn managed a less lofty appearance at number 47 on the singles chart.

Philip Oakey programmed and produced the cover of the former Deep Purple hit. Though everyone called it heavy metal, Jon Lord told me he preferred the terms 'rock 'n' roll or heavy rock. The Oakey thumbprint is all over the song's transition from bludgeoning riffology to electro. Some claim to detect his voice amongst the vocals too.

Oakey later made an appearance in the one-off pilot of Reeves and Mortimer's *The Weekenders* for Channel 4.

Loot! (1990) by Ian C. Burden
Label: Homar HOMCD6603
Release date: May 1990

After his messy departure from The Human League – conspicuously sidelined during the troubled *Crash* recording – the man who co-wrote 'The Sound Of The Crowd' and 'Love Action' recorded this solo album with a Roland D-50 – direct-to-stereo in his back room in the Endcliffe area of Sheffield. The liner notes say, 'All vocals on this album have been looted. Apologies to all those whose voices have been sampled, edited, transposed and otherwise mutilated'.

Tracklist: 1. 'Walk!' (Burden) (3:22), 2. 'Paradise' (Burden) (3:53), 3. 'See My Baby' (Burden, Martin Rootes) (3:21), 4. 'Waiting' (Burden, Ian Elliot) (3:55), 5. 'Oh No!' (Burden, Elliot) (3:25), 6. 'Wanna Shout' (Burden, Elliot, Lamont) (4:08), 7. 'Shake It Loose' (Burden, Rootes) (3:15), 8. 'Beep Beep' (Burden, Bex) (4:19), 9. 'The Loot Of The World' (Burden, Pulsford, Geoff Davis) (3:27), 10. 'I Don't Care' (Burden) (4:05)

Ian went on to work with Human League contributor Russell Dennett in a band called Deep Down Crazy, who issued the 1995 album *A Swim In The Ocean* (Inertia). Burden's 2018 solo album *Hey Hey Ho Hum* (Rutland Artspace Limited) was preceded by the single 'Let The Devil Drown', with classic electro overtones, vintage synth sounds and Ian's own breathy vocals.

Octopus by The Human League (1995)

Personnel:
Philip Oakey: vocals, synthesizers, keyboards
Joanne Catherall, Susan Ann Sulley: vocals
Neil Sutton: synthesizer
Paul Christopher Beckett, Jo Callis, Russell Dennett, Chris Hughes: playing, programming
Ian Stanley, Philip Oakey, Andy Gray: programming
Producer: Ian Stanley
Engineers: David Dodd, Pete Steart, Scott Boyce, Bob Kraushaar
Recorded at The Human League Studios (February-August 1994), Axis Studio, Sheffield Mixed at Olympic, Nomis and Metropolis Studio, London (August-September 1994)
Label: UK: East West 4509-98750-2, USA: Elektra 61788-2
Release date: UK: 23 January 1995,USA: 25 April 1995
Chart positions: UK: 6, Germany: 76, USA: Did not chart
Running time: 51:46

The Beep Goes On. New beginnings. The Human League patented British electronic pop.

Then they moved on. They moved beyond that. No theory. No hidden agenda. And no apologies. Their seemingly effortless elision of beauty, substance, subversion, discomfort and invention still sounded too experimental, too intelligent, too immaculately deep yet simple, and too timeless to be considered modern. After the termination of their Virgin contract in 1992, they decisively re-signed to the freedoms of the more-indie East West, which had links to Elektra. As though invigorated by their release from the commercial expectations imposed on them by Virgin, *Octopus* was a powerful and confident return to form, and also spawned some of the League's finest hit singles. Philip insisted, 'Whatever happens, I'm going to make ten Human League LPs. I'm going to be like Peter Hammill in my little 8-track studio. I'll beg people to put them out if needs be'.

The cover photo and those in the CD booklet emphatically show only the core trio of Philip, Joanne and Susan in heavily-shadowed profiles. Producer Ian Stanley had been a part of the hugely successful Tears For Tears, contributing keyboards and LinnDrum programming to their album *Songs From The Big Chair* (1985).

Have you ever been enamoured for longer than a decade? Have you ever loved something simply because it's there? This was the year that Philip turned 40. He'd had 18 years of the pop life. The girls were 30-somethings. They'd lived the pop life since they'd left school.

The Human League was no more Abba than Abba had been The Mamas & The Papas. It was simply that each group had operated around the interacting kissing of male and female voices to create their own unique harmony configurations. In a feature in *The Observer* titled 'Synthesizers, Psychiatry and Hairdos', Philip told journalist Miranda Sawyer: 'We watched *Romantic?* disappear without a trace. Gone – gone into the past with all you've hoped for. So you go into the studio and throw a few more songs together ... about that time, I think, I had a low-grade nervous breakdown'. He comes across as very studied, dry and dogmatic in the interview, where everything is poised between being absurdly funny and very considered. It's impossible to hear him and not believe that he takes it all so seriously. 'The Human League remains entirely sincere', Miranda concluded.

Meanwhile, new romantics never die; they just run out of eyeliner. Nick Vivian's lightweight-but-enjoyable ITV comedy/drama *Hunting Venus* (31 March 1999) featured Martin Clunes and Neil Morrissey as former members of a new romantic band whose disgruntled fans blackmailed them into reforming. Leaning heavily on 1980s nostalgia, the soundtrack has cameos from Simon Le Bon, Gary Numan, and The Human League. Then Trevor Jackson released a retro-flavoured electroclash Playgroup album *DJ Kicks: Playgroup* (2002, Studio K7 127CD), which included 'Do Or Die (Dub)' alongside reconfigured songs by The Flying Lizards and Material. The past has its immense gravitational attraction, despite the message running through the *Octopus* track 'These Are The Days'.

Possibly it's nostalgia or simple protectiveness in the face of sterile pop perfection elsewhere that makes The Human League's audience embrace their imperfections that little bit more.

'Tell Me When' (Oakey, Paul Beckett) (3:58)

With 'any waste of effort isn't part of my design' playing very much to the vocal strengths of Joanne and Susan, this synth-a-rama buzzes with the crawl of golden electric insects. When the strongly-melodic song was issued as the album's lead single (East West YZ882CD1) in December 1994 in the midst of Britpop – with a hook as basic as it was brainwashing – it soared to number 6 thanks to favourable radio support. It marked a major revival in the group's fortunes here, *and* in the US, where it reached 31 in April (East West 66147-2).

For Philip, this is the song 'that means the most to me', because 'It showed we'd survived'. Miranda Sawyer wrote in *The Observer*: 'It's all so familiar, you forget it ever went away' (15 January 1995).

The group promoted the song on *Top Of The Pops* (19 January), where it was introduced by Bruno Brookes. The video – screened on TV's *The Chart Show* – was directed by Andy Morahan, who'd previously directed the videos for 'Human' and 'Heart Like A Wheel' (not to mention Christopher Lambert's movie *Highlander III: The Sorcerer*). In the atmospheric video, people move backwards through the street, soldiers march in reverse and Philip is posed like Dolph Lundgren in some Prague hotel. Susan wears a huge pure-white fur. Joanne is in contrasting black.

A different song, also titled 'Tell Me When', had been a number seven hit for The Applejacks in February 1964. By coincidence, the beat group's bass player Megan Davies had been born in Sheffield.

The single was issued in various versions, remixed by the Utah Saints (Mix 1 (5:09); Mix 2 (6:12), Development Corporation (5:51) and Red Jerry (7:36), with B-sides including a track from the League's then-recent collaboration with Yellow Magic Orchestra: 'Kimi Ni Mune Kyun' (3:53) by YMO vs The Human League, co-written with Takashi Matsumoto. That has a fairly basic drum track, with Philip attempting lines in Japanese. Recorded at Sheffield's Fon Studios, there was a collaborative April 1993 EP issued in Asia on Alfa Records, but it included only the one song with The Human League. Also, the further non-album track 'The Bus To Crookes' (4:52) was included as a B-side. Crookes is the Sheffield suburb where singer Joe Cocker was born. It borders Broomhill and was used here as a kind of *motorvatin'* 'Autobahn' variant – the kind of instrumental The Human League seemed able to generate on a very effective whim.

'These Are the Days' (Oakey, Stanley) (5:46)

Don't look back – nostalgia is a thing of the past. Here there are Morse-code bleeps that signal a strong anthem for putting the past away and valuing what we have today. A riposte to Mary Hopkin's Paul McCartney-produced 1968 hit 'Those Were the Days', the lyric taunts 'If it was so good then, how come it didn't last?'. Oakey, at his deepest and most totalitarian, testifies this deep philosophical insight, while Joanne and Susan swish in on gorgeous, uplifting choruses, until they trade agile vocal lines with male vocal responses to build a convincing thesis, antithesis and synthesis that reverberate with a contagious danceability. The past might've had classic sitcoms and 'Those were the days, my friend/We thought they'd never end', but it also had the terrors of the Cold War. Admitting to no possibility of talkback, there's a pulse that rips from ear to ear and a descending interlude of orchestral strings. A defiant manifesto, yet not a blinkered optimism, there's a shot taken at Thatcherism's '16 years of legalized class hate' – but no, the past is not the place to be. This is a song 'that needs to be piped into every home, like running water and amusingly-awful satellite channels', said reviewer Niall Crumlish (*Hot Press*, 9 February 1995).

'One Man in My Heart' (Oakey, Sutton) (4:03)

John Phillips wrote some of his most moving songs for The Mamas & the Papas by documenting the pain his free-spirited wife Michelle caused him with her affairs. Fleetwood Mac's mega-selling *Rumours* was famously forged from the marital break-ups and shake-ups going on within the band, and Abba's hits 'Knowing Me, Knowing You' and 'The Name Of The Game' were talking through the disintegration of the foursome's marriages.

For Abba in computer land, by contrast, Philip had a relationship with Joanne that lasted for almost seven years. Later he was involved with Susan. Neither relationship seemed to have had an impact on their working arrangement. But The Human League remained the focus of their shared energies. Discussing whether they remain on friendly terms, Susan told *Smash Hits*: 'It fluctuates daily, but yeah, we are. You've got to be really. I argue the most and I cry the most'.

This is a beautifully tender song with drum programming and production assistance from Chris Hughes. Whether it's drawn from life, is something known only to those involved. After a soft electronic intro, Susan takes the first verse – a pledge of a love more fiery than the sun, 'within a universe exploding' – joined by Philip and Joanne for a verse so sweet it sets your teeth on edge. For the *Top Of The Pops* performance, she lowered her eyes in an affecting coyness as she lip-synched the line 'One man in my bed': an expression so hot it could defrost your fridge. When it moves into the following oozing instrumental break, Philip ghosts the last words in her lines, to add emphasis: 'The things we choose ... all the things you said'.

It's a work of considerably mature sophistication. Steve Sutherland wrote in his upbeat NME review: 'The true beauty of The Human League in 1995 is how they haven't become coy or bitter; how they haven't fallen out of love with pop, pure and simple ... there's an inherent understanding here of the permanent nature of pop – that it is doomed to repeat the same platitudes of grief and comfort forever' (21 January 1995).

As the album's second single (East West YZ904CD1), it deservedly climbed to a respectable 13, and spent eight weeks on the chart.

'Words' (Oakey, Dennett) (5:54)
Small particles flitter like strange rain sleeting over the surface of shadowed worlds; they spread like some viscous liquid into every corner of this track. For the Bee Gees, 'Words are all I have to take your heart away'. Philip, at his most stentorian, blends in a slow melancholy reminiscing back to when he was a child living in fear: sensitively suffused by Joanne and Susan taking harmonies and solo lines. Worlds may shatter, light-years away. Philip's throat dries, but words come back to haunt him. The strange rhyme sequence of 'Tolerating propaganda, and your girlfriend Alexandra, with her secret memoranda' seems to have strayed in from some other song. No one but The Human League could possibly get away with it, but they're all about surrendering to the moment and taking it on trust.

Mixed by Bob Kraushaar and Robin Barclay, the track closes with a fizzing of trapped particles caught in dark-matter ripples.

'Filling Up With Heaven' (Oakey, Stanley) (4:19)
Philip admitted, 'As the years had passed by, I became more cynical'. 'Once there was a vision/Once there was a glow/Once there was a certainty no chance could overthrow'. Whether that reflects his true frame of mind or merely provides a convenient lyric hook for how his new romance has renewed his sense of the possible, is something known only to him. His vocal expression

provides little clue, though Susan and Joanne inject all the inspired passion the track requires. There's a deliberately tinny old-school analogue electro quality about the whizzing effects surrounding Philip's 'Once there was a winner/Now there was a clown' and the girls chanting 'No Baby, no Baby, no Baby, no!'.

Issued in June 1995 as the album's third single (East West YZ 944CD1), it reached number 36. The CD single came with the B-side 'John Cleese: Is He Funny?', and included various 'Filling Up With Heaven' remixes – one by Neil Mclellan, a ULA remix, a hard floor vocal and dub remix.

'Housefull Of Nothing' (Oakey, Stanley, Beckett) (4:30)

A house is not a home when there's no love there. Burt Bacharach and Hal David said that. There's nothing but 'The ringing of a catchphrase from a cherished telecast', says Oakey – a similar sentiment, in an alternate accent, placed in a different context. It's a post-breakup song, and she's taken the family. In a rather downbeat review – which nevertheless awarded a 7 rating, Lisa Verrico suggested this track 'can't quite shake the aura of cheap TV sci-fi series' that so dates The Human League's trademark synth sound' (*Vox*, February 1995) – as though that cherished sci-fi telecast was a bad thing!

Philip adopts his low baritone delivery within a lattice of quantum-wave flickers as Joanne and Susan reiterate the song title, then blossoming into a close-harmony bridge, closing into, if this is a 'lost opportunity/Bring it back, bring it back, bring it back'.

'John Cleese: Is He Funny?' (Oakey) (3:59)

Well... he certainly had his moments: John Cleese, that is. Have you ever been high on laughter? – the 'Dead Parrot Sketch', 'The Ministry Of Silly Walks', *The Life Of Brian*, the *Fawlty Towers* episode 'Basil The Rat', and even the movie *Clockwise* (1986). To pose this rhetorical question, Philip contrives an appropriately eccentric instrumental that just might work as the soundtrack to a comedy routine. There are bubbling and twisting melody lines that collide with a returning earworm of a theme, spattered with curious sonic zigzags that unfurl like a torn sheet.

'Never Again' (Oakey, Callis) (4:41)

Located within the album's recurring mood of loss and regret, here's another broken romance, and Philip misses both the runaway woman's naked body and her mind. He pledges to keep himself free of future hurt, while the girls append strong chorus advice and chiding encouragement. A beautifully-brief orchestral sample in the fade catches the wistful tone.

'Cruel Young Lover' (Oakey, Dennett, Beckett) (6:56)

A hesitant reverberating introduction builds into a hoarse, bleeping yell of 'Do you hear me?', as Philip makes an appeal to his cruel young lover to relent, arguing that she can't always live on her attraction, for time will 'Take your cruel power away'. The lure of city streets is powerful. But he has feelings too, so 'Don't be unkind'. The momentum accelerates as dense machine rhythms feed-in beneath the vocals, utilising additional programming by Andy Wright. The subject matter has shifted decisively across the breadth of the album, deeper into the zone of human relationships. But the relentless 'Do you hear me?' repetitions build hypnotically towards a crescendo: ending *Octopus* on an intense high.

CD 2: The Demos, singles and edits

1. 'Tell Me When' (Demo) 2. 'These Are The Days' (Demo) 3. 'One Man In My Heart' (Demo) 4. 'Words' (Demo) 5. 'Filling Up With Heaven' (Demo) 6. 'Housefull Of Nothing' (Demo) 7. 'John Cleese: Is He Funny?' (Demo) 8. 'Never Again' (Demo) 9. 'Cruel Young Lover' (Demo) 10. 'Tell Me When' (7" edit) 11. 'The Bus To Crookes' 12. 'Stay With Me Tonight' (Single) 13. 'Behind The Mask' (Yellow Magic Orchestra vs The Human League) 14. 'Kim Ni Mune Kyun' (YMO vs THL)

LP 2: The Remixes

Side One:
1. 'Tell Me When' (Utah Saints Mix 1) 2. 'One Man In My Heart' (T.O.E.C. Nasty Sue mix) 3. 'Filling Up With Heaven' (Hardcore vocal remix) 4. 'Stay With Me Tonight' (The Biff & Memphis remix)
Side Two:
1. 'One Man In My Heart' (T.O.E.C. radio edit) 2. 'These Are The Days' (Sonic Radiation) 3. 'Filling Up With Heaven' (ULA remix) 4. 'Tell Me When' (Real Purple mix)

Related releases
'Don't You Want Me' (Callis, Oakey, Wright)
Label: Virgin VSCDT 1557
Release date: October 1995
Virgin issued new remixes of what *Select* called The Human League's 'school disco anthem'. Inevitably, it returned to the charts at an impressive number 16.

The 1995 cassette edition, VSC 1557

1. 'Don't You Want Me' (Red Jerry 7" remix) (3:43) 2. 'Don't You Want Me' (Snap 7" remix) (3:58) 3. 'Don't You Want Me' (Red Jerry 12" remix) (6:11) 4. 'Don't You Want Me' (Original version) (3:57)

The CD single (VSCDT1557) added the following

5. 'Don't You Want Me' (Snap 12" Extended remix) (6:14) 6. 'Don't You Want Me' (Red Jerry Dub) (7:01)

1995 12" edition

'Don't You Want Me' (Snap 12" Extended remix) (6:12), 'Don't You Want Me' (Red Jerry 12" remix) (6:09)

The 7" Red Jerry remix was featured on the popular compilation *Now That's What I Call Music 32* (13 November 1995). Credited with being the 23rd best-selling UK single of all time, there was a further reissue in March 2014, when 'Don't You Want Me' peaked at number 19, boosted by a Scottish social media campaign mounted by fans of Aberdeen Football Club.

There's a persistent story that Marilyn Manson recorded 'Don't You Want Me' in 2004 as a duet with Garbage singer Shirley Manson for Marilyn's *Lest We Forget (The Best Of)* compilation, but it remains unreleased.

'Stay With Me Tonight' (Oakey, Stanley) b/w various remixes
Label: East West EW 020CD
Release date: 8 January 1996

This was produced by Ian Stanley at Human League's studio in Sheffield, and was previously included on Virgin's *Greatest Hits* repackage. In the wake of the success of the *Octopus* singles, it reached number 40 in the UK.

There's a sample teaser taken from the curling photon-hail 'Love Action' intro playing throughout beneath the dance veneer. This is an unpretentious pop-strong harmony showcase, as the lovers anticipate one last night of love together – 'Hear your body call', 'Somewhere in the future will you smile when you think of me?'. The voices are merged in pleasing equilibrium, with no one predominant, in immaculate fitness for purpose.

CD single (and cassette edition)
1. 'Stay With Me Tonight' (4:01) 2. 'Stay With Me Tonight' (Space Kittens vocal mix) (8:35)

Maxi-CD
1. 'Stay With Me Tonight' (Space Kittens vocal mix) (8:35) 2. 'Stay With Me Tonight' (Space Kittens Future dub) (9:01) 3. 'Stay With Me Tonight' (Biff & Memphis remix) (6:45) 4. 'Stay With Me Tonight' (Biff & Memphis Dub) (6:46)

12" vinyl edition:
1. 'Stay With Me Tonight' (Biff & Memphis remix) (6:45) 2. 'Stay With Me Tonight' (Space Kittens vocal mix) (8:35) 3. 'Stay With Me Tonight' (Biff & Memphis Dub mix) (6:46) 4. 'Stay With Me Tonight' (Space Kittens Future dub) (9:01)

Related Album Release: Pickled Eggs And Sherbet (1999) by The All-Seeing I
Label: London 3984 29241-2
Release date: 1999

The All-Seeing I was a Sheffield techno trio made up of Dean Honer, Jason Buckle and DJ Parrot (Richard Barratt) who tended to operate as a Sheffield heritage collective. Singer Tony Christie featured on their hit 'Walk Like A Panther' (London/Earth FFRR-FCD351), and they also occasionally collaborated with Jarvis Cocker, Babybird and Philip Oakey. The album track 'First Man In Space' portrays a disillusioned Major Tom bewailing the lack of a ticker-tape welcome. It was written by Jarvis Cocker, effectively combining The Hollies with The Sweet ('Love Is Like Oxygen'), with 'Sometimes all I need is the air that I breathe/And the air that I breathe is so thin I get high'. Philip Oakey provides the deadpan vocal 'Darling, come quick/You can see our house from here' over a rhythm track vaguely resembling that of Squeeze's 'Take Me I'm Yours'. Of course, the real first man in space had been Yuri Gagarin, as pictured on the cover of 'The Dignity Of Labour' all those years ago. When the track was released as a single in September 1999 (FFRR-FCDP 370), Oakey appeared in the official promo video – sitting high in an umpire's chair watching a frisbee/tennis game. He appeared live with the unit when they performed at the London Brick Lane Music Hall.

Dean Honer went go on to form the electronic duo I Monster, who produced The Human League album *Credo* in 2011. Richard Barratt formed the duo Sweet Exorcist with Richard H. Kirk.

Secrets by The Human League (2001)

Personnel:
Philip Oakey: vocals, synthesizers, keyboards
Joanne Catherall, Susan Ann Gayle (formerly Susan Ann Sulley): vocals
Neil Sutton: keyboards
David Beevers: Technical Secrets
Robin Hancock, Ross Callum, Jamie Callum, Pete Davis: programming
Cover Design: Peacock
Producers: Toy (David Clayton, Kerry Hopwood)
Label: UK: Papillon BTFLYCD0019, USA: Ark 21 186-810-075-2
Release date: UK: 6 August 2001, USA: 30 October 2001
Chart position: UK: 44
Running time: 51:46

It was more confrontational this time, with little of the *Octopus* sweetness. Electro was still a force to be reckoned with, as Depeche Mode proved with their album *Exciter* (May 2001), which not only peaked at 8 in America and 9 in the UK but themed the band's most successful tour. The Prodigy were ratcheting up the decibels, and Chemical Brothers had just logged their second UK number one album *Surrender* (1999), which spawned the contagious number-3 single 'Hey Boy Hey Girl'. The Orb had branched out into more conventional ambient trip hop song content for their *Cydonia* (February 2001), while Orbital had peaked and released their last significant album for the FFRR label: *The Altogether* (2001). Moby and Armand Van Helden were strategically name-dropping The Human League as significant influences.

David Clayton had been a part of the extended ABC lineup on their *Alphabet City* (1987) and *Up* (1989) albums, which revolved around the duo of Martin Fry and Mark White. So it was not unnatural that Clayton should be involved in The Human League's eighth studio album. Kerry Hopwood had been influenced by early-Depeche Mode and Human League when he first joined Tim Simenon in the sample-based Bomb The Bass, so there's a pleasing symmetry in that he worked with Tim (and Dave Clayton) on the Depeche Mode album *Ultra* (1997), and then on The Human League's *Secrets* too.

The cover shows the three core members – short-haired Philip with boho chin-stub goatee, full-faced, but eclipsed by Joanne with heavily-shadowed eyes closed, eclipsed in turn by side-face Susan in the iconic Abba style: red lips collaged together into a single cupid bow shape.

Papillon – a troubled subsidiary of Chrysalis Records – failed to adequately support or promote the album. Critical reception was also mixed. Neil Spencer in *The Observer* said, 'Cue churning beats from antique synths, Phil Oakey intoning like a sing-your-weight machine, while his two erstwhile cocktail waitresses coo alongside'. More upbeat, online writer Krister Malm praised the album's 'witty and clever lyrics, perfected retro, yet very modern-sounding production full of quirky and noteworthy details – all with that trademarked and undeniable Human League sound. This proves to be yet another truly remarkable comeback of the seemingly forever young synth-popsters from Sheffield'.

'All I Ever Wanted' (Oakey, Sutton) (3:31)

There's a grating feed into building synths, then Philip takes the first verse before Susan and Joanne eclipse his voice in an alternation that continues as echoed lines and growls are submerged in the busy mix. Originally titled 'New Start', and with a lyric that is 'Snow pure, demure', there's nothing here that's radically new because it had taken the rest of the scene this long to catch up with what The Human League had been doing all along.

It was extracted as the album's first single, with various 12" remixes by Oliver Lieb and Vanity Case, taking the album cut as raw material for the further regulation extended mixes 'Toy'(3:52), and the more spacey and percussive 'Alter Ego' (6:51) – mixes that take the track into and out of jittery dub house realms.

Despite its many positive features, the single reached only 47 on the charts. It seems there was a widely-held perception that The Human League had fallen between the demographic stools that delineate the Radio 1 youth focus and the Radio 2 heritage-artist orientation. Writer Jon Katz pontificated: 'A generation ago, almost everyone shared common media. That universality has been shattered, probably for good. Information now splits along demographic, political and cultural fault lines' (*Wired*, December 1994). The politics of music can be complicated at times.

'Nervous' (Oakey, Sutton, Toy) (2:05)

This is the first of what are described as 'Instrumental transitional tracks', with a snaky noodling synth outline broken by crashing and rippling interjections in long slow strokes of silver gashes; a blend of hard and soft. Despite all the changes and evolutions that had taken place over the years and projects between, there is a clear conceptual continuity connecting these experiments with ideas from the days of *The Golden Hour Of The Future*. The track fades, leaving only the sense of a ghostly passing.

'Love Me Madly?' (Oakey, Sutton) (4:08)

This originally grew out of the 'Nervous' demo – which can be heard on a bootleg CD called *New Start (Secrets Demos)*. The bpm accelerates as the playful lyrics go off the scale: 'You're like the woman out of Species/I think I'm gonna go to pieces' – *Species* being the 1995 sci-fi movie with H. R. Giger special effects and Natasha Henstridge as the alien with a mating urge. When Joanne and Susan make the accusation, 'You never do right for doing wrong', they're plugging directly into an old Yorkshire aphorism.

There was a high-energy Dave Bascombe mix and an even-more-danceable Cuzco remix (7:49), with dub effects and what resembles a looped burp. 'Is this supposed to be romantic?' enquires Philip helpfully.

'Shameless' (Oakey, Sutton) (3:57)

Philip's voice is treated in a flange-like audio effect, setting every nerve alight. The lyric tells of temptation where 'a person of such principles' falls into some kind of dark infidelity where 'I'd forgotten wrong and right'. For writer Simon Reynolds, 'The squeaky-clean synths, crisp beats and chittering 16th-note bass lines make you flash on 'Computer World' and the Moroder-produced Sparks of 'Beat The Clock' and 'The Number One Song In Heaven' (*Uncut*, September 2001). Perhaps – but these are also unfamiliar hieroglyphs in a blue sound wash, where Susan and Joanne's voices chime in a rich, silky euphoria.

'122.3 BPM' (Oakey, Sutton, Toy) (1:39)

Musicians improvise – it's what they do. They play around with musical phrases and ideas, then follow them to see where they lead. Jazz musicians improvise with horns; rock musicians improvise with guitars. Electronic musicians are no different. They set up a drum-machine pattern to provide a bottom – maybe with a 122.3-bpm setting – and they follow where the ideas take them. For writer Neil Spencer, 'The handful of instrumentals that pepper proceedings offer some curt nods to latter-day club culture'. And this is another 'instrumental transitional track' – one with a robotic voice saying the title with a cold precision that nods at Sheffield's other electronic legacy – the label Warp Records: later the London-based home of LFO and Aphex Twin.

'Never Give Your Heart' (Oakey, Sutton) (3:48)

Why this is called 'Vince' for the original demo, is not immediately obvious, though Philip attempts the kind of falsetto that stresses his range in unconvincing Bee Gees disco territory. Wisely, the girls – predominantly Susan – take the vocals on the album version, with sweet, easy harmonies, while Philip simply adds ghost words and phrases here and there, over bubbling, burbling electronica. 'Never never give your heart to a runaway/You can never make them stay', they caution repeatedly.

'Ran' (Oakey, Sutton) (0:49)

A transitional instrumental track that links from 'Never Give Your Heart', and briefly extemporises around its main synth figure. Technology comparatively permits electronica producers to simply throw a switch in order to add *swing* to their tracks; computers can be sequenced to give the music feel by factoring in small rhythmic irregularities. Paradoxically, what makes the League human – and sometimes superhuman – is their rigidity and deliberate stiffness.

'The Snake' (Oakey, Sutton) (4:25)

The path of least resistance looks all the way back to *Reproduction*. This song has nothing to do with Al Wilson's snaky encounter and everything to do with the bleak Snake Pass on the A628 leading west out of Sheffield towards Hyde.

It's an unusual travelogue, rifted with Peak District geography. The 'Come and join us' line has its roots in the wassail tradition, delivered with Philip's sonorous gravity winding all the way to its destination in the final cadence.

'Ringinglow' (Oakey, Sutton, Toy) (3:18)

This is a lengthy exercise in tweeting and buzzing in hard electro dislocations. As a transitional instrumental track, it works in the kind of hard, relentless weirdness The Human League had not produced since Martyn Ware and Ian Craig Marsh figured in the lineup.

For those who are wondering, Ringinglow is a village to the west of Sheffield. It gets a masked mention halfway through (continuity-sampled from previous track 'The Snake').

'Liar' (Oakey, Sutton) (3:17)

A mesh of hard-edged tweaked electro sounds are ripped by flashes of distortion. Philip takes the verse with a contrasting melodic flair. Joanne and Susan give accusatory harmony choruses, with the comments 'You're a liar' and 'Such a liar' thrown in as if to stress the point. Their venom sustains the track in a near-complete symbiosis. Reviewer Neil Spencer calls this (along with 'You'll Be Sorry' and 'Sin City') – a 'straight homage to the golden age of synth-pop (*The Observer*, 5 August 2001).

'Lament' (Sutton) (1:12)

A brief but effective instrumental transitional track that opens like the cosmic music of the spheres, charting the background radiation configurations left by the Big Bang before a sprinkle of vibraphone shimmers across swirls of forming-nebulae – the voice of time itself, searching for the numinous.

'Reflections (Demons Of The Mind)' (Oakey, Steve Fellowes) (6:35)

This brew simmers in a Devil's cauldron where fragments of meaning surface and dissolve. Philip's voice is treated with narrative menace, while a sampled movie voice intones 'Demons of the mind', offset by the girls' redemptive sunshine. Its weirdness almost recalls aspects of *Reproduction*. *Demons Of The Mind* was a supernatural Hammer movie from 1972 starring former-Manfred Mann vocalist Paul Jones, Patrick Magee and Robert Hardy.

'Brute' (Oakey) (2:26)

Single-word titles have always served The Human League well – but why 'Brute'? Maybe it was chosen on the random I-Ching principle, signifying nothing. It's a transitional instrumental track with deep 90-bpm throbs in a robotic lower register and a high scatter of silver notes run over its event horizon. It could be argued there are bits of Tangerine Dream within the organic pulse.

'Sin City' (Oakey) (4:23)

The Human League had driven a long satnav-guided way from 'Toyota City', yet the pledge to shiny techno tomorrows is still intact, even with 'No more visions left to sell'. Synths wail like sirens over the futuristic cityscape, with vocoder as the cyclic intro voices. There's an uncompromising electro-bleakness 'like an etching of death' that eerily anticipates the 2005 movie based on Frank Miller's graphic noir novel series *Sin City*. 'Is it time for release, for an end to this sham?', Philip asks. No, there's more richness to come.

'Release' (Sutton) (1:59)

This is another transitional instrumental track in a geometry of electrophile clicks constructed around a catchy trilling synth figure. This is no unfinished backing track awaiting a vocal – it's a complete entity in its own right, functioning with pocket-watch precision. As Peter Kane pointed out in his *Q* magazine review, it's 'Shinier and spunkier than it has any right to be' (August 2001).

'You'll Be Sorry' (Oakey, Sutton) (4:01)

There's a raw unreleased 1996 East West demo subtitled 'Thank God' (5:45), which strips this track back to a 1960s beat-group simplicity – 'You'll be sorry in the morning if you leave me in the evening, today' – but for the two chiming instrumental breaks. There are additional layers of complexity and interwoven harmony on the album version. 'You'll be sorry, you'll be sorry', chide Joanne and Susan, providing the light to Oakey's darkness, though they are absent on the demo. It's an intriguing lesson, showing the track's growth and evolution. There's also a Marc Anthony Radio mix (3:29), which seems to lean on Giogio Moroder for its more-accelerated rhythmic synth basis. The retro-analogue feel of the demo has a pleasing, attractive rawness too.

Contemporary Single
'All I Ever Wanted' (Oakey, Sutton)

Label: UK: Papillon DJFLY153, Canada: Papillon LMCD 0302-1
Release date: 23 July 2001
Chart position: UK: 47
12" vinyl edition:
'All I Ever Wanted' (Oliver Lieb's main mix) (7:41), 'All I Ever Wanted' (Oliver Bieb's alternative mix) (7:10), 'All I Ever Wanted' (Vanity Case mix) (6:02), 'All I Ever Wanted' (Vanity Case instrumental) (5:59)
Two CD single formats:
1. 'All I Ever Wanted' (Dave Bascombe album mix) (3:32) (Album remix, faster with more instrumentation) 2. 'Tranquility' (3:28) 3. 'All I Ever Wanted' (Vanity Case mix) (6:02)
1. 'All I Ever Wanted' (Original) (3:55) (Mix on Greatest Hits (2003) 2. 'All I Ever Wanted' Oliver Lieb main mix) (7:41) 3. 'All I Ever Wanted' (Video) (3:33)

The Golden Hour Of The Future by The Human League (2002)

Personnel:
Philip Oakey, Martyn Ware: vocals, synthesizer
Ian Craig Marsh: synthesizer and devices
Adi Newton: vocals, tapes, loops, treatments
Producer: Richard X
Label: Black Melody MEL4
Cover design: Designers Republic
Release date: 20 October 2002
Running time: 76:53

As soon as the Beatles hit it big, earlier unreleased material by the fab four was released. 'Ain't She Sweet' recorded in Germany with Tony Sheridan under the production gaze of Bert Kaempfert, became an unlikely chart entry, and a low-fidelity 1977 album recorded on a domestic Grundig tape machine for Ted 'Kingsize' Taylor – *Live! At The Star-Club In Hamburg, Germany, 1962* has regularly re-emerged.

The same thing happened for The Human League when *Dare* conquered the world. With Ian and Martyn's assistance, various early rehearsal tapes, incomplete tracks and demos were assembled as *The Future Tapes*, with Virgin backing and an announcement about its imminent release tacked onto the sleeve of *Penthouse And Pavement*, showing a potential October-1981 release date. However, the album could not be released without the official approval of The Human League, around whom the marketing would orbit. Suspicious of the motives behind the project, Philip declined to give his approval. As such, the release was cancelled. Martyn told me at the time: 'You will hear the album as soon as Philip Oakey decides to lift his ban on releasing some of the tracks'. Of course, Philip was not on all of *The Future Tapes*, but the band 'used to perform to backing tapes', and the first tour they did as The Human League was 'like a small tour, and we used some of the old tapes. We used some of the stuff we'd done before Philip joined as backing tapes for certain songs. And he's using that as a legal argument to try and stop us putting them out'.

Much later, Philip gave his consent to the release – first of the 'Dance Like A Star' EP, then the fully-reconfigured *The Golden Hour Of The Future* album, which drew in further previously-unknown material, with assistance from Human League members past-and-present, studio engineer David Beevers, and Sean Turner: creator and curator of the excellent Blind Youth website. It was remastered and given a CD reissue in September 2008.

Live At The Dome by The Human League (2005)

Personnel:
Philip Oakey, Joanne Catherall, Susan Ann Gayle: vocals
Neil Sutton: keyboards
Errol Rollins: percussion, electronic drums
Nic Burke: keyboards, guitar
David Beevers: programming
Recorded at the Brighton Dome, 19 December 2003
Label: Secret Films SMADVD201X, USA: Secret Films DR 4461
DVD directed by Dave Meehan
Cover art: Stig Olsen
Release date: 18 July 2005 (as enhanced digipak CD SMACD 904)
Running Time: 62:03

From electronic skiffle through to the bebop of rock, to remaking the future…

This live Human League CD documents the final night of their 2003 tour and exceeds expectations. The DVD edition *Live At The Dome* was issued simultaneously, and includes the full concert plus good-value bonus footage – an interview conducted by 'Jet' Martin Celmins (55:11), a five-page band biography, a fly-on-the-wall featurette 'Access All Areas' (19:23), plus a 35-picture photo gallery of the event, with audio options.

The Brighton Dome is an arts centre containing the Concert Hall, the Corn Exchange and the Studio Theatre. 'What a lovely place to finish a tour', oozed Philip about 'this beautiful venue'.

But something had gone seriously wrong with music. This was not the future that was supposed to be. History had warped out of shape. Oasis were luminous. They made wonderful classic platinum-selling albums, and they set the course for Britpop to dominate the 1990s in the UK. But the business model they used was trad rock. Britpop's unique selling point was its familiarity. Though it took its energy from punk, its essential form was pre-punk. It was revisionist. It was retrograde. This wasn't the way the future was supposed to be. The Human League were still the alternate history of the present.

The Human League never revived because they never split. They took periodic five-year hibernations in Sheffield out of boredom or laziness. But they never actually split. In 1998, they toured as part of The Big Rewind Tour on a bill with Culture Club and ABC. Philip told *Metro* that they 'were dropped by the record label. So we did some tours we wouldn't have done otherwise, with Culture Club and a few others, to make some money while we got some demos together to get a new deal' (30 July 2001).

I caught them at their Sheffield Arena gig on 12 December 1998, doing an abbreviated 11-song set – Philip, Joanne and Susan were backed by Neil Sutton and Adam Everard (synthesizers), Steve Williams (percussion), Lyndon Connah (synth, guitar, percussion), with David Beevers (technical). Theirs was a clean white set with the Kraftwerk purity of a machine-only empty-stage opener of 'Being Boiled'. Then came a colour-coordinated frieze of white, a croaky Oakey as hooded Obi-Wan-Kenobi, and blonde Susan in huge furs and shades – pale and immobile as a showroom dummy – for 'The Sound Of The Crowd'. Those who slag off Susan and Joanne's hugely exaggerated handbag-dancing antics, miss the point. Within their mail-order fashion catalogue poses and caricatured dance antics, lies a sharp pop-art prescience. Seldom has cheap tat come with such class. And their harmonies on the immaculate 'One Man In My Heart' are faultless. Plus, we got Oakey's pierced nipple, and Catherine's inadvertent nipple during a swift costume stage too. Revival? Hell no. Despite the 1990s resurgence of retro guitar bands via Liam-'n'-Noel, The Human League still seemed to me what music would look and sound like in the 21st century, even though they could be accused of impersonating themselves.

In 2004, The Human League supported Basement Jaxx at V-Festival at Weston Park in Staffordshire (22 August) and Chelmsford's Hylands Park (21 August).

'Medley: Hard Times/Love Action (I Believe In Love)' (Burden, Wright, Callis, Oakey) (8:21)
There's an endlessly-looped extended synth opening as searchlights prowl and stab the blue-drenched stage with jerky trip-treated interventions. Philip wears bug shades and a long high-neck embroidered coat as he stalks from stage-front to the riser clasping a radio mic with all the menace of a pantomime villain, his hair razored to the skull. Stage-left, Susan and Joanne gyrate in slender glitter and black trouser suits, chanting the 'Hard Times' motif. The extended edit (13:50) reduces down to a solo programmed drum rhythm at one point, then builds again, but every pulse of the song remains anthemic.

'Mirror Man' (Burden, Callis, Oakey) (4:27)
'Greatest Hits In Concert' it says in the top-right of the cover. Joanne and Susan's shrills are prominent, and Philip's voice stands strong against the pile-driver backing. At the time of *Dare*, the British Musician's Union were scared that burgeoning technology meant that real musicians were already being phased onto the endangered species list; that The Human League were leading us into a promised land of digital leisure where guitars would be nothing more than weird museum exhibits. When is 'live in concert' more programmed than spontaneous? Maybe it was, or maybe it wasn't. There may be sequenced elements here, but who cares when the performance is never less than intensely of-the-moment live on a set beamed directly from the gleaming deck of the USS Enterprise where banks of computers glimmer with flashing diodes. 'Thank you very much. Hello Brighton', says Philip, adding instant immediacy.

'Louise' (Wright, Callis, Oakey) (5:04)
'Our bus station song', said Philip, in another context. For a song essentially structured as an introspective internal dialogue – a hit in a minor (not a major)

key – 'Louise' survives its transition to mega-stadium status remarkably intact, with Joanne and Susan cooing decorously in the background as Philip delivers the talk-singing soap opera lines with faultless drama; only the 'la la la' wind-down sounds a tad laboured. Yet, as part of this live package of gorgeous hits, it feels as though we never appreciated what we had until it was gone. Philip quipped: 'Five years ago, the only place you could get something to eat in Sheffield on a Sunday, was at the bloody bus terminal'.

'The Snake' (Sutton, Oakey) (4:22)
'This is a song about going over the Snake Pass between Sheffield and Manchester', Philip explains helpfully. Opening to ragged applause, the invitation 'Join us, come and join us' is warmly received as the group take the 'path that's crystal clear'. Because this is a more-recent song (from the 2001 *Secrets* package) and maybe not performed to such numbing repetition as some of the other material, this 'journey of the mind' sounds remarkably fresh. Even the instrumental break has a detonation-precision sharpness.

'Darkness' (Wright, Callis) (3:54)
'Don't turn out the lights', chant Joanne and Susan in warning as Philip pledges never to read those books again. When it was originally released, this song was a standout change of pace for *Dare*, and it retains the potential to unsettle: there's an acceleration at the 2:37 point. It retains all the scrubbed, spruced, pristine textures and metronomic precision of the best Martin Rushent production, upholding the spirit of 1981 with the bass sound and electronic percussion of the lost futures of electropop. It's still so far ahead of its time, that it has achieved timelessness.

'All I Ever Wanted' (Sutton, Oakey) (4:04)
Whizzing electric fireworks, Philip's treated voice leads into a slick interpretation of the *Secrets* lead track. The singles sales performance failed to fully realize its chart potential, which was surely an error on the part of the great British record-buying public rather than any fault with the song or production. In this live context, with the voices buzzing in fluorescent circles, it sounds exactly like a hit should sound – the chemical reaction of sex and stance; the equilibrium linking naivety to pop knowing.

'Open Your Heart' (Callis, Oakey) (4:03)
Philip gives a nod to John Foxx and Louis Gordon, who provided 'the best support we have ever had' for the tour, promoting their duo *Crash And Burn* album. 'Open Your Heart ' is one of the strongest hits from *Dare*. It was craftily crafted and fashionably well-fashioned, tailor-made for radio by a band both knowing and in the know, and it survives its transition into the new century remarkably intact, betraying only a slight vocal flatness in places along its convoluted melodic path.

'The Lebanon' (Callis, Oakey) (4:16)

'Here's another song about a war', says Philip by way of offhand introduction. Unlike live albums by some other more-improvisational bands, there's little that's unexpected for The Human League in concert; no radical re-workings, no innovative new interpretations of the songs, and no experiments with new untried material. These are the hits, and they follow the blueprint laid down by the albums. This track is a litmus paper test. Nic Burke replicates the original Jo Callis guitar lines with less explosive emphasis – more veracity than inspiration – and the song loses something of its edge, being robbed of that spontaneity and frozen in time. It could be argued that way.

The other test case zaps back in time to 1979 for the well-versed absurdity of *Reproduction*'s 'Empire State Human' – 'Here's a song from our very first album', Philip announces as the sole continuity from that lineup. Although performed on the DVD, it's omitted from the CD, with Joanne and Susan absent, and no one doing Ian and Martyn's vocal parts. Nic Burke throws in some extravagant guitar-hero poses while Philip winds the track down by strangling sound distortion from a big white guitar synth. Compare and contrast with Martyn's Roland V-Synth bleeps and interjections during the live Heaven 17 version of the same song from 4 September 2021 at the Sheffield City Hall, with Glenn Gregory energetically acting out the lyric; or, with the radically spacey reinvention for Heaven 17's *Naked As Advertised* album (2008), opening with the lyric recitation as a story-poem.

'Human' (James Harris III, Terry Lewis) (4:21)

There are heartbeat synth pulses, and Philip rallies a depth of emotional response that almost breaks at the highest-note point – 'No one else could ever take your place' – he's flesh and blood, a man, after all! This was the song that returned The Human League to the top of the American charts, and they perform it with due reverence. Philip's authoritative pleading is matched by Joanne's naively blunt confessional talk-over, added with equal gravity. It's a sob story with a sting in the tail; pure Hollywood.

'The Things That Dreams Are Made Of' (Wright, Oakey) (3:48)

This is the song that captures all the freshness of a great 1981 adventure that was now 20 years in the past; bright bubbles of ephemeral pop music that refuse to burst even across decades. These are strictly materialist, fun, consumer dreams of the advertiser's glittering game-show prizes; no dreams of love, world peace, an end to poverty, a cure for cancer or Aids; a pop-art irony about the acquisitive society that might just lose something in time's translation across the years from *Dare*. But in a moment of sober reflection, it's useful to recall that The Beatles' recording career involved an arc of little over eight years. Elvis Presley's active recording career for RCA – from 'Heartbreak Hotel' in 1956 until his death in 1977 – barely exceeded 20 years. For The Human League, it was 20 years and counting.

'(Keep Feeling) Fascination' (Callis, Oakey) (4:01)

The original video featured a Sheffield corner house painted red like a pandemic total-exclusion zone. Simple ideas work best on small screens. When the original single was issued, reviewer Mark Brennan said, 'It's pretty obvious that the biggest dare facing Human League, is to actively seek that new direction, rather than passively contemplate it; to take a chance and love and dance in an unfamiliar way' (*Melody Maker*, 16 April 1985). It's arguable whether that challenge was ever fully met. Here, what a hoarse Philip calls 'Human League 2003', is a fairly faithful replication of the original 'song from 1984', complete with his deep 'Hey hey hey hey' and the riff that still slashes as lethal as a laser knife.

It's an uneasy pleasure, displaying little evidence that 'Looking, learning, moving on' has taken place.

'Don't You Want Me' (Wright, Callis, Oakey) (3:59)

In their separate arena incarnations, Cliff Richard still performs 'Living Doll', and The Rolling Stones still do '(I Can't Get No) Satisfaction'. This is where the memories lie. This is the defining hit – the song where all of the audience knows the words and get to sing the chorus back, making a playground of their reciprocal mutual past; a shout-along for all the Sharons and Kevins of the Newtown designer pub cocktail set. It's the millstone that weighs the band down in relentless regurgitation and the reward of unqualified adoration. Susan wears a lurid lipstick-red dress. After the first time they played the V festival, she said, 'We were all very nervous and new to the festival scene. During 'Don't You Want Me', I didn't sing at all, because the audience sang my part so loud. It had never happened before, and it made me cry'. As Noël Coward once said, it's 'extraordinary how potent cheap music is'. These songs touch lives. That is no small thing. More practically, Jo Callis said, 'You don't put out a song that's not got a chorus if you want to go to number 1. It's just basic thinking'.

'Together In Electric Dreams' (Moroder, Oakey) (4:48)

For Philip Oakey of Sheffield, opportunity knocks! What had begun as the Giorgio Moroder movie-theme collaboration had been fully integrated into The Human League set – with added Nic Burke guitar-riffing and a hoarse flawed vocal from Philip, as though he's straining to hit the higher notes. It's softened by Joanne and Susan's backing harmonies, providing an attainable glamour tweaking pastiche into passion. Philip closes with, 'Thank you very much, Brighton'.

The song was used as the theme for the 2021 John Lewis Christmas campaign featuring a silver alien visitor.

CD enhanced video bonus tracks

'Mirror Man' (4:27), 'Human' (4:21), '(Keep Feeling) Fascination' (4:01)

Extended DVD running order

1. 'Intro' 2. 'Hard Times' 3. 'Love Action (I Believe In Love)' 4. 'Mirror Man' 5. 'Louise' 6. 'The Snake' 7. 'Heart Like A Wheel' 8. 'Darkness' 9. 'All I Ever Wanted' 10. 'Open Your Heart' 11. 'The Lebanon' 12. 'One Man In My Heart' 13. 'Human' 14. 'The Things That Dreams Are Made Of' 15. 'Love Me Madly?' 16. '(Keep Feeling) Fascination' 17. 'Tell Me When' 18. 'Don't You Want Me' 19. 'Empire State Human' 20. 'Together In Electric Dreams' 21. 'The Sound Of The Crowd'

Related Releases
Hands by Little Boots

Released: June 2009 (679 Recordings, Atlantic 2564689052)

Highest UK chart position: 5

The debut album by Victoria Hesketh under her Little Boots alias features Philip Oakey dueting with her on just one track, 'Symmetry' (4:30), written by Victoria with Anu Pillai and Roy Kerr. Philip also talk-sings the lines, 'So tell me your dreams and I'll tell you my fears, so ask me your questions, what you want to hear.' It's a smooth exercise in electro-dance that shows to what extent Human League innovations have been seamlessly absorbed into the Pop mainstream.

DVD: Made In Sheffield: The Birth Of Electronic Pop 1977-1982 (2001)

DVD, 2004, Sheffield Vision SV001 (2005, Plexifilm 017)
Director: Eve Wood
Richard Heap: Cinematography and Film Editing
Sheffield Vision and Slackjaw Film Ltd
Artwork: The Designers Republic
Release date: 24 October 2001
Running time: 52:00

This is an informed and informative *bleepumentary* history of Sheffield music by first-time Dutch director Eve Wood. It covers the 1970s and early-1980s, when the famous, almost-famous, and not-famous-at-all bands Cabaret Voltaire, The Human League, ABC, Def Leppard, Heaven 17, Pulp, I'm So Hollow, Artery, The Extras, 2.3, Clock DVA and The Comsat Angels became integral to a 'new aesthetic' that exploited electronic music in a post-punk avant-garde revolutionary sonic terrorism. 'Their dream was to destroy rock music', with integral trips to Boots' makeup counter. It catches the raw experimental edge of early Sheffield electro exactly as I remember it; the open try-anything attitude to sound that – as Ian Craig Marsh phrases it – 'not only you hadn't heard before, but maybe other people anywhere in the world hadn't heard that sound before'. It includes interviews with members of The Extras, Pulp, The Human League and others – Paul Bower, Jarvis Cocker, Andy Gill, John Lake, Robin Markin, Ian Craig Marsh, Adi Newton, Philip Oakey, John Peel, Martin Ware, Stephen Singleton and Chris Watson. As with the writing of this book – in Eve's words, 'We felt that to document how these bands came about, we needed to give an idea of the whole scene. Each band and individual, famous or not, played an important part in the development of the scene and, therefore, also the success of the bands'.

Assembled with an appropriately low-budget DIY ethos, sequences include Intro & Steel City, Meatwhistle, Formation of Cabaret Voltaire, Kraftwerk & Electronics, The Future, Punk, Formation Of Early Human League, Gunrubber, Early Human League, The Extras, Cabaret Voltaire & Vice Versa, 1978: More Bands Enter Scene, Artery, Vice Versa at Now Society, Artery Live, The Limit, 2.3: First to get signed, DIY & Neutron Records, Extras go to London, Start of ABC, Split: Early Human League, Chris leaves Cabaret Voltaire, Split: Artery, 2.3 & Extras, ABC at *Top Of The Pops*, Success: New Human League & Heaven 17 – with bonus live footage of Vice Versa ('Democratic Dancebeat', 'Genetic Warfare', plus photo gallery), Artery ('Afterwards') and I'm So Hollow ('Touch').

Credo by **The Human League** (2011)

Personnel:
Philip Oakey: vocals, synthesizers, keyboards
Joanne Catherall: vocals
Susan Ann Sulley (reverted from Gayle October 2007): vocals
augmented by
Nic Burke: guitar and keyboards
Jarrod Nicholas Gosling: percussion
Mike Ward (aka Mick Somerset): saxophone
Neil Sutton: keyboards
Dean Thomas Honer: writer
Arrangements: Robert Matthew Barton
Management: Simon Watson for Sidewinder Management Ltd.
Produced by I Monster
Recorded at The Human League, Pig View and The Bowling Green (Dean Honer), engineered at The Human League by David Beevers, mastered by Mike Marsh at The Exchange
Label: Wall Of Sound WOS085CD, PIAS Entertainment Group, Europe; USA digital, CD MB3 Records MB3 009 (16 and 23 August 2011)
Release date: 21 March 2011
Chart position: UK: 44

'There are no walls in cyberspace', said David Chaum (*Wired*, December 1994). The ninth studio album – trailing almost ten years after *Secrets* (2001) – emerged into a shifting musicscape of streaming and downloads. Molloy Woodcraft wrote in *The Observer* about 'Oakey's strident baritone intoning over synths and stark harmonies. It's a post-house, post-electro revival world, so the beats have been updated courtesy of Sheffield producers I Monster, but the doomy wordscapes and wayward modulations, remain' (20 March 2011).

Keeping it local, the duo who make up I Monster are Sheffield's Dean Honer and Jarrod Gosling, who take both their collective identity name and their label name Twins Of Evil from old Peter Cushing horror movies. The Sheffield music scene had moved on, but was still actively innovative. Dean also operated as part of the All Seeing I, who collaborated with other local artists from Jarvis Cocker and Tony Christie to Philip Oakey!

A 'credo' is a statement of belief, of principles. This album is a reaffirmation. The mission continues – love, and dancing.

'Never Let Me Go' (Oakey, Barton, Honer, Gosling) (3:33)

There was a stripped-back 'Aeroplane dance mix' (7:47) and 'Italo Connection' remix (5:42) for this the album's second single, issued in March 2011. It takes full advantage of the band's gender balance, with Joanne and Susan alternating passages well to the fore with 'I'm the one you want/I'm the one you need', leaving Philip largely confined to the harmony chorus title statements. And it's all wrapped in a bright melody line interfaced to attractive vocoder production trip-effects, fusing the best of the old League with vital new energies. All the way is far enough.

'Night People' (Oakey, Barton) (5:29)

There's a deeply addictive rumbling of electric storms – an overwhelming energy rush that hits like diamond light. In the long history of pop culture, there's always been the in-crowd and the place where the in-crowd go. Maybe there's a self-mocking sense of irony here in 'Gather up your skirts and trousers/put on your best frock and blouses', referring back to a night out at the Crazy Daisy rather than the ultra-hip metropolitan glitterati celebrity haunts. Disco music for people who can't dance. But that collision of trash with flash has always been part of the Human League métier, and this track works, even if it's interpreted as a satirical dance meme. In a John Doran interview on the *The Quietus* website, Philip admitted the track 'was not designed to go on the radio. It was designed to go into clubs, to have remixes, but suddenly it's a single and it got played on Radio 2' (14 February 2011). 'Night People' is an unapologetic delight; a guiltless pleasure.

'Sky' (Oakey, Barton) (3:11)

There are a drizzle of notes, saturated in blurry white noise as two worlds align, with Philip adopting senses he'd not previously employed in order to seek out a transient girl on a blazing day. The lyric has a distant narrative connection to 'Louise', with an occasional vocal-line distortion. It's part of a recurrent male fantasy in which there's the magical visitation of the perfect dream lover, who bestows sensual gifts without guilt or commitment, only to vanish without trace, leaving only a sweet aftertaste. For The Byrds, she was the 'Child Of The Universe', 'giving freely of herself, leaving man her cosmic love'. For Cliff Richard, it was 'The Day I Met Marie'. For The Human League, she is Sky. An encounter more transfiguring than a one-night stand placed in an urban setting, 'I drained my glass and turned to see'. There's an intangible sense of threat, undefined that she's in danger. He knows a place of sanctuary. Though 'The day of my birth was her last day on Earth', life goes on after Sky. The song was issued on 25 July 2011 as the album's third single but disappeared as surely as she did.

'Into The Night' (Oakey, Barton) (3:46)

This is a message directed at startled simians, charming helions and darling bohemians – don't fear the darkness; the future is still out there waiting. Maybe the 'Wake me, shake me/Just let me know/Take me, make me, hungry to go' carries faint trace echoes of The Four Tops' 'Shake Me, Wake Me When It's Over', or maybe not. There's admittedly a certain formulaic pattern that has settled around the structure and arrangements of tracks; a reassuring if-it-ain't-broke familiarity. Although, within the style variants, this song oozes more smoothly, with a use of left-and-right panning on the 'Will you turn the key' line, followed by an effective gradual fade-out. I'm too chic to dare to disagree.

'Egomaniac' (Oakey, Barton) (4:01)

Dancing like a diamond in the sun! At this stage, it would be absurd to expect any of the chilling precision of *Dare*'s darker moments or the obdurate experimental obscurity of 'The Dignity Of Labour'. Instead, there's a cunning revised vocabulary wrapped in some freshly-minted spurious semiotics: 'A new direction in an old familiar way'. If not exactly re-contouring electronic dance into new shapes, it runs various synth-tronics on top of a deep sonorous bass figure. Issued as a single on 4 March 2011 in Germany, Austria and Switzerland, this track nudges the edges of the template in jerky disruptive ways, with an echo-treated voice repeating the title and the shimmery earworm of a spiralling synth riff that trips through the mix. 'When you're the best, who needs the rest?'. Thy will be done.

'Single Minded' (Oakey, Barton) (3:52)

I see no right, I see no wrong. Truth reduced down to one concentrated nucleus. A little joy, a little pain. There's an early demo version called 'Biller 10' on the *A Very British Synthesizer Group* compilation, which hints at the track's evolution. Twittering synths that sigh and quiver, piping behind and around the voice interactions, the track quietens around the 2:33 mark, for Philip to talk-sing through a middle-eight break before it swirls back into single focus. For this album in total, there's not necessarily any advancement on what had come before, but there's no noticeable disimprovement either. They're reaffirming old allegiances while hunting for a future. It might be going nowhere, but it's an entrancing place to stand.

'Electric Shock' (Oakey, Barton, Honer) (4:56)

Electric music for the mind and the body, tangled up in electric dreams. 'Electric' is an adjective that usefully prefixes a noun in order to denote excitement, modernity and energy. Mary Shelley's character Victor Frankenstein harvests the spark of lightning to animate a corpse, and ever since that moment, civilization has mainlined on its megawatt generation. It's entirely appropriate when applied to this relentless programmed drum track, reinforced by the remorseless chittering electro riff looped endlessly into the crescendo. But this track also opens with the same gentle rising ascending curve that opens 'One Man In My Heart' – the static hits, ozone and electricity. It's a beautiful philosophy.

'Get Together' (Oakey, Barton) (3:48)

Nothing good comes easily. Human hearts are so fragile. Philip urges collective action; mutual aid: 'Find the courage to make a difference/Hold your head up high'. He advocates cooperative strategies in order to combat negativity. Journalist Colm O'Hare finds contrasting impulses in that 'despite the otherworldly electronic backdrop' of the social consciousness-raising 'Get Together', 'there was always something quintessentially suburban and domestic about The Human League' (*Hot Press*). Nevertheless, this track works as a stirring anthem.

'Privilege' (Oakey, Barton) (3:41)

Gruff. Granite hard. This is a welter of aggressive discord that rails against financial wrongdoings – 'Overpower privilege/Seize the hour of privilege/Storm the tower of privilege' – inflicting some of the most confrontational effects they've dropped into the mix since *Travelogue*. A brief hint of squiggly 'Love Action' synths and a lock-stock-and-two-smoking-barrels of illicit activity opens with a vivid series of lyrical flash-images – the tough guy in his stolen Jaguar driving past the lights of Birmingham until that threat from far away is standing on your drive. Philip's voice is warped into an electronic edge of menace.

'Breaking The Chains' (Oakey, Barton) (4:02)

An alien swirl of bleeping signals direct from extrasolar systems. He's a rebel, wild at heart, bound by nobody's rules. But in a real theatrical fury, he's got a wire on you, so you can't disappear. There are suggestions of surveillance, conspiracy theory – an Orwellian big-brother monitoring of unstable free radicals. A midpoint breakdown dissolves into broken digital code. Nic played synth guitar on the demo, which was retained for the studio session, while knob-twiddler supreme Jarrod Gosling contributes Mellotron strings. The results are pleasingly strange.

'When The Stars Start To Shine' (Oakey, Barton) (3:49)

There's an odd percussive start played on tribal drums and other hollow objects, with a distorted-undertow voice before a groundswell of a catchy sing-along verse, breaks into the more-conventional Human League template of the Philip-Joanne-and-Susan back-and-forth dialogue. Then there's another quirky break. It proves The Human League are still capable of springing tongue-in-cheek surprises. They urge 'Keep on moving', and there's a reiteration of the uplifting 'Get Together' message to 'Hold your head up' – as if to stress a positive confirming tone that's maybe intended as a response to 'The Stars Are Going Out' from *Romantic?*. It's been a lovely day …

Contemporary Releases
'Night People' (Digital single)

Label: Wall Of Sound WOS092D
Release date: 22 November 2010 (12": 6 December 2010)
Jarrod Gosling commented that, as the first single, 'Many mixes and tweaks were done here. This one had to appeal to the clubbers'.

12" single:

1. 'Night People' (3:45) 2. 'Night People' (Radio edit) (3:00) 3. 'Night People' (Cerrone Club remix) (5:21) 4. 'Night People' (Mylo remix) (6:09) 5. 'Night People' (Emperor Machine remix) (9:07) 6. 'Night People' (Villa remix) (7:02)

'Never Let Me Go' (Digital and CD single)

Label: Wall Of Sound WOS103D
Release date: 21 March 2011
1. 'Never Let Me Go' (Radio edit) (2:48) 2. 'Never Let Me Go' (Single) (3:30) 3. 'Never Let Me Go' (Album) (4:55)

There was also a US (RCRD LBL) 'Aeroplane' download remix. Again, for Jarrod, there was 'tweaking, tweaking and extra tweaking in every department. Edits, and big edits they were, due to the album version being much longer and the arrangement quite unusual'.

Susan and Joanne trade vocals, with Philip joining for the chorus. The bio-metamorphosis video is genuinely disturbing, with faces blurring and merging like a mutant experiment in genetic engineering. As in 'Night People', 'We are people, not just creatures/We can rearrange our features'.

Epilogue

In Sheffield, music had moved on. The Arctic Monkeys, Pulp and Richard Hawley continue to be high-profile but were not related to that unique electronic tradition of which The Human League were a formative part. Cabaret Voltaire had arguably been the first. Following their Some Bizzare period with Virgin, they up-switched to EMI for the critically well-received *Code* (1987) (produced by On-U Sound dub mixer Adrian Sherwood, and featuring input from Bill Nelson and Mark Brydon): super cool for maximum efficiency. But there was dissension within their wide-eyed and wilfully-obscure technophilia and solo projects that diverted energies while creating an extensive cult following. The album *Groovy, Laidback And Nasty* (1990, Parlophone) constituted a move into house music, recorded in Chicago with Marshall Jefferson. Then *Body And Soul* (1991) from the Belgian Les Disques du Crépuscule became the last to feature Stephen's lead vocals. They were supercontinents that collided and then came apart. After a pause, Richard revived the Cabaret Voltaire brand in 2009, recording new work at Western Works – a revival brought to an untimely halt only when Richard died in September 2021 at the age of 65, leaving a hugely influential back catalogue.

Following their last album for Virgin – *Teddy Bear, Duke & Psycho* (1988) – Heaven 17 went through a quiet period, concentrating on B.E.F. and Martyn Ware production work for the likes of Terence Trent D'Arby, Marc Almond and Erasure, while the Brothers In Rhythm remix of 'Temptation' re-established their chart presence. 'We're totally out of the mainstream and far apart from anything that's categorisable. We are a very odd group', rationalised Martyn (*Melody Maker*, 1 October 1988). *Bigger Than America* (1996) and *Before After* (2005) (which featured a strange cover of Blue Oyster Cult's 'Don't Fear The Reaper') were their final products to include Ian Craig Marsh, who subsequently quit music. Glenn and Martyn continued to tour as Heaven 17, joining The Human League and ABC as part of the December 2008 Steel City tour. They recorded new versions of 'Being Boiled' and 'Empire State Human' as part of their album *Naked As Advertised* (2008, Just Music), before performing the entire *Reproduction* and *Travelogue* albums live on stage in September 2021.

For ABC, the immense critical and commercial success of *Lexicon Of Love* had proven difficult to follow. Stephen Singleton left to concentrate on production work after *Beauty Stab* (November 1983), allowing a complete image redesign ('Me, I go from one extreme to the other') into real-life cartoon figures for *How To Be A... Zillionaire!* (1985). The single 'Be Near Me' took them into the American top 10, followed by the sublime 'When Smokey Sings' – an eloquent tribute to Smokey Robinson, which peaked at 5 in the US in September 1987. Working as the duo of Martin Fry and Mark White, they issued *Up* (1989) – their final project for Polygram – until Martin recorded *Skycraping* (1997) using the ABC name as a solo flag of convenience, augmented by Glenn Gregory and Carol Kenyon. 1980s nostalgia packages – including the 2008

Regeneration tour with The Human League, Belinda Carlisle and A Flock Of Seagulls – led to *Lexicon Of Love II* (2016), which was a deliberate replication of the grand style of their debut album with Anne Dudley orchestrations, which returned Martin to number 5 on the UK album chart. Mark White and Stephen Singleton compiled the comprehensive four-LP box-set *Electrogenesis 1978-1980* (2014, VOD Records). which collected everything released and previously unreleased by Vice Versa.

Adi Newton reactivated Clock DVA in 1987 with Dean Dennis and Paul Browse as a more extreme experimental art-installation project involving cyberpunk sampling and operating from a more Eurocentric base, where they'd always enjoyed a more fanatical following. By the time of *Man-Amplified* (1992) and the instrumental *Digital Soundtracks* (1992), Browse had quit, and following *Sign* (1993), Dean left the lineup too. Adi Newton continues to produce challenging new electronic music across European festivals, as reissues and critical re-evaluation increases the group's retrospective reputation.

Once Box had run its course, vocalist Pete Hope (his voice sired by Howlin' Wolf during a voodoo eclipse, then wrenched from the larynx with a claw hammer) collaborated with Richard H. Kirk for *Hoodoo Talk* (1987), and has continued to release confrontational electro-industrial projects across a wide spectrum, with The Exploding Mind (*Hot Crow On The Wrong Hand Side* (2015)) and David Harrow (*Blue Electric* (2016)).

While The Human League simply continue – still far weirder than most of the current music that people stream on their devices – they tour, and play festivals, such as the Electric Picnic, Camp Bestival, the Ostend W-Festival 2021, the Rewind Festival 2018 at Henley-on-Thames, the Liverpool Sound City Festival (2017), the V-Festival (2014), and various Rewinds.

Philip Oakey:

I've got an interesting theory which I haven't yet brought to anyone's attention. I think time started going backwards. As soon as we reach the right point – 1982 or 1983 – The Human League will be huge again. That point might be now.

Human League Compilation Albums

Human League: Greatest Hits (1988) (Vinyl, CD and cassette)
Label: UK: Virgin HLCD1-2593555-222, USA: A&M SP-5227
Release date: 31 October 1988
Chart position: UK: 3
1. 'Mirror Man' (3:49, from Fascination!) 2. '(Keep Feeling) Fascination' (3:43, from Fascination!) 3. 'The Sound Of The Crowd' (3:56, from Dare) 4. 'The Lebanon' (3:43, from Hysteria) 5. 'Human' (3:46, from Crash) 6. 'Together In Electric Dreams' (3:53, from Philip Oakey & Giorgio Moroder, also Electric Dreams) (Omitted from US edition of the album.) 7. 'Don't You Want Me?' (3:57, from Dare) 8. 'Being Boiled' (3:38, single) 9. 'Love Action (I Believe In Love)' (3:50, from Dare) 10. 'Louise' (4:55, from Hysteria) 11. 'Open Your Heart' (3:55, from Dare) 12. 'Love Is All That Matters' (4:06, from Crash) 13. 'Life On Your Own' (4:05, from Hysteria)

It may be hard, today, to appreciate the politics of dance: the brave new world these songs once promised. The adamant use of synthesizers to produce emotional epics was perhaps the last great bid and statement for modernity before pop re-succumbed to the factory mentality it had resisted since the '50s.
Steve Sutherland (*Melody Maker*, 29 October 1988)

Greatest Hits (1995)
Label: Virgin CDV 2792-724384094621
Release date: 6 November 1995
Chart position: 28
In order to benefit from renewed interest in The Human League sparked by the success
of the *Octopus* album on East West Records, Virgin hastily repackaged the 1988 *Greatest Hits* compilation with bonus tracks and issued it on CD and cassette.

1. 'Don't You Want Me?' (3:59, from Dare) 2. 'Love Action (I Believe In Love)' (3:52, from Dare) 3. 'Mirror Man' (3:52, from Fascination!) 4. 'Tell Me When' (4:43, from Octopus) 5. 'Stay With Me Tonight' (4:01, a 1996 East West single) 6. 'Open Your Heart' (3:56, from Dare) 7. '(Keep Feeling) Fascination' (3:45, from Fascination!) 8. 'The Sound Of The Crowd' (3:57, from Dare) 9. Being Boiled' (3:39, non-album single) 10. 'The Lebanon' (3:43, from Hysteria) 11. 'Love Is All That Matters' (4:06, from Crash) 12. 'Louise' (4:57, from Hysteria) 13. 'Life On Your Own' (4:05, from Hysteria) 14. 'Together In Electric Dreams' (3:53, from Philip Oakey & Giorgio Moroder and Electric Dreams) 15. 'Human' (3:49, from Crash) 16. 'Don't You Want Me' (Snap! 7" remix) (3:58, previously unissued)

Soundtrack To A Generation (1996)
Label: Netherlands: Disky VI 875302
Release date: I November 1996

1. 'Human' (4:28) 2. 'Kiss The Future' (4:14) 3. 'Together In Electric Dreams' (3:53) 4. 'Are You Ever Coming Back?' (4:53) 5. 'Betrayed' (4:03) 6. 'Hard Times' (5:11, 12" A-side) 7. 'Get It Right This Time' (4:13) 8. 'I Need Your Loving' (3:45) 9. 'Do Or Die' (5:24) 10. 'Rebound' (5:24) 11. 'Soundtrack To A Generation' (4:35) 12. 'Empire State Human' (3:13) 13. 'The Real Thing' (4:18) 14. 'Don't You Know I Want You?' (3:09)

The Best Of The Human League (1997)
Label: UK: Virgin SITHCD1, Canada: Virgin SITHCD1
Release date: 5 January 1997
1. 'Love Action (I Believe In Love)' (3:49) 2. 'Mirror Man' (3:48) 3. 'Open Your Heart' (3:53) 4. 'The Sound Of The Crowd' (3:55) 5. 'Don't You Know I Want You?' (3:06) 6. 'Life On Your Own' (4:04) 7. 'Seconds' (4:58) 8. 'Hard Times' (4:52) 9. 'Do Or Die' (5:23) 10. 'Heart Like A Wheel' (4:27) 11. 'The Lebanon' (3:45) 12. 'Get It Right This Time' (4:12) 13. 'Louise' (4:55) 14. 'Kiss The Future' (4:13) 15. 'Human' (3:47) 16. 'Let's Get Together Again' (4:59)

The Very Best Of The Human League (1998)
Label: US: Ark 21 61868-10034-2
Release date: 14 July 1998
1. 'Don't You Want Me?' (3:56) 2. 'Love Action (I Believe In Love)' (3:49, single) 3. 'Mirror Man' (3:48) 4. '(Keep Feeling) Fascination' (3:40) 5. 'Tell Me When' (4:42, single) 6. 'Stay With Me Tonight' (4:00) 7. 'Human' (3:45, single) 8. 'Together In Electric Dreams' (3:53, by Giorgio Moroder with Philip Oakey) 9. 'Heart Like A Wheel' (4:28) 10. 'One Man In My Heart' (4:05) 11. 'Being Boiled' (3:39, stereo mix) 12. 'The Lebanon' (3:44, single) 13. 'Don't You Want Me?' (3:58, Snap 7" remix) (14). (Hidden Track) (9:40 interview taken from American promo interview-CD 'Sixty Minutes Of Conversation And Music', East West PRCD 9185-21995)

The Very Best Of The Human League (2003)
Label: UK: Virgin 2CD 7243-5-92646-22, USA: Caroline CAR92645
Release date: 15 September 2003
Chart position: UK: 24

Disc 1
1. 'Don't You Want Me?' 2. 'Love Action (I Believe In Love)' 3. 'Open Your Heart' 4. 'The Sound Of The Crowd' 5. 'Mirror Man' 6. '(Keep Feeling) Fascination' 7. 'The Lebanon' (Single) 8. 'Life On Your Own' 9. 'Together In Electric Dreams' 10. 'Louise' 11. 'Human' (Single) 12. 'Heart Like A Wheel' 13. 'Tell Me When' (Single) 14. 'One Man In My Heart' 15. 'All I Ever Wanted' 16. 'Being Boiled' (Stereo mix) 17. 'Empire State Human'

Disc 2 – Remixes
1. 'Don't You Want Me' (7:47, Majik J Original Booty Vocal Mix) 2. 'Open Your Heart' (6:48, Laid Remix) 3. 'The Sound Of The Crowd' (7:20, Trisco's PopClash Mix)

4. 'Love Action (I Believe In Love)' (7:09, Brooks Red Line Vocal Mix) 5. '(Keep Feeling) Fascination' (6:48, Groove Collision TMC Mix) 6. 'Empire State Human' (5:31, Chamber's Reproduced Mix) 7. 'The Things That Dreams Are Made Of' (5:04, Jimmy 19 The A509 PWC Remix) 8. 'The Sound Of The Crowd' (6:11, Freaksblamredo) 9. 'Open Your Heart' (5:24, The Strand Remix) 10. 'The Sound Of The Crowd' (4:27, Riton Re-Rub) 11. 'Love Action (I Believe In Love)' (7:13, Fluke's Dub Action Remix)

Original Remixes & Rarities (2005)
Label: Virgin CDV3011
Release date: 7 November 2005
1. 'Being Boiled' (4:16, 1980 version) 2. 'The Sound Of The Crowd' (6:28, 12")
3. 'Hard Times' (4:53, 'Love Action' B-side) 4. 'Non-Stop' (4:16, 'Open Your Heart' B-side) 5. 'Don't You Want Me' (7:28, Extended Dance Mix) 6. 'Mirror Man' (4:20, 12") 7. 'You Remind Me Of Gold' (3:36, 'Mirror Man' B-side) 8. '(Keep Feeling) Fascination' (6:10, 12" Improvisation mix) 9. 'Total Panic' (3:29, '(Keep Feeling) Fascination' B-side) 10. 'The Lebanon' (5:52, 12") 11. 'Life On Your Own' (5:45, 12") 12. 'Together In Electric Dreams' (6:22, 12") 13. 'Human' (5:02, 12") 14. 'Heart Like A Wheel' (6:49, 12")

Dare/Fascination (2012)
Label: Virgin CDV2192
Release date: 6 April 2012
Bonus tracks:
'The Sound Of The Crowd' (Instrumental), plus both an extended Dance Mix and an alternate version of 'Don't You Want Me'

Greatest Hits On CD and DVD (2012)
Label: EMI Gold 5099962436328
Release date: 24 August 2012

All The Best (2-CD compilation) (2012)
Label: UK: Virgin 721-8232 EU: Universal 0600753462669 (Issued as Gold)
Release date: UK: 26 November 2012, EU: 28 November 2013

A Very British Synthesizer Group (2016)
Label: UK: Virgin 5702581, USA: Virgin/Ume B0025709-02
Release date: 18 November 2016
Issued in 2-CD and three-LP formats. A deluxe edition features a third CD of demos and early versions, and a DVD featuring promo videos and TV clips from *Top Of The Pops*, *Wogan*, and *Later... with Jools Holland*.

CD1
1. 'Being Boiled' (3:50, Fast version, single 6/78) 2. 'The Dignity Of Labour, Part 3' (3:51, EP 4/79) 3. 'Empire State Human' (3:13, single 10/79) 4. 'Only After Dark'

(3:47, listed as single edit, but is LP version, 5/80) 5. 'Nightclubbing' (2:57, from EP 'Holiday 80', 4/80) 6. 'Boys And Girls' (3:14, single 2/81) 7. 'The Sound Of The Crowd' (4:12, B-side instrumental, 5/81) 8. 'Hard Times' (4:55, B-side 'Love Action' 12", 8/81) 9. 'Love Action (I Believe In Love)' (3:51, single, 8/81) 10. 'Open Your Heart' (3:56, LP version, 10/81) 11. 'Don't You Want Me' (3:58, LP version, 10/81) 12. 'Mirror Man' (3:51, single, 11/82) 13. 'You Remind Me Of Gold' (3:37, 'Mirror Man' B-side) 14. '(Keep Feeling) Fascination' (4:58, extended single mix, 4/83) 15. 'The Lebanon' (3:43, 7", 4/84) 16. 'Louise' (4:07, DJ edit, 11/84)

CD2

1. 'Life On Your Own' (4:11, listed as single edit, but is LP version, 5/84) 2. 'Human' (5:06, extended version, 8/86) 3. 'I Need Your Loving' (2:52, DJ edit, 11/86) 4. 'Love Is All That Matters' (2:58, edit) 5. 'Heart Like A Wheel' (4:52, William Orbit Remix) 6. 'Soundtrack To A Generation' (4:03, single edit, 10/90) 7. 'Tell Me When' (4:09, radio edit, 12/94) 8. 'One Man In My Heart' (4:05, single, 3/95) 9. 'Filling Up With Heaven' (4:20, single, 6/95) 10. 'Stay With Me Tonight' (4.01, single, 1/96) 11. 'All I Ever Wanted' (3:31, radio edit, 7/01) 12. 'Night People' (3:02, radio digital single edit, 12/10) 13. 'Never Let Me Go' (4.56, LP version) 14. 'Sky' (3:12, radio digital single edit, 7/11)

CD 3: CD and DVD

1. 'The Path Of Least Resistance' (3:23, early version, 1979) 2. 'No Time' (3:53, early version of 'The Word Before Last', 1979) 3. 'Being Boiled' (4:12, State of the Art Mix, 1980) 4. 'Stylopops You Broke My Heart' (3:45, early version of 'Marianne', 1980) 5. 'I Am The Law' (4:16, early version, 1981) 6. 'Darkness' (4:17, early version, 1981) 7. 'Louise' (4:55, early version, 1984) 8. 'The Real Thing' (4:00, early version, 1986) 9. 'Love On The Run' (3:51, early version, 1986) 10. 'A Doorway' (4:28, early version, 1990) 11. 'F.M.' (4:24, early version of 'Soundtrack To A Generation', 1990) 12. 'Happening Woman' (3:25, early version of 'Filling Up With Heaven', 1995) 13. 'Give It Back' (4:39, early version of 'Houseful Of Nothing', 1995) 14. 'New Start' (4:06, early version of 'All I Ever Wanted', 2001) 15. 'SH5' (5:41, early version of 'Liar', 2001) 16. 'Biller 10' (3:51, early version of 'Single Minded', 2011) 17. 'Jupiter 4C' (5:57, early version of 'Sky', 2011)

CD3: The Music Videos

1. 'Circus Of Death' (3:49, 1978) 2. 'Empire State Human' (3:10, 1979) 3. 'Love Action (I Believe In Love)' (3:49, 1981) 4. 'Open Your Heart' (3:42, 1981) 5. 'Don't You Want Me' (3:27, 1981) 6. 'Mirror Man' (3:13, 1982) 7. '(Keep Feeling) Fascination' (3:45, 1983) 8. 'The Lebanon' (3:35, 1984) 9. 'Life On Your Own' (4:07, 1984) 10. 'Louise' (4.07, 1984) 11. 'Human' (3:51, 1986) 12. 'I Need Your Loving' (3:44, 1986) 13. 'Love Is All That Matters' (2:56, 1988) 14. 'Heart Like A Wheel' (4:28, 1990) 15. 'Soundtrack To A Generation' (3:59, 1990) 16. 'Tell Me When' (4:09, 1994) 17. 'One Man In My Heart' (3:58, 1995) 18. 'Filling Up With Heaven' (3:52, 1995) 19. 'All I Ever Wanted' (3:26, 2001) 20. 'Night People' (3:45, 2010) 21. 'Never Let Me Go' (3:33, 2011)

Live at the BBC

22. 'The Path Of Least Resistance' (3:23, Mainstream, 6 November 1979)
23. 'Empire State Human' (also listed as from Mainstream, but omitted) 24. 'Rock 'N' Roll, Part 2' (2:46, Top Of The Pops, 8 May 1980) 25. 'The Sound Of The Crowd' (3:01, Top Of The Pops, 21 May 1981) 26. 'The Sound Of The Crowd' (2:57, Top Of The Pops, 30 April 1981) 27. 'Love Action (I Believe In Love)' (3:25, Top Of The Pops, 6 August 1981) 28. 'Open Your Heart' (3:38, Top Of The Pops, 8 October 1981) 29. 'Don't You Want Me' (3:28, Top Of The Pops, 21 December 1981) 30. 'Love Action (I Believe In Love)' (3:26, Top Of The Pops, 25 December 1981) 31. 'Love Action (I Believe In Love)' (3:26, Multi-Coloured Swap Shop, 30 May 1982) 32. 'Mirror Man' (3:30, Top Of The Pops, 18 November 1982) 33. '(Keep Feeling) Fascination' (3:35, Top Of The Pops, 5 May 1983) 34. 'The Lebanon' (3:20, Top Of The Pops, 3 May 1984) 35. 'Life On Your Own' (3:52, Top Of The Pops, 1984) 36. 'I'm Coming Back' (4:13, The Oxford Road Show, 25 August 1984) 37. 'Rock Me Again And Again And Again And Again And Again And Again (Six Times)' (2:56, The Oxford Road Show, 25 August 1984) 38. 'Human' (3:38, Wogan, 13 August 1986) 39. 'Human' (3:35, Top Of The Pops, 23 September 1986) 40. 'Heart Like A Wheel' (3:32, Wogan, 13 August 1990) 41. 'Heart Like A Wheel' (3:02, Top Of The Pops, 23 August 1990) 42. 'Tell Me When' (2:53, Top Of The Pops, 22 December 1994) 43. 'Tell Me When' (2:54, Top Of The Pops, 5 January 1995) 44. 'One Man In My Heart' (2:57, Top Of The Pops, 16 March 1995) 45. 'The Stars Are Going Out' (4:19, Later... with Jools Holland, 25 November 1995) 46. 'The Sound Of The Crowd' (4:00, Later... with Jools Holland, 25 November 1995)

Essential (3-CD box set) (2020)

Label: Spectrum UMC 5390976
Release date: 5 June 2020
Chart position: 13

CD1:

1. 'Don't You Want Me' (3:56, 1981) 2. '(Keep Feeling) Fascination' (4:52, extended, 1983) 3. 'The Sound Of The Crowd' (4:03, LP version, 1981) 4. 'Open Your Heart' (3:54, 1981) 5. 'Life On Your Own' (4:04, 1984) 6. 'Louise' (4:56, 1984) 7. 'Hard Times' (4:48, 'Love Action (I Believe In Love)' B-side, 1981) 8. 'You Remind Me Of Gold' (3:36, 'Mirror Man' B-side, 1982) 9. 'I Love You Too Much' (3:27, 1984) 10. 'The Things That Dreams Are Made Of' (4:12, 1981) 11. 'I'm Coming Back' (4:11, 1984) 12. 'Let's Get Together Again' (5:00, 1990)

CD2:

1. 'Love Action (I Believe In Love)' (4:58, LP version, 1981) 2. 'Mirror Man' (3:48, 1982) 3. 'The Lebanon' (3:43, single, 1984) 4. 'Love Is All That Matters' (7:45, extended, 1987) 5. 'Heart Like A Wheel' (4:52, William Orbit Remix, 1990) 6. 'I Need Your Loving' (7:12, extended, 1986) 7. 'Love On The Run' (3:54, 1986) 8. 'Are You Ever Coming Back?' (4:52, 1986) 9. 'Soundtrack To A Generation' (6:03,

William Orbit mix, 1990) 10. 'Kiss The Future' (4:13, 1990) 11. 'Men Are Dreamers' (3:54, 1990) 12. 'Rebound' (3:56, 1990) 13. 'The Stars Are Going Out' (4:05, 1990) 14. 'Dreams Of Leaving' (5:48, 1980)

CD3:

1. 'Together In Electric Dreams' (6:22, extended, 1984) 2. 'Human' (5:00, extended, 1986) 3. 'Being Boiled' (4:21, 1980 version) 4. 'Empire State Human' (3:12, 1979) 5. 'Boys And Girls' (3:14, single, 1981) 6. 'The Path Of Least Resistance' (3:28, 1979) 7. 'Blind Youth' (3:17, 1979) 8. 'Morale... You've Lost That Loving Feeling' (9:30, 1979) 9. 'Marianne' (3:15, 1980) 10. 'Rock 'N' Roll/ Nightclubbing' (6:21, 'Marianne' B-side, 1980) 11. 'Only After Dark' (3:46, 1980) 12. 'WXJL Tonight' (4:36, 1980) 13. 'Crow And A Baby' (3:39, 1980) 14. 'I Don't Depend On You' (4:33, single by The Men, 1979) 15. 'Tom Baker' (3:58, 'Boys And Girls' B-side, 1981)

Bibliography

https://www.facebook.com/80s-futuristic-electronics-forever-132826693461449/
History and music by The Human League and information on the
New Wave and Post Punk period. https://www.facebook.com/groups/
NewWaveAndPostPunkOnly/
http://www.discog.info/human-league.html
Roger Quail's archive of Sheffield music https://www.mylifeinthemoshofghosts.
com/
Made In Sheffield: The Birth Of Electronic Pop 1977-1982 (Director: Eve Wood)
(Sheffield Vision & Slackjaw Film Ltd, DVD, 2005, Plexifilm 017)
Mendez, F. (Ed.), *Cabaret Voltaire: A Collection Of Interviews 1977-1994*
(DL:SA 294-2021)
Gambaccini, P., Rice, T., Rice, J., *The Guinness Top Forty Charts* (GRR
Publications, 1992)
Thanks to: Stephen Singleton and Mark White
Tim Lott in *Record Mirror* 'Syn-Rock Is Here', 24 November 1979
Lynn Barber in *Melody Maker*, 3 October 1981
Pete Frame and Tony Mitchell in *Sounds*, 25 June 1983
Colin Irwin in *Melody Maker*, 9 June 1984
Carole Linfield in *Sounds*, 10 August 1985
Ted Mico in *Melody Maker*, 29 October 1988
Jim Shelley in *New Musical Express*, 5 November 1988
Miranda Sawyer in *The Observer*, 15 January 1995
Roger Morton in *New Musical Express*, 18 November 1995
Neil McCormick in *Hot Press*

On Track series

Alan Parsons Project – Steve Swift 978-1-78952-154-2
Tori Amos – Lisa Torem 978-1-78952-142-9
Asia – Peter Braidis 978-1-78952-099-6
Badfinger – Robert Day-Webb 978-1-878952-176-4
Barclay James Harvest – Keith and Monica Domone 978-1-78952-067-5
The Beatles – Andrew Wild 978-1-78952-009-5
The Beatles Solo 1969-1980 – Andrew Wild 978-1-78952-030-9
Blue Oyster Cult – Jacob Holm-Lupo 978-1-78952-007-1
Blur – Matt Bishop – 978-178952-164-1
Marc Bolan and T.Rex – Peter Gallagher 978-1-78952-124-5
Kate Bush – Bill Thomas 978-1-78952-097-2
Camel – Hamish Kuzminski 978-1-78952-040-8
Caravan – Andy Boot 978-1-78952-127-6
Cardiacs – Eric Benac 978-1-78952-131-3
Eric Clapton Solo – Andrew Wild 978-1-78952-141-2
The Clash – Nick Assirati 978-1-78952-077-4
Crosby, Stills and Nash – Andrew Wild 978-1-78952-039-2
The Damned – Morgan Brown 978-1-78952-136-8
Deep Purple and Rainbow 1968-79 – Steve Pilkington 978-1-78952-002-6
Dire Straits – Andrew Wild 978-1-78952-044-6
The Doors – Tony Thompson 978-1-78952-137-5
Dream Theater – Jordan Blum 978-1-78952-050-7
Electric Light Orchestra – Barry Delve 978-1-78952-152-8
Elvis Costello and The Attractions – Georg Purvis 978-1-78952-129-0
Emerson Lake and Palmer – Mike Goode 978-1-78952-000-2
Fairport Convention – Kevan Furbank 978-1-78952-051-4
Peter Gabriel – Graeme Scarfe 978-1-78952-138-2
Genesis – Stuart MacFarlane 978-1-78952-005-7
Gentle Giant – Gary Steel 978-1-78952-058-3
Gong – Kevan Furbank 978-1-78952-082-8
Hall and Oates – Ian Abrahams 978-1-78952-167-2
Hawkwind – Duncan Harris 978-1-78952-052-1
Peter Hammill – Richard Rees Jones 978-1-78952-163-4
Roy Harper – Opher Goodwin 978-1-78952-130-6
Jimi Hendrix – Emma Stott 978-1-78952-175-7
The Hollies – Andrew Darlington 978-1-78952-159-7
Iron Maiden – Steve Pilkington 978-1-78952-061-3
Jefferson Airplane – Richard Butterworth 978-1-78952-143-6
Jethro Tull – Jordan Blum 978-1-78952-016-3
Elton John in the 1970s – Peter Kearns 978-1-78952-034-7
The Incredible String Band – Tim Moon 978-1-78952-107-8
Iron Maiden – Steve Pilkington 978-1-78952-061-3
Judas Priest – John Tucker 978-1-78952-018-7
Kansas – Kevin Cummings 978-1-78952-057-6
The Kinks – Martin Hutchinson 978-1-78952-172-6
Korn – Matt Karpe 978-1-78952-153-5
Led Zeppelin – Steve Pilkington 978-1-78952-151-1

Level 42 – Matt Philips 978-1-78952-102-3
Little Feat – 978-1-78952-168-9
Aimee Mann – Jez Rowden 978-1-78952-036-1
Joni Mitchell – Peter Kearns 978-1-78952-081-1
The Moody Blues – Geoffrey Feakes 978-1-78952-042-2
Motorhead – Duncan Harris 978-1-78952-173-3
Mike Oldfield – Ryan Yard 978-1-78952-060-6
Opeth – Jordan Blum 978-1-78-952-166-5
Tom Petty – Richard James 978-1-78952-128-3
Porcupine Tree – Nick Holmes 978-1-78952-144-3
Queen – Andrew Wild 978-1-78952-003-3
Radiohead – William Allen 978-1-78952-149-8
Renaissance – David Detmer 978-1-78952-062-0
The Rolling Stones 1963-80 – Steve Pilkington 978-1-78952-017-0
The Smiths and Morrissey – Tommy Gunnarsson 978-1-78952-140-5
Status Quo the Frantic Four Years – Richard James 978-1-78952-160-3
Steely Dan – Jez Rowden 978-1-78952-043-9
Steve Hackett – Geoffrey Feakes 978-1-78952-098-9
Thin Lizzy – Graeme Stroud 978-1-78952-064-4
Toto – Jacob Holm-Lupo 978-1-78952-019-4
U2 – Eoghan Lyng 978-1-78952-078-1
UFO – Richard James 978-1-78952-073-6
The Who – Geoffrey Feakes 978-1-78952-076-7
Roy Wood and the Move – James R Turner 978-1-78952-008-8
Van Der Graaf Generator – Dan Coffey 978-1-78952-031-6
Yes – Stephen Lambe 978-1-78952-001-9
Frank Zappa 1966 to 1979 – Eric Benac 978-1-78952-033-0
Warren Zevon – Peter Gallagher 978-1-78952-170-2
10CC – Peter Kearns 978-1-78952-054-5

Decades Series
The Bee Gees in the 1960s – Andrew Mon Hughes et al 978-1-78952-148-1
The Bee Gees in the 1970s – Andrew Mon Hughes et al 978-1-78952-179-5
Black Sabbath in the 1970s – Chris Sutton 978-1-78952-171-9
Britpop – Peter Richard Adams and Matt Pooler 978-1-78952-169-6
Alice Cooper in the 1970s – Chris Sutton 978-1-78952-104-7
Curved Air in the 1970s – Laura Shenton 978-1-78952-069-9
Bob Dylan in the 1980s – Don Klees 978-1-78952-157-3
Fleetwood Mac in the 1970s – Andrew Wild 978-1-78952-105-4
Focus in the 1970s – Stephen Lambe 978-1-78952-079-8
Free and Bad Company in the 1970s – John Van der Kiste 978-1-78952-178-8
Genesis in the 1970s – Bill Thomas 978178952-146-7
George Harrison in the 1970s – Eoghan Lyng 978-1-78952-174-0
Marillion in the 1980s – Nathaniel Webb 978-1-78952-065-1
Mott the Hoople and Ian Hunter in the 1970s – John Van der Kiste
978-1-78-952-162-7
Pink Floyd In The 1970s – Georg Purvis 978-1-78952-072-9
Tangerine Dream in the 1970s – Stephen Palmer 978-1-78952-161-0
The Sweet in the 1970s – Darren Johnson 978-1-78952-139-9

Uriah Heep in the 1970s – Steve Pilkington 978-1-78952-103-0
Yes in the 1980s – Stephen Lambe with David Watkinson 978-1-78952-125-2

On Screen series
Carry On... – Stephen Lambe 978-1-78952-004-0
David Cronenberg – Patrick Chapman 978-1-78952-071-2
Doctor Who: The David Tennant Years – Jamie Hailstone 978-1-78952-066-8
James Bond – Andrew Wild – 978-1-78952-010-1
Monty Python – Steve Pilkington 978-1-78952-047-7
Seinfeld Seasons 1 to 5 – Stephen Lambe 978-1-78952-012-5

Other Books
1967: A Year In Psychedelic Rock – Kevan Furbank 978-1-78952-155-9
1970: A Year In Rock – John Van der Kiste 978-1-78952-147-4
1973: The Golden Year of Progressive Rock 978-1-78952-165-8
Babysitting A Band On The Rocks – G.D. Praetorius 978-1-78952-106-1
Eric Clapton Sessions – Andrew Wild 978-1-78952-177-1
Derek Taylor: For Your Radioactive Children – Andrew Darlington
978-1-78952-038-5
The Golden Road: The Recording History of The Grateful Dead – John Kilbride
978-1-78952-156-6
Iggy and The Stooges On Stage 1967-1974 – Per Nilsen 978-1-78952-101-6
Jon Anderson and the Warriors – the road to Yes – David Watkinson
978-1-78952-059-0
Nu Metal: A Definitive Guide – Matt Karpe 978-1-78952-063-7
Tommy Bolin: In and Out of Deep Purple – Laura Shenton 978-1-78952-070-5
Maximum Darkness – Deke Leonard 978-1-78952-048-4
Maybe I Should've Stayed In Bed – Deke Leonard 978-1-78952-053-8
The Twang Dynasty – Deke Leonard 978-1-78952-049-1

and many more to come!